Sexual Abuse in Youth Sport

Cases of sport-related child sexual abuse have received increasing news coverage in recent years. This book documents and evaluates this important issue through a critical investigation of the research and theory on sexual violence and child sex offending that has emerged over the past 30 years.

Based on life history interviews with male and female 'survivors' of child sexual abuse in sport, this text offers a deeper appreciation for the experiences of those who are sexually victimized within sports and school sport settings. Drawing on a wide range of sources, it also provides a new theoretical framework through which child sexual abuse in sport may be explored. Offering a critique spanning psychology, sociology and criminology, this book challenges existing theories of sex offending while advocating an alternative epistemology to help better understand and address this social problem.

Presenting an original sociological approach to this field of study, *Sexual Abuse in Youth Sport* is important reading for any researcher, policy maker or practitioner working in youth sport, physical education, sports coaching, sport policy, child protection or social work.

Michael J. Hartill is Senior Lecturer in Sociology of Sport at Edge Hill University, UK. He has conducted research into child sexual exploitation in sport for over a decade, working on a number of significant national and international projects aimed at preventing abuse of children in sport.

Routledge Research in Sport, Culture and Society

Sexual Abuse in Youth Sport

A sociocultural analysis

Michael J. Hartill

Routledge
Taylor & Francis Group

LONDON AND NEW YORK

First published 2017
by Routledge
2 Park Square, Milton Park, Abingdon, Oxon OX14 4RN

and by Routledge
711 Third Avenue, New York, NY 10017

First issued in paperback 2017

Routledge is an imprint of the Taylor & Francis Group, an informa business

British Library Cataloguing-in-Publication Data
A catalogue record for this book is available from the British
Library

Library of Congress Cataloging-in-Publication Data
Names: Hartill, Mike, author.
Title: Sexual abuse in youth sport : a sociocultural analysis /
Michael J. Hartill.
Description: Abingdon, Oxon ; New York : Routledge is an
imprint of the Taylor & Francis Group, an Informa Business,
[2017] | Series: Routledge research in sport, culture and society ;
65 | Includes bibliographical references and index.
Identifiers: LCCN 2016015208| ISBN 9781138848504 (hardback) |
ISBN 9781315726113 (ebook)
Subjects: LCSH: Child sexual abuse in sports. | Sports for
children–Social aspects.
Classification: LCC HV6570 .H37 2017 | DDC 362.76–dc23
LC record available at https://lccn.loc.gov/2016015208

ISBN 13: 978-1-138-49424-4 (pbk)
ISBN 13: 978-1-138-84850-4 (hbk)

Typeset in Sabon
by Wearset Ltd, Boldon, Tyne and Wear

For Sharon

Contents

Acknowledgements

First, my sincere thanks go to all the individuals who generously agreed to be interviewed for this research and participated so graciously in interviews of the most intrusive kind. Their contribution to this work is by far the most significant, and I hope they feel their time and effort is justified by what follows.

Celia Brackenridge has been an immense source of inspiration to me for the duration of my work in this field, and I am very grateful to her for the guidance and support she has given.

Specific mentions must also go to my colleagues at Edge Hill University, especially Phil Prescott who broadened my thinking on child maltreatment and provided the support which enabled me to pursue research in this field. Thanks also to Paul Reynolds, Leon Culbertson, John Diamond and Melanie Lang who continue to offer much needed critical discussion and professional support as well as friendship. I am also grateful to the Edge Hill University Research Investment Fund, which supported some of the data collection for this work, and the Department of Sport and Physical Activity, including many students, which has enabled me to pursue investigations in this field over the past 15 years.

This work has brought me into contact with many colleagues in the UK and across the globe, especially in Europe and North America, and I am grateful for the interest and support they have shown me and the friendships that have developed over the years. Particular mention goes (in no particular order) to Colette Eden, Bettina Rulofs, Montserrat Martin, Tom Perry, Tine Vertommen, Nick Ashley, Joel Donnelly, Joe Moore, Duncan Craig, Sylvie Parent, Gretchen Kerr, Kari Fasting, Nadezda Knorre, Jan Toftegaard Nielsen, Ani Chroni, Maria Papaefstathiou, Agnes Kainz, Gitta Axmann, Meike Schröer, Anno Kluss, Karen Leach, Anne Tiivas, Sally Proudlove, Daniel Rhind, Joca Zurc, Sheila Taylor MBE, Steve LePore, Liz Pike, Jan Holze, Rebekka Kemmler-Mueller, Vyacheslav Melnyk, Cecile Veldman, Michael Leyendecker, Alexandra Hoffmann, Paul Gruber, Paolo Adami and Elena Lamby.

I am also grateful to Simon Whitmore at Routledge for his support and conviction to publish this work and to Cecily Davey for her support in the production of this book.

Above all I am deeply grateful to my family and friends who have supported me in more ways than they could know and have given me the love – and time – needed to complete this work.

Introduction

Since ancient times, stories of great feats of skill, strength, speed and endurance have been a fundamental feature of human culture. In the twenty-first century, stories generated from our sporting endeavours are now more prominent than ever before. Sport stories are woven into the fabric of families, schools, villages, towns, cities, regions and nations. They are now dispersed quickly and widely and feature prominently in societies across the globe. Indeed, sport, and the stories generated from our engagement in it, often form a central pillar of our collective sense of community and identity, bonding us further with every re-telling of the endeavours of local, national and international athletes; small but significant acts of commemoration, in which we affirm, to ourselves and others, who we are. Therefore, as in other areas of late twentieth and early twenty-first century life, the intrusion of child sexual abuse in sport, and the relatively recent recognition that this isn't a practice confined to social outcasts, pulls at the fabric of our lives because it threatens to undermine deeply held convictions and long-established 'truths'.

Although rather peripheral, the culture of storytelling within and around the world of sport includes more challenging and complex stories, such as those focused on racism, violence, doping and corruption. As with other popular coverage of the much-referenced 'dark-side' of sport, in some countries at least, stories of sexual violence in sport have been worthy of national news coverage, if not headline news, for the past two decades. In the UK, coverage of the Paul Hickson arrest, trial and conviction between 1992 and 1995 (Donegan, 1995) – also covered extensively in a docudrama by BBC television (BBC, 1998) – in fact followed nearly a decade of advocacy and research from academic Celia Brackenridge OBE, who had faced years of vehement criticism, within and without sport, for suggesting that sport was also the site of child sexual abuse (CSA) (see Brackenridge, 2001). There is, then, a history of sexual violence within sport that is as old as sport itself. Yet it is only since the early 1990s that stories of sexual abuse in sport began to emerge (see Lang and Hartill, 2015). A persistent feature of investigations into these cases is that other people – coaches, officials, parents – were aware of the abuse but failed to report it. Therefore, it is a dimension of sports cultural history that has been, not simply unrecognized, but also concealed. The sociology of sport has played a significant role in revealing this problem (see Fasting, 2015).

While this book represents a qualitative investigation, quantitative research in this field is of course crucial, not least to combat the charge that measures to protect children from sexual violence (and other forms of maltreatment) are, as one Spanish coach put it, 'a bomb to kill flies', or as a research respondent in the UK said 'a sledgehammer to crack a nut' (Hartill and Prescott, 2007). Fasting (2015: 438) reports that 'the prevalence of sexual harassment (which sometimes includes abuse) in sport varies between 19 and 92% and the prevalence of sexual abuse between 2 and 49%.' It is important to point out, then, the most recent findings from prevalence research. From a representative sample of 4,043 individuals from the Netherlands and Flanders, with varying levels of sports participation, Vertommen *et al.* (2016) found:

> Almost 38% indicated at least one incident of psychological violence, 11% at least one event involving physical violence, while 14% had experienced sexual violence at least once … Ethnic minority, lesbian/gay/bisexual (LGB) and disabled athletes, and those competing at the international level report significantly more experiences of interpersonal violence in sport.

Parent *et al.* (2015) found 0.5 per cent of 14–17 year olds had experienced sexual abuse by a sports coach from a representative sample within the general population in Quebec; within the group identified as 'athletes' the prevalence figure was 0.8 per cent. Thus, prevalence research in this field is in its infancy, and there is nothing approaching an agreed prevalence figure for 'sport'. As Fasting (2015) notes, variations in the terms and definitions applied in the field effect measurement and, therefore, prevalence rates. There are a range of concepts and definitions to choose from, 'but central in most definitions of gender, sexual harassment and abuse (GSHA) is that the behaviour experienced is unwanted or threatening, troublesome, insulting or offensive and an abuse of power' (Fasting, 2015: 438). However, it is useful to note Brown and Walklate's (2012: 489) recent reworking of Liz Kelly's (1988) definition of 'sexual violence':

> Sexual violence is defined in terms of the frequency (either high or low) with which any act having explicit or implicit sexual content comprising any actual or threatened behaviour, verbal or non-verbal aimed at an individual that (in)directly hurts, degrades, frightens or controls her/him at the time of the act or at any time in the future.

Kelly's (1988) definition failed to account for sexual abuse against males reflecting the dominant paradigm of 'male perpetrator-female victim' that guided early approaches to this problem, including in sport (Crosset, 1986; Tomlinson and Yorganci, 1997).

This work focuses on the experiences of children (defined as anyone under 18 years), therefore, the terms 'child sexual abuse' (CSA) and 'child sexual exploitation' (CSE) are particularly relevant. Full definitions of these, according to current statutory guidance issued by the UK government, are provided separately (Appendix 1) but, briefly, CSA refers to forced or coerced sexual activity with a child, and CSE is a form of abuse where the child receives something in return for sexual activity.

Alongside ground-breaking research (e.g. Brackenridge, 1992; Fasting et al., 2002; Kirby et al., 2000; Toftegaard Nielsen, 2001), first-hand accounts of sexual exploitation in sport by ex-professional athletes have also begun to emerge. One of the most significant is that of Sheldon Kennedy, a Canadian hockey player and now high-profile activist and educator on the issue of sexual abuse. Kennedy's autobiography *Why I Didn't Say Anything* (Kennedy with Grainger, 2006) tells of his experiences of sexual abuse by his coach Graham James and his difficulties coping with this. Publication of Kennedy's story, and also a feature film (*The Sheldon Kennedy Story*, 1999), was followed by that of another 'survivor' of Graham James, Theo Fleury (Fleury with McLellan, 2009). Others have followed, for example: Leonard (2011); Moore (2010); Sjöberg (2011). Thus, while much of the early research in this field focused on the sexual exploitation of female athletes, some of the most high-profile disclosures (and media attention) have come from male athletes over the past decade. Nevertheless, research in the general population repeatedly shows higher prevalence rates of sexual abuse for females than males, and this also appears to be the case in sport (Alexander et al., 2011; Parent et al., 2015; Vertommen et al., 2016). That said, it remains that there is almost no research focused on the sexual exploitation of males in sport (Parent and Bannon, 2012), and this text also helps to address this absence. In addition, it is important to recall that 'in many countries, sexual harassment and abuse in sport is still ignored … and there is both a denial of the issue and a lack of evidence-based knowledge' (Fasting, 2015: 440).

First and foremost, this book is about men and women who were sexually exploited as children within a sport-related setting. It prioritizes their first-hand accounts of the experience of being subjected to sex by an adult in whose care they were entrusted. Therefore, central to this research endeavour has been the provision of sufficient and appropriate time and space in which their stories can be told. I offer the accounts of men and women who have been subjected to sexual violence in childhood through their engagement in, and passion for, sport. These individuals have given their stories willingly and generously with one clear goal in mind: that it contributes to efforts to prevent others from suffering the same experience.

Equally, I bring these stories to the reader in the hope that the insights they offer may prove beneficial to prevention efforts. It is also the hope of my research participants, and myself, that these stories may reach someone who is experiencing, or has experienced, sexual abuse and that they may provide some support for them in their efforts to either liberate themselves from victimization or from the effects of it. From my work with young people in sport, both as an academic and within the community, I feel confident that the stories presented possess this potential, and I hope they can be shared widely within the sports community and beyond. Equally, I hope they will encourage the telling of, and analysis of, further stories of sexual exploitation in sport.

However, an additional but also central purpose for writing this book is to articulate and address some theoretical questions or dilemmas raised by Brackenridge's (2001) seminal text 'Spoilsports'. Indeed, in my early considerations of the problem of CSE in sport, my major concern was not, and is not, the determination of the *extent* of the experience in sport, but rather the *conceptualization* of the problem. This does not mean simply how we define it, but rather how the problem should be approached – thought about – theoretically, epistemologically and conceptually. This is a wider issue for the field in general, thus, in their recent review, Smallbone and McKillop (2015: 180) observe that 'the field has not yet established an agreed, coherent theoretical framework or overarching prevention model'.

However, if, as feminist theory has argued for many years, sexual violence is fundamentally about power rather than simply sexual gratification, then the way we conceptualize power has implications for how we come to understand and explain sexual violence and abuse within sport. In short, it effects how we theorize sexual violence and, thus, how we address it. Brackenridge considered this explicitly, arguing that 'it is desirable to address both the structural and cultural parameters of sexual exploitation in sport' (Brackenridge, 2001: 85), and Rulofs (2015) reaffirms the importance of this approach. This position presents particular demands for research in developing cohesive, robust and authentic accounts of sexual violence and abuse in sport and indicates that explanatory accounts must go well beyond studying the motivations of offenders. Therefore, Brackenridge (2001: 102–103) notes 'sport researchers need to seek theoretical relevance from a bewildering array of possible sources.' The epistemological and theoretical means by which researchers approach the problem of sexual violence, abuse and exploitation in sport, then, has important ramifications for the development of knowledge in the field and this book addresses this issue explicitly.

The motivation to produce this book, then, is based on four fundamental points:

1 That the sexual exploitation of children is an entrenched and wide-spread problem that must be persistently challenged by all communities;

2 That the goal of prevention requires all contexts, or fields, to critically examine their own cultures, principles and processes for the antecedents of sexual violence;

3 That (sports) communities can benefit significantly from the stories of those who have experienced sexual violence in sports and should actively encourage the disclosure of 'victim'/'survivor' accounts; and

4 That a wider range of theoretical perspectives should be explored in our efforts to better understand and conceptualize this social problem.

References

Alexander, K., Stafford, A. and Lewis, R. (2011) *The experiences of children participating in organised sport in the UK*. Edinburgh: Dunedin Academic Press.

Brackenridge, C.H. (2001) *Spoilsports: understanding and preventing sexual exploitation in sport*. London: Routledge.

Crosset, T. (1986) Male coach/female athlete relationships. *Paper presented at the first international conference for sport sciences*, Sole, Norway, 5–6 November.

Donegan, L. (1995) Olympic coach jailed for rapes. *The Guardian*, September 28.

Fasting, K. (2015) Assessing the sociology of sport: on sexual harassment research and policy. *International Review for the Sociology of Sport*, 50(4–5): 437–441.

Fasting, K., Brackenridge, C.H. and Walseth, K. (2002) Coping with sexual harassment in sport: experiences of elite female athletes. *The Journal of Sexual Aggression*, 8(2): 16–36.

Fisher, A., Gillum, M. and Daniels, D. (2012) *Silent no more: victim 1's fight for justice against Jerry Sandusky*. New York: Ballantine.

Fleury, T. with McLellan, K. (2009) *Playing with fire*. Illinois: Triumph.

Hartill, M. and Prescott, P. (2007) Serious business or 'any other business?' Safeguarding and child protection in British Rugby League. *Child Abuse Review*, 16: 237–251. DOI: 10.1002/car.990.

Kennedy, S. with Grainger, J. (2006) *Why I didn't say anything: the Sheldon Kennedy story*. Toronto: Insomniac Press.

Kirby, S.L., Greaves, L. and Hankivsky, O. (2000) *The dome of silence: sexual harassment and abuse in sport*. London: Zed Books.

Leonard, S.R. (2011) *The big fight: my life in and out of the ring*. New York: Viking.

Moore, B. (2010) *Beware of the dog: Rugby's hard man reveals all*. London: Simon and Schuster.

Parent, S. and Bannon, J. (2012) Sexual abuse in sport: what about boys? *Children and Youth Services Review*, 34(2): 354–359.

Parent, S., Lavoie, F., Thibodeau, M-E., Hebert, M., Blais, M. and Team PAJ (2015) Sexual violence experienced in the sport context by a representative sample of Quebec adolescents. *Journal of Interpersonal Violence*. Published online before print 13 April 2015, DOI: 10.1177/0886260515580366.

Rulofs, B. (2015) Assessing the sociology of sport: on gender-based violence and child maltreatment in sport. *International Review for the Sociology of Sport*, 50(4–5): 580–584.

Sjöberg, P. with Lutteman, M. (2011) *Det du inte såg [What you did not see]*. Stockholm: Norstedts.

Smallbone, S.W. and McKillop, N. (2015) Evidence-informed approaches to preventing sexual violence and abuse. In P.D. Donnelly and C.L. Ward (eds) *Oxford Handbook of Violence Prevention*, 177–181.

The Sheldon Kennedy Story (1999) Directed by Norma Bailey. Calgary, Canada: Alberta Filmworks [Film].

Toftegaard Nielsen, J. (2001) The forbidden zone: intimacy, sexual relations and misconduct in the relationship between coaches and athletes. *International Review for the Sociology of Sport*, 36(2): 165–183.

Tomlinson, A. and Yorganci, I. (1997) Male coach/female athlete relations: gender and power relations in competitive sport. *Journal of Sport and Social Issues*, 21(2): 134–155.

Vertommen, T., Schipper-van Veldhoven, N., Wouters, K., Kampen, J.K., Brackenridge, C.H., Rhind, D.J.A., Neels, K. and Van Den Eede, F. (2016) Interpersonal violence against children in sport in the Netherlands and Belgium. *Child Abuse and Neglect*, 51: 223–236.

Chapter 1

Perspectives, theories and models of sex offending and child sexual abuse

Tony Ward, a prominent researcher and theorist on sex offending, argues that many researchers do not take theory development seriously and that 'the theoretical landscape is characterized by lack of communication and fragmentation' (Ward, 2014: 137). Within sport research, Celia Brackenridge (2001) has led the way, incorporating theoretical analyses from the start, however, there has been a distinct lack of theory development since her seminal text 'Spoilsports'.

Early accounts of child sexual abuse are dominated by perspectives that construe child sex offending in pathological terms. For example, Groth *et al.* (1982) argue a child sex offender is 'an immature individual whose pedophilic behaviour serves to compensate for his relative helplessness in meeting bio-psycho-social life demands' (in Herman, 1990: 183). However, for Jenks (2005b: 94–95) such explanations are 'sadly simplistic ... stemming from the face-value positivism at the heart of their grasp of the issue.' This is an important and substantive criticism that helps to frame the debate around the theorization of sexual violence and sex offending. Cowburn and Myers (2015: 672) provide an important overview, separating the field into '*psychological approaches*' – that 'focus on working with individual offenders' – and '*sociological perspectives*' – that 'locate sexual offences and sex offenders within a wider social context'. Using this broad template, the purpose of this chapter is to introduce some of the key perspectives and debates in the field while making no claim to a comprehensive review.

Psychology-based theories of sexual offending

Psychological approaches to sex offending against children have dominated research and theory development relating to 'causation'. Ward and colleagues, especially Anthony Beech, have been particularly influential in promoting and expanding theory. Ward *et al.* (2006) identify three levels of theory on sex offending: Level 1: multifactorial theories offer a complex account of the etiology and continuance of sex offending; Level 2: single factor theories focus on one issue to account for the etiology and continuance of sex offending; Level 3: micro-level or offense process theories give particular attention to an aspect of offending behaviour. Cowburn and Myers (2015) observe that multifactorial theories have commanded greatest influence within psychological approaches and 'a key aspect of these theories is that they have been developed from analyses of empirical studies of sex offenders, their personal histories, and their offense patterns' (Cowburn and Myers, 2015: 674–675). It is not possible or necessary to review the full range of theories developed within (social) psychology, however, I will focus on two of the most influential multifactorial theories: Finkelhor and Araji's (1986) 'Four Factor Model' and Ward and Beech's (2006) 'Integrated Theory of Sexual Offending' (ITSO).

Finkelhor and Araji's (1986) 'Four Factor Model' of explanations of pedophilia[1]

David Finkelhor's contribution to the field of sexual violence research, policy and practice has been profound. According to Ward *et al.* (2006: 19) despite being 'relatively old ... Finkelhor's theory is currently thriving and is used by countless practitioners in the course of their day to day practice.' Critical of 'inadequate' single factor explanations, Finkelhor and Araji (1986: 147) argued for 'a more complicated model that integrates a variety of single factor explanations in a way that accounts for the many different kinds of pedophilic outcomes.'[2]

Finkelhor and Araji (1986: 147) summarize previous causal theories 'as trying to explain one of four factors' which they categorize as: (1) *Emotional congruence* – which 'conveys the idea of a fit between the adult's emotional needs and the child's characteristics' (148); (2) *Sexual arousal to children* – referring to 'explanations of how a person comes to find children sexually arousing' (149); (3) *Blockage* – referring to 'explanations of why some individuals are blocked in their ability to get their sexual and emotional needs met in adult heterosexual relationships' (categorized as 'normal development' (153)); and (4) *Disinhibition* – theories about 'why conventional inhibitions against having sex with children are overcome or are not present in some adults' (154). They refer to this as a 'four factor model' of paedophilia (Finkelhor *et al.*, 1986) which included social factors (drawn particularly from feminist research, e.g. Rush, 1980) as well as personal/psychological factors. In addition, Finkelhor (1984) describes four 'pre-conditions' or the 'necessary conditions for abuse' (Howells, 1995: 201). The first precondition is *motivation*, which incorporates the four factors identified from previous theory (above). The second relates to 'overcoming *internal* inhibitions against acting on the motivation'; third, 'overcoming *external* impediments to committing sexual abuse'; and fourth, 'overcoming a *child's resistance* to sexual abuse' (Finkelhor, 1984).

Colton and Vanstone (1996: 21–22) argue a key strength of the model is that 'it combines psychological and sociological explanations' and is sufficiently general 'to integrate all forms of intra- and extrafamilial sexual abuse.' This is clearly a model of process rather than an explanation or theory and noticeably absent from Finkelhor and Araji's (1986) review is any substantial critique of the research from which their four factors are generated; rather, their model 'is merely constructed around them' (Cossins, 2000: 72–73). There are a number of critical evaluations of Finkelhor's preconditions model (e.g. see Colton and Vanstone, 1996; Cossins, 2000; Howells, 1995; Ward et al., 2006). Ward et al. (2006: 26) argue that Finkelhor's desire to draw together theory from different perspectives leaves the model 'with a set of conflicting and mutually exclusive ideas ... in other words it lacks *internal coherence*'.

Cossins's (2000: 74–82) presents a range of weaknesses in Finkelhor's argument clustered around the criticism that any theory that takes CSA to be a product of abnormal or deviant male psychopathology must demonstrate that offenders are psychologically distinct from the wider male population that do not offend. She claims that Finkelhor fails to recognize this and, therefore, 'he has, at the outset, accepted the dichotomy between so-called normal and deviant masculine sexual behaviour' (Cossins, 2000: 74). Thus, Finkelhor's theory is based upon essentialist claims to distinct psychological characteristics, such as a lack of empathy, but 'fails to analyse the extent to which child sex offending is congruent with normative masculine sexual practices' (Cossins, 2000: 74). She argues:

> Such unsupported supposition [regarding male, biological sex drive] leaves the model looking like an artificial device that could be moulded to explain any type of sexual behaviour without adding to an understanding of why child sex offending is predominantly a male phenomenon ...
>
> (Cossins, 2000: 81–82)

Nevertheless, Finkelhor's model remains influential.

Ward and Beech's (2006) 'Integrated Theory of Sexual Offending' (ITSO)

As Cowburn and Myers (2015: 674) point out, 'from a psychological perspective, the works of Ward and colleagues are of key importance'. Ward et al. (2006) offer an impressive overview and assessment of the most prominent theories of sex offending. They utilize Ward and Hudson's (1998) 'meta-theoretical framework for classifying theories based on their level of generality of focus' (Ward et al., 2006: 12) separating theories on sex offending into three distinct levels, according to scope and complexity, as noted at the start of this chapter. Like all 'objective' and 'scientific' systems of classification, however, the categories selected to describe the field are, of course, products of the ontological and epistemological perspectives of those devising them. As Ward (2014: 139) later notes, 'science is a value-laden enterprise', thus, as Bourdieu (1989: 19) observes 'nothing classifies somebody more than the way he or she classifies'.

Ward and Beech (2006) acknowledge substantive progress in the field of sexual offending research, but they are critical of previous attempts to develop comprehensive theories:

> ...a key flaw in the majority of theories is that they tend to focus on the surface level of symptomology and fail to take into account the fact that human beings are biological or embodied creatures. What references there are to the causal (underlying) properties of sexual offenders and their environments are typically simply general descriptions of observable factors. They are convenient labels for summarizing behavior masquerading as causal mechanisms. The danger with such theorizing is that it may simply recycle ideas from everyday 'commonsense' views of human behavior (i.e., folk psychology), which fail to capture the causal origins of dysfunctional sexual behavior.
>
> (Ward and Beech, 2006: 45)

There is much to agree with here, however, Ward and Beech (2006) also reveal the underlying ontological assumption in their project: that sexual offending equates to 'dysfunctional sexual behaviour' perpetrated by dysfunctional or *malfunctioning* individuals. Ward and Beech state their goal is:

> ...to knit together a number of factors and processes thought to be causally implicated in the occurrence of sexual abuse into an Integrated Theory of Sexual Offending (ITSO) ... meant as a general theory of sexual offending.
>
> (Ward and Beech, 2006: 45)

They identify their sources for this theory as 'neuropsychology, ecology, psychopathology, and clinical assessment' (Ward and Beech, 2006: 45). Despite a chapter devoted to feminist theories of sex offending in their comprehensive review (Ward *et al.*, 2006: 167–180; see also Purvis and Ward, 2006), Ward and Beech (2006) appear to largely dismiss feminist approaches, claiming they offer little in regard to effective treatment and, therefore, are of limited value to theory development.

According to the *ITSO* 'there are a number of types of causes plausibly associated with sexual crimes': *genetic predispositions*; *adverse developmental experiences*; *psychological dispositions/trait factors*. In addition, they cite '*cultural structures and processes*; and *contextual factors*' (Ward and Beech, 2006: 45). Thus, importantly, Ward and colleagues explicitly acknowledge that 'sexual offending emerges from a network of relationships between individuals and their local habitats and niches, and is not simply the consequence of individual psychopathology' (Ward *et al.*, 2006: 336). Nevertheless, the neuropsychological level is critical to '... understanding the psychological vulnerabilities of sexual offenders ... It is this level of analysis that directly informs researchers of the mechanisms generating offenders' psychological symptoms and problems (Ward and Beech, 2006: 48).

Explicit here is the assertion that sexual offending is a manifestation of psychological *vulnerabilities*; vulnerabilities that *generate* offenders 'symptoms and *problems*' (my emphasis). Again, there is very explicit acknowledgement of the sociocultural dimension and its role in sex offending. However, this is frequently addressed through scenarios or examples of negative (social) experiences, such as witnessing domestic violence in childhood, that *may* result in impaired brain functioning. The individual is reduced to an organism constituted by various interrelated systems of the brain and sex offending is the product of impaired functioning, in other words 'brain damage'. 'Sociocultural factors' are simply recruited in the service of this paradigm but are not considered worthy of theorization in themselves.

Within the Unified Theory, then, the *social* remains largely uninterrogated. As a consequence the individual is not a social *agent* but rather a mechanism of interrelated brain systems that are impacted, or driven, by internal (e.g. 'genetic inheritance') or external (e.g. 'ecological niche') stimuli (Ward and Beech, 2006: 52–53). Therefore, the 'offender' in Ward and Beech's theory appears to be 'acting under the influence'; that is, their action is the result of forces – malfunctioning brain systems – beyond the control of the individual, or rather, beyond the control of reason.

Within this type of theory construction, a relationship is created whereby subjecting a child to a sexual encounter can only be associated with (as a product of) negative psychological/personal circumstances. Thus:

> According to the unified theory, psychological functioning – in conjunction with the offender's ecology – creates the clinical phenomena typically noted in sexual offenders: emotional problems, social difficulties, deviant arousal and cognitive distortions ... these clinical phenomena ... are likely to lead the individual concerned to commit a sexual offence, depending of course on the availability and accessibility of a potential victim (an ecological variable).
>
> (Ward *et al.*, 2006: 338–339)

Again, this serves to establish that it is not possible to come to an under-standing of the practice of sexually subjecting a child in the way we may come to an understanding of other widespread social practices (that many/ most people *don't* engage in) such as riding a motorbike, 'body-building' or entering beauty pageants. This prompts the question: at what *point* does social action become the product of negative psychological/personal experi-ence? When it becomes illegal? Or does this only apply to behaviour that is especially taboo? Equally, does all legally-sanctioned behaviour correlate with 'normal' psychology, genetic credits (rather than deficits) and 'positive' personal experiences? This seems highly unlikely, but such ques-tions emerge from biological and neuroscientific perspectives on sex offending.

Ultimately the ITSO is not so much a theory as a model. Indeed, Ward *et al.*, (2006: 340) acknowledge this on the final page of their book: 'the unified theory is really an abstract framework for thinking systematically about sexual offending and its constituent causal variables'. In a more recent review of theory development in the field of sex offending, Ward (2014) laments the neglect of theory development in recent years, observ-ing that 'existing level 1 theories ... do not appear to have significantly influenced research and practice' (Ward, 2014: 131). It also appears that Ward's thinking has developed somewhat from earlier work:

> A preoccupation with measurement may trap us into surface level explanations ... attention to individuals' experiences, values and beliefs should be a priority and we ought not to regard this level of analysis as unworthy of research. Qualitative methodologies provide a rich array of cognitive tools for incorporating phenomenology and agency issues into interlevel theories.
>
> (Ward, 2014: 140)

Ward's inclination towards building theory through inter-disciplinary means and collaboration is important. However, 'theory knitting', or 'integrative pluralism' (Ward, 2014) may sound like a fruitful strategy for the development of 'unified theory' but it may also be a recipe for episte-mological incoherence and theoretical confusion. The following comment perhaps provides a good illustration of current thinking in the field of sex offending:

> While there may not be a gene(s) for rape or child sexual offending, there is a growing conviction that the cognitive neurological systems of sex offenders may be functionally abnormal in some way and that therefore understanding the nature of such malfunctioning mechanisms may be our best bet for prevention and effective management.
>
> (Ward, 2014: 132)

This 'conviction' has in fact been a persistent feature of theorizing that has dominated the sex offending literature (and as a consequence popular discourse on sex offenders) and is more closely associated with the disciplinary expertise and epistemological leanings of those formulating hypotheses and proposing theoretical arguments than any widespread agreement among the academic community.

Indeed, this summary demonstrates the lack of substantive engagement by clinical and psychological approaches with the theoretical developments within feminism and sociology (see Brown, 2012 for an exception to this) and this is reflected in the nature of the literature and concepts that inform them. Thus, while key theoretical developments include reference to the importance of 'sociocultural' factors (e.g. Finkelhor and Araji, 1986; Marshall and Barbaree, 1990, 2000) and the 'ecological niche' (Ward *et al.*, 2006) in fact they do little more than pay lip-service to the idea that CSA is a *social* phenomenon. Thus, Cowburn and Myers (2015: 676) argue that:

> ... while such theorists note the importance of the social context and cultures wherein offending occurs, this is given little or no sustained attention in their theories of sex offending or therapeutic programs ... Given that sexual offences occur in social contexts that may contribute substantially to their onset, development, and maintenance, a comprehensive theory must incorporate social and cultural issues and aim to improve not only therapy but also social/public policy responses to sex crime.

In other words, there must be a much greater appreciation for the 'sex offender' as a thoroughly *social* agent, and this requires theoretical and conceptual frameworks that enable the social to be fully captured within theorizing (rather than being largely superfluous to it) without losing sight of the individual social agent. Furthermore, a key element of all the theories discussed above is that they focus exclusively on the perpetrator: that is, they construct all sexual offending as an action carried out by an individual within a one-sided power relation rather than as an encounter, or relation, between *two* 'social agents'. The effect is that the *child* is virtually absent in any meaningful sense, sometimes reduced simply to an 'opportunity' or 'situational factor' and thus objectified. Given that most sexual abuse is perpetrated by those known to the child, this seems unsatisfactory. I intend to demonstrate that by drawing from a broader range of theoretical perspectives and going beyond the established theorizing of those who take paedophilia/CSA as their focus, the relative contribution of medical and psychological approaches can be more appropriately positioned when considering childhood sexual exploitation and abuse. The main opposition to these approaches has come from feminism.

Feminist approaches to sexual violence and abuse

Feminist approaches are often simultaneously sociological approaches, but not exclusively. Therefore, I discuss them separately from sociological perspectives. This also serves to acknowledge the significant contribution they have made to the recognition of child sexual abuse as a serious social problem and one that extends well beyond notions of criminality.

For Cossins (2000: 41) 'it is possible to discern an ongoing tension in academic work between feminist explanations and non-feminist psychological and biological theories of men's sexual attraction to children'. Indeed, in response to her work, Purvis and Ward (2006: 309) state 'perhaps one of the most notable shortcomings of feminist literature on child sexual abuse is the feminist tendency to dismiss the value of psychological research'. Unsurprisingly, psychology-based work conducted by researchers with a close interest in the therapeutic context place great value on the necessity for any theory to have a 'clinical utility', and this emphasis lies at the heart of psychology's approach to sexual offending. Thus, Purvis and Ward (2006: 304) claim 'the difficulty for a radical feminist perspective [of CSA] is that it does not provide a clinical framework for changing the dispositions and behavior of sexually aggressive men'. Of course, the focus of the therapist/clinician is perfectly reasonable and pragmatic. One of their key functions is to assist the individual offender to reduce offending behaviour. Thus, the more that is known about offending behaviour (arguably) and offence patterns, including knowledge of offending 'pathways' and recidivism (Jones, 2012) the better we are able to understand the individuals that present themselves in treatment and counselling programmes. Yet this does not imply that such approaches offer the conceptual tools required for a comprehensive theoretical account of the social phenomenon of rape, or the sexual abuse of children. Nor should it be assumed that the ultimate test for a *theory* of sexual offending against children is whether it can prescribe a clinical solution or treatment that will 'fix' the individual perpetrator. Furthermore:

> Theories that do not look beyond clinical utility are limited because sex offending is not confined to a discrete population of offenders, whose risk can be reduced and who can be supported in their desistance from offending. While some sex offenders may receive effective help, there is always a new population emerging.
>
> (Cowburn and Myers, 2015: 676)

Feminist theory, then, situates sexual violence within wider inequalities and gendered power relations and looks well beyond the individual motivations and proclivities of the male sex offender and, indeed, beyond those that engage in behaviour considered to be deviant and/or criminal.

Following quickly on the heels of feminist analyses of rape (e.g. Brown-miller, 1975; Griffin, 1971) feminist activists and researchers have played the most significant role in politicizing the issue of childhood sexual abuse (e.g. Rush, 1980). The work of Florence Rush (1980) was pivotal and offers a crucial insight into the development of attitudes to adult-child sex over the past four decades:

> It is difficult to be patient with contemporary attitudes toward the sexual abuse of children. A current inclination to view child-adult sex as harmless and a reluctance to hold molesters responsible for their behaviour has encouraged sexual liberationists to insist that in matters of sex 'children aren't always children anymore', that pedophilia is a victimless crime and, comes the sexual revolution, 'the taboo of pedo-philia will fall away'. This new morality has also spurred organized pedophiles to come forward and claim sex with children as a civil right, and encouraged some professionals to 'scientifically' defend the practice.
>
> (Rush, 1980: 1)

Thus, Ken Plummer's comments, a year later, are noteworthy: 'pedophilia cannot, in sociological terms, be seen as inherently deviant; it must be seen as a stigmatizing categorization historically produced in certain kinds of societies' (1981: 236). This perhaps also reveals tensions between (fem-inist) activism and (male) intellectual endeavours within the academy. Arguably, the male-dominated theorizing of sexual offending within the 'hard' sciences (e.g. neuroscience, psychology and criminology), which con-tinue to substantively ignore feminist arguments, is also an illustration of continuing tensions within the field that have much more to do with per-sonal values and beliefs than the objective collection of 'scientific facts'. Thus, Cowburn (2005: 221) observes that feminist 'voices have largely been ignored in forensic consideration of male sex offenders'.

Feminist theories of sexual violence

Cowburn and Dominelli (2001: 402) illustrate the feminist (and socio-logical) critique: 'medico-legal discourses minimize sexual violence by individualizing and pathologizing this kind of behaviour, thereby divert-ing attention from addressing its underlying social causes and links to hegemonic masculinity'. Generally, then, feminist perspectives on CSA are critical of individualist accounts that entirely or substantively ignore the evident gender aspect of CSA. According to Doan (2005: 304) 'fem-inist understandings ... compel an analysis that connects [CSA] to the hegemonic constructions of family and masculinity that support it'. Thus, 'the feminist perspective examines child sexual abuse within its wider social context' but 'there exists no single feminist theory' (Seymour, 1998: 415–416).

Feminist theory, unsurprisingly, locates gendered power relations at the centre of theorizing on sexual violence and identifies widespread sexist and misogynist attitudes as fundamental for an understanding of sexual violence. Sexual abuse and exploitation is, then, 'intrinsic to a system of male supremacy' (Herman, 1990: 177–178) where 'males are socialized to adopt a predatory approach to sexuality and to use sex to assert power over females' (Seymour, 1998: 416). Thus, Scully (1990: 166) argues, men are sexually violent 'not because they are idiosyncratic or irrational, but because they have learned that in this culture sexual violence is rewarding'. According to Herman (1990: 177–178):

> If … the social definition of sexuality involves the erotization [*sic*] of male dominance and female submission, then the use of coercive means to achieve sexual conquest may represent a crude exaggeration of prevailing norms, but not a departure from them … It is a commonplace notion that men who commit sex crimes must be 'sick'. Feminists contend, rather, that these men are all too normal.

Arguably, the medical-model approach stems from the fact that sexual activity with children has recently been classified as a 'serious social problem' (Kempe, 1978)[3] that for neuro-scientists, psychiatrists and psychologists translates to a 'serious psychological dysfunction' or 'disorder'. This starting point – the hegemonic perspective in the field – has served to immediately distance the man who seeks sexual activity with children from the 'normal' male population, assisted by media coverage which continues to reinforce the narrative of the 'evil' paedophile and the 'monster paedo' (e.g. Chippindale, 2015; ITV1, 2009; see Critcher, 2002) which in turn trains the general perception that child sex offenders are 'nothing like us', or 'nothing like normal men'.

Building on early feminist perspectives on sexual violence (e.g. Herman, 1981), Kelly (1988) developed the notion of a *continuum of sexual violence* which emphasizes and illustrates it's relation to the 'everyday aspects of male behaviour' (Kelly, 1988: 75). This conceptualization of sexual violence remains influential (Cowburn and Myers, 2015).

Kelly's Continuum of Sexual Violence

Liz Kelly's contribution to the field of sexual violence has been profound. She notes that when she began researching the area of sexual violence 'many key feminist texts continued to differentiate men who used violence from the majority of "normal" men' (Kelly, 1988: xvii). Kelly (1988) offers a definition of sexual violence that (regrettably) excludes male victims:

Sexual violence includes any physical, visual, verbal or sexual act that is experienced by the woman or girl, at the time or later, as a threat, invasion or assault, that has the effect of hurting or degrading her and/ or takes away her ability to control intimate contact.

(Kelly, 1988: 41)

Official statistics continue to demonstrate that females are more likely to experience sexual violence and abuse and that males are overwhelmingly (but certainly not exclusively) the perpetrators (Brown and Walklate, 2012). Such a definition, however, excludes male experiences of sexual violence and is, therefore, clearly inadequate (as noted in the introduction, Brown and Walklate (2012) correct this).

However, importantly, Kelly introduced the concept of a continuum to 'enable women to make sense of their own experiences by showing how "typical" and "aberrant" male behaviour shade into one another' (Kelly, 1988: 75). The continuum comprises 11 forms of violence generated from research interviews with 60 women. It is deliberately not presented as a hierarchy, but instead 'moves from experiences which were most common in women's lives to those which were least common' (Kelly, 1988: 78); as follows: (1) threat of violence; (2) sexual harassment; (3) pressure to have sex; (4) sexual assault; (5) obscene phone calls; (6) coercive sex; (7) domestic violence; (8) sexual abuse; (9) flashing; (10) rape; (11) incest. In Brown and Walklate's (2012) recent celebration and critique of her work, the categories of Kelly's continuum have been criticized as excluding many forms of sexual violence (e.g. female genital mutilation), however, Kelly (2012, *preface*) observes that there is 'no reason in principle why the continuum concept cannot accommodate them'.

For Brown (2012: 174) 'sexually violent behaviours arise from both normative and pathological routes'. She argues that the categories of Kelly's continuum 'are not mutually exclusive and some are higher order categories which can themselves be broken down into more specific behaviours' (Brown, 2012: 159). Drawing on the work of David Canter in particular (e.g. Canter, 2000; Canter and Youngs, 2009) Brown (2012: 170) argues that Kelly's continuum can be reconceptualized by differentiating between 'core behaviours of sexual violence' and more specific 'behaviour patterns associated with different classes of sexual violence' (Brown, 2012: 170). She then presents a 'model differentiating subclasses of sexual violence' which 'hypothesises that each subclass of sexual violence [e.g. rape, sexual harassment] would have behaviours that are typical of all classes of sexual violence' as well as 'distinguishable behavioural patterns associated with different types' (Brown, 2012: 172). Brown (2012: 174) claims her model 'offers a means to differentiate offenders/perpetrators with a view to assessing risk factors ... designing programmed interventions with offenders, aiding detection, and assessing and treating them'.

Brown focuses on criminal behaviour (excluding CSA) and her development of Kelly's continuum clearly focuses on the psychology of 'offenders' and the goal of prediction, detection and effective treatment, rather than 'the connections between sexual violence and other aspects of male dominance and women's subordination' (Kelly, 1988: 231). However, it will be interesting to see if research in sport finds value in applying her model to develop theory. Kelly's (1988) original call for the necessity of collective action to bring about cultural change had a substantial impact, however, she recently observed that 'decades of reform, new policy and practices have made such little difference in the overall picture' (Kelly, 2012, *preface*).

Seymour's (1998) 'Extended Feminist Perspective'

Feminists (e.g. Seymour, 1998) and non-feminists (e.g. Purvis and Ward, 2006) alike have argued, 'the feminist perspective has tended to develop as a critique of other theories rather than as a theory in itself' (Seymour, 1998: 418). Consequently, the question of why it appears that only *some* males take advantage of a gender order that socializes them as sexual predators and constructs them as dominant, has gone largely unanswered. In attempting to address this issue, Seymour (1998) 'extends' the feminist account.

Seymour (1998) accepts the accuracy of the feminist approach to sexual violence but is critical of feminist approaches that provide descriptions of patriarchy while failing to consider 'what motivates offenders, and why that motivation is directed through sexuality' (Seymour, 1998: 418). Seymour draws upon social learning theory to argue that the social construction of masculinity – characterized by emotional illiteracy, a low capacity for empathy, and a moral code that prioritizes domination and conquest (all in contrast to female socialization patterns) – should be at the centre of any attempt to understand why men sexually abuse children. Utilizing a feminist, psychoanalytical approach, Seymour goes on to address the specifically *sexual* component of CSA arguing that male *sexual* socialization 'encourages males to validate their masculinity through sexuality' (1998: 423). In addition, males are socialized to 'sexualize the expression of non-sexual emotions'; to 'be sexually responsive separate from the context of a relationship'; and 'to become sexually aroused in the absence of feelings of intimacy' (1998: 424). Seymour provides a strong general account of the social and cultural context in which patriarchal forces prioritize a particular notion of masculinity and male sexual practice and how 'hegemonic masculinity' (Connell, 1995) can be understood as the backdrop to the sexual abuse of children. She argues:

> No one aspect of socialization can by itself explain child-sexual abuse but, considered together, they offer an explanation. Patriarchy

provides males with the social opportunity for abuse. Male socialization provides the motivation for abuse. Male sexual socialization provides direction for expression of the motivation for abuse.

(Seymour, 1998: 425)

While I find much in her account to agree with, she also presents, men, as a group, singularly lacking a fundamental psychological capacity:

Because of the relative inability of males to distinguish between sexual and non-sexual expressions of affection, they may be more likely to perceive friendly and affectionate behaviour of children as having sexual connotation and invitation.

(Seymour, 1998: 424)

Furthermore, it seems as though the offender is in some way an individual (male) who turns to sex with a child on the basis of a particular psychological inadequacy or flaw:

...a male who feels insecure about his masculinity may compensate for these feelings by acting in an excessively masculine manner ... The offender punishes himself by punishing the child ... Thus by sexually dominating the child with whom he identifies, the offender counters his own inadequacy.

(Seymour, 1998: 419–420)

Therefore, while Seymour maintains a focus on the wider patriarchal culture and its effects on male psychology as a whole, in the final calculation the act of abuse is reduced to the actions of an individual (male) who is insecure, impaired or misguided, in some way. Thus, again, sexual offending is a manifestation of dysfunction, weakness and abnormality. So while the social context, or structure, is emphasized, her account lacks a clear or determinate theory of agency so that the man who sexually abuses a child is ultimately reduced to a malfunctioning offender.

Feminist writers and researchers, then, have revealed and contested the ideological and political ground upon which the sexual violence and abuse of women and children (particularly female children) sits and they have argued effectively for political action to generate cultural change. Indeed, a similar pattern occurred within the context of organized sport, a decade or so after the first feminist contributions to the general problem of child sexual abuse, when Celia Brackenridge challenged male-dominated sports governing bodies to reflect more critically on the environments they were responsible for and the dangers inherent for the female athlete within them (Brackenridge, 1986, 1992, 1994).

Brackenridge's Contingency Model of Sexual Exploitation in Sport

Brackenridge's (2001) *Spoilsports* represents by far the most extensive investigation of sexual exploitation and abuse in sport. Her body of work sets the direction of research in this field for many years to come and is compulsory reading for any student or researcher wishing to pursue studies in this area (and indeed anyone connected to sport wishing to provide a safer environment for children). Brackenridge approaches the problem of sexual exploitation and abuse principally from a feminist standpoint, however, she combines both psychological and sociological perspectives, drawing on a vast array of literature from within and especially beyond the study of sport.

According to Brackenridge (2001: 126) 'pathologising sexual abuse distracts from other much more useful areas of risk analysis and management to do with individual agency and the athlete, and perhaps, most importantly, the gender culture of sport.' She argues that 'all instances of sexual exploitation arise from expressions of agency within structural limits and cultural contexts … sport researchers [must] link their analyses of structure, culture and agency to case-studies and ethnographies of real-world settings' (Brackenridge, 2001: 135). Brackenridge (2001) provides a critical analysis of masculinity in sport and its relationship to sexual violence which underpins her work in this field. Attempting to provide an explanatory account that could 'capture three-dimensionally the multidimensional complexities of sexual exploitation in sport' (Brackenridge, 2001: 145), she introduces a 'contingency model of sexual exploitation in sport' (Brackenridge, 2001: 140) where (high or low) levels of *risk* of, and *resistance* to, sexual exploitation are contingent upon three interacting dimensions: (a) coach inclination; (b) sport opportunity; and (c) athlete vulnerability. This model represented a 'work-in-progress towards finding a comprehensive theory of sexual exploitation in sport' (Brackenridge, 2001: 145). At time of writing there appears to have been very little testing or development of Brackenridge's model. She concludes that 'any theoretical resolution will have to incorporate both the organizational sexuality of sport and its interpersonal sex-gender relations in ways which expose the problem of men' (Brackenridge, 2001: 241). Brackenridge's perspective has greatly influenced my approach to sexual exploitation in sport and I return to her ideas throughout the book.

A sociological critique

According to Jones (2012: 181) 'sociology can offer historically and culturally informed discussions from a range of perspectives to open the door on the once secret world of sexual violence'. Sociological perspectives (which includes much feminist writing) have often been critical of psychology's approach to the problem of sexual violence. According to Cossins (2000: 177):

> Although not explicitly stated in the psychological literature, sexual deviance is not an objective scientific measure but merely constitutes a subjective evaluation of what researchers consider, from their own subjective standpoints, to be socially unacceptable sexual behaviour.

This illustrates well the manner in which sociological perspectives determinedly problematize categories used to conceptualize and define the object of concern. Thus, for Bourdieu, the research act is an act of construction; in the act of carrying out research, researchers construct the object with which they are concerned and the labels, categories, definitions that are generated are the manifestations of this process of construction.

For Jenks (2005b: 96) explanations of child abuse should originate not within malfunctioning individuals but 'within the context of changing social structures' and from the perspective of 'a childhood historicity'. He claims 'it is not essentially that the character or pattern of our actions towards children has altered but that our threshold of tolerance of potentially 'abusive' conduct has lowered' (2005b: 99). Jenks (2005b) argues 'the source of blame for this abuse ... should really be sought in the way that we have, over time, come to organize our social relationships' (114); thus, the potential for abuse 'resides within the differentials of both power and status' (93). While Jenks does not refer to the earlier work of Gil (1975) it would seem that such an analysis owes at least some debt to Gil's early comments on the origins of child abuse. Originally published in the *American Journal of Orthopsychiatry*, it is the foundation upon which a number of key theorists have built. According to Gil (1975):

> The most fundamental causal level of child abuse consists of a cloister of interacting elements, to wit, a society's basic social philosophy, its dominant value premises, its concept of humans; the nature of its social, economic, and political institutions, which are shaped by its philosophy and value premises and which in turn reinforce that philosophy and these values; and, finally, the particular quality of human relations prevailing in the society, which derives from its philosophy, values, and institutions.
>
> (In Donnelly and Oates, 2000: 65)

For Gil, then, it is the nature of society's basic approach to human relations, and particularly adult-child relations, that serve as indicators of child abuse. Gil (1975) refers to three 'levels of manifestation' which 'identify the agents and the settings in which children may experience abuse': (1) the familial (or home) level; (2) the institutional level; and (3) the societal level.

Prior to Gil's (1975) analysis, discussions of child maltreatment focused on the family environment and the role of parents in perpetrating abuse; crucially, Gil 'expands the definition of child maltreatment' and 'adds many forms of institutional abuse' (Donnelly and Oates, 2000: 61). My approach is closely aligned with Gil and the 'ecological approach' to child maltreatment (e.g. Belsky, 1980; Kenny and Wurtele, 2012) where 'child abuse is understood to be a product of the characteristics of the environments in which it occurs rather than simply being the result of the actions of certain individuals' (Jack, 2001: 185). In this fashion, Gil (1975) argues:

> ...any human phenomenon, at any moment, involves both social and individual elements. In real life, these elements are inseparable ... child abuse, at any level of manifestation, may be understood as acts or inactions of individuals, on their own or as institutional agents, whose behaviour reflects societal forces mediated through their unique personalities.
>
> (In Donnelly and Oates, 2000: 65)

As I will discuss below, such an approach bears a striking resemblance to the sociological theory of Pierre Bourdieu (e.g. 1977; 1998). Thus, for Gil and others, in explaining child abuse, the social and the cultural is fundamental. Nigel Parton (1979, 1981, 1985) built on the work of Gil, drawing attention to the culture of institutions over traditional concerns with the individual and the family, arguing that the causes of CSA 'may reside elsewhere in the social structure' (Parton, 1985: 168). Similarly, for Kitzinger (1997: 185):

> Debates about the sexual abuse of children are deeply embedded in discourses about childhood – what it is and what it should be. However, much of the 'pro-child' discussion, even many of the most radical 'child-centred' or 'empowerment' approaches, have succeeded in *problematizing child sexual abuse without problematizing childhood as a structural position within society* ... Ultimately, it is childhood as an institution that makes children 'vulnerable' ... The risk of abuse is built into childhood as an institution itself ... Child abuse is not an anomaly but part of the structural oppression of children (my emphasis).

Therefore, according to Wyness (2000: 65) 'we cannot rule out the possibility that a starting point for the analysis of child sexual abuse is the social structural position of childhood'.

Yet, as discussed above, it is frequently the 'anomalous' (Jenks, 2005b) 'demonized' (Young, 1999) malfunctioning individual who is drawn to the heart of the issue, rather than the commonplace features of the society and specific social contexts within which they are situated. Parton (2006) helps to develop this debate, framing the discussion in terms of an essentialist response to social anxiety, wrought by the transition from modern to late-modern society that emphasizes individualism. He argues that late modernity has wrought an 'ontological insecurity' (see Giddens, 1991) where traditional and secure certainties are undermined (Bauman, 2000; Young, 2009). Essentialist reductionism helps to resolve this insecurity. According to Young (1999) essentialism is 'the necessary prerequisite for the demonization of parts of society [which] allows the problems of society to be blamed upon "others" usually perceived as being on the edge of society' (quoted in Parton, 2006: 58). Thus, 'the monstrous is construed and experienced as "outside us" and is thus a quality possessed by monstrous others' (Parton, 2006: 58). Parton (2006) argues that we are in a period of 'uncertainty' and that during such times, notions of 'good' and 'evil' become prominent. Indeed, in the UK currently hardly a news report goes by without the mention of 'paedophilia' or 'child sexual abuse' and it appears that the paedophile (along with the 'Islamic Fundamentalist') has come to represent the embodiment of 'evil' in the West. As many commentators have noted, the prominence and persistence of the 'stranger danger' discourse (supported by science that reduces sexual violence to individual pathology) is contradicted by the empirical evidence on child abuse, yet remains 'significant in drawing our attention away from thinking of abuse within familiar settings' (Wyness, 2000: 60).

Drawing on the work of Laws (1994), Cowburn (2005: 226) argues that the difference between *normal* men and sex offenders 'continues to be unclear in research that examines the attitudes about, and proclivities towards, sexual violence in populations of normal adult men'. Nevertheless, notions of the damaged/malfunctioning individual obstruct recognition that men who seek sex with children are indeed *normal* men. The unintended consequence (although clearly convenient for many) has been to mask the sexual abuse of many children. That is to say, if the dominant narrative constructs sex offenders as monstrous misfits, there is no reason to think that men in positions of influence and prestige could be abusing children. In the UK and across the globe, the flawed nature of this thinking is now abundantly clear as a steady stream of powerful, esteemed men are found guilty of multiple sex offences against children over many years.

Liddle's (1993) consideration of what a sociological account might offer is important to note:

> ...[a] sociological account of the male preponderance in child sexual abuse offers not only to give theoretical prominence to macro-level factors, such as those so effectively highlighted within feminist and other recent works on gender, but also to allow for a *theoretical*

linkage of these with the more local details of everyday sexual politics, and with the emotional and other complexities which seem to occasion matters of sexual desire and attachment (my emphasis).

(Liddle, 1993: 105)

The 'theoretical linkage' Liddle (1993) refers to is in fact a long-standing problem for social science, often referred to as the 'structure-agency' debate (Bourdieu and Wacquant, 1992; Marshall, 1998: 10). This debate has been central to sociology and feminist social theory (McNay, 2000) where theorists 'must straddle the space between recognizing macro-conditions, while also having some understanding of how such macro-conditions are lived out ... at the level of very different individuals' (Whitehead and Barrett, 2001: 14). The same 'straddling' is also a require-ment for any sociological analysis of childhood sexual abuse. Anne Cossins (2000) takes up this challenge in her theory of the *male* perpetration of sexual offending against children.

Cossins' (2000) 'Power-Powerlessness Theory of Child Sexual Abuse'

Cossins (2000: 111) focuses on 'those elements of masculine sexuality that are common to all forms of masculinity' that she refers to as 'exploitative masculine sexuality'. Cossins (2000: 88) argues:

> ...different masculinities contain normative sexual elements that are reproduced and affirmed by child sex offenders in a cultural environ-ment where the objects of culturally normative masculine sexual desire are constructed by reference to characteristics such as passivity and receptivity ... and because of the historical and cultural variability of men's sexual practices (such as heterosexuality, homosexuality, bisexu-ality and transvestism), sexual practices with children are related to that variability and, are, therefore, a particular sexual choice for some men ... this argument raises the uncomfortable possibility that sexual practices with children could be a sexual choice that child sex offend-ers make, in much the same way as other men make choices about engaging in sexual practices with adults.

This argument may be uncomfortable but it seems eminently sensible. Building on the work of Colton and Vanstone (1998: 514–515) who argue 'abuse can be seen as a re-assertion of masculinity and the maintenance of the ideal male role of dominance', Cossins (2000: 134) claims:

> Child sex offenders are actively involved in a 'masculinising practice' in that because of the centrality of sexuality for establishing relations

of power between men, child sex offending is a specific sexual practice for the accomplishment of masculinity by some men in a cultural environment where men's lives are characterised by a combination of power and powerlessness.

Thus, Cossins firmly acknowledges the feminist perspective that sexual offending is overwhelmingly a male offence permitted and approved through the patriarchal privileging of male over female. She also takes on the point made by masculinity scholars, such as Connell (1995, 2000), and Kimmel and Messner (2001) that men may well occupy a structural position of dominance but that does not always accurately characterize men's subjectivity, i.e. they might *feel* power*less* even while *being* power*ful* (Kimmel, 1994). While I agree with much of Cossins's (2000) perspective, the application of her theory to the life histories of perpetrators in order to explain why they, and *all* male perpetrators, abuse children, is not so convincing.

In her 're-analysis' of Colton and Vanstone's (1996) interviews with (male) offenders, Cossins considers the narratives of five perpetrators. One is 'Ronnie', a homosexual man who reports struggling with his sexuality as a boy and experiencing 'emotional rejection and constant criticism' from his father and who as a young man experienced a fear of 'going into pubs, clubs, places where male-orientated dominated' and an inability to form sexual relationships with adults (Cossins, 2000: 226). According to Ronnie:

> I think that, in my case, the fact that I found it difficult to make relationships with … adult males, and how easy it was to make a relationship with non-adults … my ego was definitely given a boost that these people wanted my company … I had a tremendous comfort out of that, if only I hadn't gone the full way in sexual abuse. I'm sure perhaps I could have had that comfort, which in a way we all do need.
> (Colton and Vanstone, 1996: 121)

Ronnie seeks to rationalize, or justify, his offences by recourse to his own inadequacy (inability to 'make relationships with adults'[4]) previously explained through an emotionally abusive family structure (a rejection of his homosexual identity). He also refers to the realization (as a 24-year-old) that he would never be a father: 'in time you get used to something … you accept that. But I suppose I crept into abuse through that need' (Colton and Vanstone, 1996: 121). Thus, he explains his behaviour as the product of a misguided attempt to find 'comfort' and the 'need' to be a father – a prospect denied to him as a homosexual man – in other words, Ronnie experiences very natural/normal needs which he chooses to meet through inappropriate means. Yet Cossins says little about the self-serving nature of Ronnie's narrative, arguing instead:

...it is possible that his fear of adult male relationships can be attributed to his previous experiences of powerlessness as a boy. Arguably, one way that these experiences were able to be alleviated was by engaging in sexual practices with socially inferior boys in circumstances where he exercised the public power of a school teacher.

(Cossins, 2000: 227–228)

Colton and Vanstone (1998: 517) note how the perpetrators they interviewed 'invariably seek psychologically rather than sociologically defined explanations for their behaviour'. Yet in seeking evidence for her 'power-powerlessness' thesis, Cossins (2000) appears to understate the fact that the men's accounts are often served up as tacit rationalizations for their offences, essentially founded on the 'cycle of abuse' and the narrative of psychological malfunction, intended to diminish their culpability.

Thus, we also hear David's account, a Catholic priest, who 'describes a childhood in which he was the youngest of a large family ... in which he was the "last in the pecking order" and describes relationships of power between himself and other members of his family, in particular his older brothers' (Cossins, 2000: 231). He goes on to describe a 'macho' working-class upbringing where 'you had to be very street-wise and very hard' and emotions had to be 'suppressed' (Colton and Vanstone, 1996: 67) as did his academic ability. According to Colton and Vanstone (1998: 521) this:

Exemplifies how a particular definition of masculinity creates distortion in what, on the face of it, appears to be acceptance rather than denial of harm. By defining masculinity as cold and callous and to do with physical power, the abuser, even when acknowledging the concept of victim, can minimize his behaviour.

Again, the perpetrator casts himself as a victim, misunderstood – emotionally exceptional – through which he rationalizes his actions, and asks others to do the same. He extols us to understand his abusive actions through the narrative of victimhood (emotional abuse), in other words, it was not his fault, or at least *not really*. As David states:

...very much to do with being isolated from friends, family ... suddenly being on your own and actually craving company. I believe that the abuse developed through this craving company ... And then progressing that need for company into fulfilling other needs within yourself.

(Cossins, 2000: 234–235)

Thus, while obviously unable to deny the sexual activity, constructed as 'other needs' – that is, needs common to all – he constructs himself as suffering a very natural/normal reaction ('craving company'). Therefore, he constructs his actions as misguided attempts to alleviate an emotionally distressing situation – crucially, a situation that anyone would find distressing. In other words, it was not how he would have behaved if factors beyond his control had not placed him in such an understandable state of anxiety. Thus, he constructs a narrative whereby his abusive actions were determined by things external to him and, crucially, as an individual who was the victim of circumstance. However, according to Cossins (2000: 235): 'It can be argued that David's experiences of powerlessness as a man were likely to have been a necessary pre-condition for his subsequent sexual behaviour with children…'

Thus, Cossins (2000: 125–6) argues '…it can be said that child sex offending allows a man to accomplish masculinity and overcome experiences of powerlessness *when his power is in jeopardy* [e.g. 'lack of sexual potency'] as a result of his relationships with other men…' (my emphasis). I would not discount such a possibility and Cossins's (2000) emphasis on normative masculine sexuality is important, however, constructing these men's actions as a reaction to stressful situations couched within a psychology of weakness, lack, deficit, etc., seems to move the debate back towards the perpetrator with pathological failings.

Cossins (2000) argues, following many feminist and pro-feminist writers, that sexual activity is one important way (perhaps *the* most important) in which men engage with, or express, the struggle to 'do masculinity'. However, the 'theoretical linkage' that Liddle (1993) argues for is not apparent. While Cossins (2000) argues that men *choose* to commit sexual abuse, this choice appears to be driven by psychological weakness or malfunction, because of their (apparent) inability to live up to normative masculine standards. Thus, she concludes:

> Some offenders, in particular those who practised homosexual masculinity, appeared to experience chronic levels of powerlessness in their lives … most offenders discussed how they had been shamed by hegemonic masculine culture.
>
> (236–237)

Again, a causal explanation is sought and constructed on the basis that sexually subjecting a child must emanate, fundamentally, from an experience resembling trauma and anxiety. Thus, it is important to ask (of Cossins, and others) how is social action conceived within this theory? How is choice, resistance and agency theorized within this power/powerlessness scheme? Is all men's action explicable by reference to powerlessness or only the act of sexually abusing a child? If 'experiences of powerlessness, as a result of their relationships with other men, are central to understanding a man's motivation for child sex offending' (Cossins,

2000: 238) does it underpin all 'deviant' sexual acts? Does it hold across cultures and across time? In addition, do the principles of the theory also apply to female perpetrators? While Cossins (2000) works hard to locate CSA within normative masculine sexual practice and gender relations, she ultimately relies on apparent pathological failings within individual men to explain their offending.

Criminological approaches

In summarizing the current situation in research on sexual violence and abuse prevention, Smallbone and McKillop (2015: 180) argue that 'the two dominant approaches seem to be a feminist model, which frames the problem at the broadest sociocultural level, and a clinical model, which typically frames the problem at the narrowest individual level'. Wortley and Smallbone (2010: 11) note that 'many researchers and clinicians working in the sexual offending area have continued to focus attention on the personal, intrapsychic dimensions of the behaviour and to overlook the contributions of immediate circumstances'. More particularly, Nigel Parton (2014: 192) recently argued that '…we need to recognize that child maltreatment has cultural, institutional and structural dimensions as well as individual ones and that these must be taken seriously and addressed'. Wortley and Smallbone (2010: 11) argue that research has recently 'challenged the view that most sexual offenders are dedicated, serial offenders driven by irresistible sexual urges' and point to a range of research findings that 'suggest that immediate environmental factors were important in many cases'. These are condensed below:

1   *Late onset of the behaviour*: it seems men are most likely to abuse children after the age of 30, suggesting they are not psychologically predisposed to abuse children…

2   A *low incidence of chronic sexual offending*: contrary to popular belief, once identified, sex offenders tend not to re-offend…

3   A *high incidence of previous non-sexual offences*: suggests that sex offenders are offenders first, sex offenders second…

4   A *low incidence of stranger abuse*: convenience seems to be a major determinant in which children an adult abuses…

5   A *low incidence of networking among offenders*: very few offenders are part of a 'paedophile subculture'…

6   A *low incidence of child pornography use*: the significant majority of offenders do not display interest in 'child pornography'…

7   A *low incidence of paraphilic (sexually deviant) interests*: very few offenders could be diagnosed with a paraphilia other than paedophilia…

(Wortley and Smallbone, 2010: 11)

Recently, then, some researchers have suggested that 'situational' approaches offer a more productive line of investigation. Wortley and Smallbone (2010) enjoined other researchers to consider the 'situational prevention of child sexual abuse' which they describe as a:

> ...criminological model that shifts the focus from supposed deficits of offenders to aspects of immediate environments ... It is based on the premise that all behaviour is the result of an interaction between the characteristics of the actor and the circumstances in which an act is performed. The immediate environment is more than a passive back-drop against which action is played out; it plays a fundamental role in initiating and shaping that action...
>
> (Wortley and Smallbone, 2010: 8)

Clearly, this strongly resembles perspectives within feminist and sociological approaches. However, Wortley and Smallbone (2010) claim that situational crime prevention is underpinned by two theoretical perspectives. First, the rational choice perspective where 'offenders are portrayed as active decision makers who undertake cost-benefit analyses of the crime opportunities' they are presented with (Wortley and Smallbone, 2010: 9). Prevention, therefore, focuses on manipulating environments to reduce opportunities, 'making crime more risky, increasing the effort [required] to commit crime, and reducing the rewards of crime' (Wortley and Small-bone, 2010: 9). The second perspective underpinning the situational approach derives from 'research in behavioural, social and environmental psychology [where] there is a subtle and intimate relationship between individuals and their immediate environments' (Wortley and Smallbone, 2010: 9). Here, the 'behaviour of an individual may be highly variable from one situation to the next' with the immediate environment seen as playing an 'instigating role' (Wortley and Smallbone, 2010: 10). This seems a promising development and provides potential grounds for the development of theory from previously disparate and oppositional perspectives.

It appears, then, that influential researchers on sex offending, previously working from within individualist-orientated or offender-focused frameworks, are now beginning to focus more attention on the environment in which CSA occurs and, crucially, to conceptualize it as a key factor in the commission of sexual crimes. 'Situational crime prevention, then, is about creating safe environments rather than creating safe individuals ... the criminal event rather than the offender becomes the unit of analysis' (Wortley and Smallbone, 2010: 8). This seems to offer the potential for much greater dialogue between sociology and psychology in considering CSA. Such dialogue is also needed within the field of research into sexual violence in sport. This development also resonates with child protection policy in sport, which is, in essence, a situational prevention approach aimed at creating safe sport environments (Boocock, 2002). More recently, Smallbone and McKillop (2015: 178) advocate a public health model which adopts a 'social ecological framework' that:

> ...situates individual offenders and victims within their natural ecological context, and locates risk and protective factors at various levels of the ecological systems in which the individual develops and lives. Thus the causes of SVA [sexual violence and abuse] exist not just within individuals, but also within the family, peer, organizational, neighbourhood, and sociocultural systems within which they are embedded.

This is a well-established position within sociology and resonates with the underpinning approach adopted here. However, it does seem to require a fuller working out of social action and the individual(s) who acts within these systems, as I will discuss below.

Summary

In this chapter, I have discussed key contemporary theories of sexual offending against children. The main weakness in theoretical accounts of sex offending, especially offending against children, appear to be an absence of a determinate theory of agency that connects the individual to the social in an authentic fashion. Typically the sex offender (regardless of the specific offence) is constructed not as an individual, autonomous agent, but as an automaton, mechanically reacting to internal or external cues. Particularly, while the role of the social environment (or 'ecological niche') is widely acknowledged, it is largely untheorized other than to note that some negative environments (abusive families, war) can be psychologically harmful and lead to neurological and psychological problems. Where the social context is approached critically, the individual male that commits sexual violence either substantively disappears from accounts or is again constructed as acting from a 'lack'. However, recent criminological perspectives draw on 'rational actor theory' which seems to indicate a shift in focus within the field of sex offending research (discussed further in Chapter 2). Finally, and despite the apparent shift to acknowledge the importance of the interaction between the offender and the environment (Wortley and Smallbone, 2010), the child and young person that is sexually subjected is also mostly absent from theorizing and appears simply as a 'victim', often described as being selected due to particular vulnerabilities. Celia Brackenridge's (2001) focus on sexual exploitation in a specific social space (namely sport) insists that theoretical accounts incorporate not simply the offender and the environment, but also the child/young person.

In other words, her 'contingency model' and her wider theoretical discussion of sports culture, emphasize a *relational* approach to attempts to understand and explain sexual exploitation.

I conclude by setting down three principle conditions for theoretical development:

1 Sociocultural environments must be approached critically and these critical accounts must be incorporated *within* theories of sexual violence;
2 Explanatory accounts must provide the 'theoretical linkage' between the macro and the micro (the structural and the individual);
3 The gendered nature of sexual violence and child sexual abuse must be accounted for, while not precluding female offending.

A coherent articulation of social action which can meet these conditions must underpin any attempt to theorize sexual violence, and it is to this problem that I will now turn.

Notes

1 Also Finkelhor's 'Four Factor Model' (Finkelhor *et al.*, 1986: 124–137).
2 'Paedophile' first appeared in 'The Times index ... only in 1977 and was used in scholarly works, at the time, to refer to a lone male sexually interested in children' (Parton, 2006: 117–118).
3 Although psychiatric research on sex offending against children goes back to at least the mid-1950s with the term 'sexual abuse' appearing in the title of a research paper by D.W. Swanson as early as 1968 (see Virkkunen, 1981).
4 A common theme within the research literature (Finkelhor, 1986) and virtually monolithic within popular discourse.

References

Bauman, Z. (2000) *Liquid modernity*. Cambridge: Polity.
Belsky, J. (1980) Child maltreatment: an ecological integration. *American Psychologist*, 35(4): 320–335.
Boocock, S. (2002) The child protection in sport unit. *The Journal of Sexual Aggression*, 8(2): 99–106.
Bourdieu, P. (1977) *Outline of a theory of practice* [translation: R. Nice]. Cambridge: Cambridge University Press.
Bourdieu, P. (1989) Social space and symbolic power. *Sociological Theory*, 7(1): 14–25.
Bourdieu, P. (1998) *Practical reason: on the theory of action*. Cambridge: Polity Press.
Bourdieu, P. and Wacquant, L.D. (1992) *An invitation to reflexive sociology*. Cambridge: Polity Press.
Brackenridge, C.H. (1986) *Problem? What problem? Thoughts on a professional code of practice for coaches*. Unpublished paper presented to the Annual Conference of British Association of National Coaches, Bristol, England, December.

Brackenridge, C.H. (1992) Sexual abuse of children in sport: a comparative exploration of research methodologies and professional practice. *Pre-Olympic Scientific Congress*. Malaga, Spain, (14–19 July).

Brackenridge, C.H. (1994) Fair play or fair game: child sexual abuse in sport organisations. *International Review for the Sociology of Sport*, 29(3): 287–299.

Brackenridge, C.H. (2001) *Spoilsports: understanding and preventing sexual exploitation in sport*. London: Routledge.

Brown, J.M. (2012) Psychological perspectives on sexual violence: generating a general theory. *Handbook on sexual violence*. Oxon: Routledge, 156–179.

Brown, J.M. and Walklate, S.L. (eds.) (2012) *Handbook on sexual violence*. Oxon: Routledge.

Brownmiller, S. (1975) *Against our will: men, women and rape*. New York: Simon and Schuster.

Canter, D. (2000) Offender profiling and criminal differentiation. *Legal and Criminological Psychology*, 5: 23–46.

Canter, D. and Youngs, D. (2009) *Investigative psychology: offender profiling and the analysis of criminal action*. Chichester: Wiley.

Chippindale, M. (2015) Lord Brittan refused to ban evil peado ring. *Daily Star*, 30 May. Accessed at: www.dailystar.co.uk/news/latest-news/445277/Lord-Brittan-Home-secretary-pedophiles-evil-men.

Colton, M. and Vanstone, M. (1996) *Betrayal of trust: sexual abuse by men who work with children – In their own words*. London: Free Association Books.

Colton, M. and Vanstone, M. (1998) Sexual abuse by men who work with children: an exploratory study. *British Journal of Social Work*, 28: 511–523.

Connell, R.W. (1995) *Masculinities*. Cambridge: Polity.

Connell, R.W. (2000) *The men and the boys*. Cambridge, Polity.

Cossins, A. (2000) *Masculinities, sexualities and child sexual abuse*. The Hague: Kluwer Law International.

Cowburn, M. (2005) Hegemony and discourse: reconstruing the male sex offender and sexual coercion by men. *Sexualities, Evolution & Gender*, 7 (3): 215–231.

Cowburn, M. and Dominelli, L. (2001) Masking hegemonic masculinity: reconstructing the paedophile as the dangerous stranger. *British Journal of Social Work*, 31: 399–415.

Cowburn, M. and Myers, S. (2015) Sex offenders. In J. Wright (editor-in-chief) *International encyclopedia of the social and behavioural sciences* (2nd ed.). London: Elsevier, 672–677.

Critcher, C. (2002) Media, government and moral panic: the politics of paedophilia in Britain 2000–1. *Journalism Studies*, 3(4): 521–535.

Deer, C. (2012) Doxa. In M. Grenfell (2012) (ed.) *Bourdieu: key concepts* (2nd ed.). London: Routledge, 114–125.

Doan, C. (2005) Subversive stories and hegemonic tales of child sexual abuse: from expert legal testimony to television talk shows. *International Journal of Law in Context*, 1(3): 295–309. DOI: 10.1017/S1744552305003046.

Donnelly, A.C. and Oates, K. (2000) *Classic papers in child abuse*. Thousand Oaks, CA: Sage.

Finkelhor, D. (1984) *Child sexual abuse: new theory and research*. New York: Free Press.

Finkelhor, D. and Araji, S. (1986) Explanations of pedophilia: a four factor model. *Journal of Sex Research*, 22(2): 145–161.

Finkelhor, D. and Associates with Araji, S., Baron, L., Browne, A., Peters, S.D. and Wyatt, G.E. (1986) *A sourcebook on child sexual abuse*. London: Sage.

Giddens, A. (1991) *Modernity and self-identity: self and society in the late modern age*. Cambridge: Polity.

Gil, D.G. (1975) Unraveling child abuse. *American Journal of Orthopsychiatry*, 45(3): 346–56.

Griffin, S. (1971) Rape: the all-American crime. *Ramparts*. September: 26–35.

Groth, N.A., Hobson, W., and Gary, T. (1982) The child molester: clinical observations. In J. Conte and D. Shore (eds.) *Social work and child sexual abuse*. New York: Haworth, 129–144.

Herman, J.L. (1981) *Father-daughter incest*. Cambridge: Harvard University Press.

Herman, J.L. (1990) Sex offenders: a feminist perspective. In W.L. Marshall, D.R. Laws and H.E. Barbaree (eds.) *Handbook of sexual assault: issues, theories and treatment of the offender*. New York: Plenum Press, 177–193.

Howells, K. (1995) Child sexual abuse: Finkelhor's precondition model revisited. *Psychology, Crime and Law*, 1(3): 201–214.

Jack, G. (2001) An ecological perspective on child abuse. In P. Foley, J. Roche and S. Tucker (2001) (eds.) *Children in society: contemporary theory, policy and practice*. Basingstoke: Palgrave in association with the Open University, 185–194.

Jenks, C. (2005b) *Childhood* (2nd ed.). London: Routledge.

Jones, H. (2012) On sociological perspectives. In J.M. Brown, and S.L. Walklate, (eds.) *Handbook on sexual violence*. Oxon: Routledge, 181–202.

Kelly, L. (1988) *Surviving sexual violence*. Cambridge: Polity.

Kelly, L. (2012) Preface: standing the test of time? Reflections on the concept of the continuum of sexual violence. In J.M. Brown and S.L. Walklate (eds.) *Handbook on sexual violence*. Oxon: Routledge, xvii–xxvi.

Kempe, H.D. (1978) Sexual abuse: another hidden paediatric problem. *Pediatrics*, 62(3): 382–389.

Kenny, J.C. and Wurtele, S.K. (2012) Preventing childhood sexual abuse: an ecological approach. *Journal of Child Sexual Abuse*, 21(4): 361–367.

Kimmel, M. (1994) Masculinity as homophobia: fear, shame and silence in the construction of gender identity. In H. Brod and M. Kaufman (eds.) *Theorizing masculinities*. Thousand Oaks, CA: Sage, 119–141.

Kimmel, M.S. and Messner, M.A. (2001) *Men's lives* (2nd ed.). New York: Macmillan.

Kitzinger, J. (1997) Who are you kidding? Children, power and the struggle against sexual abuse. In A. James and A. Prout (eds.) *Constructing and reconstructing childhood: Contemporary issues in the sociological study of childhood*. London: Falmer Press, 165–189.

Laws, D.R. (1994) How dangerous are rapists to children? *The Journal of Sexual Aggression*, 1(1): 1–14.

Liddle, A.M. (1993) Gender, desire and child sexual abuse: accounting for the male majority. *Theory, Culture, and Society*, 10: 103–126.

Marshall, G. (1998) *Oxford dictionary of sociology*. Oxford: Oxford University Press.

Marshall, W.L. and Barbaree, H.E. (1990) An integrated theory of the etiology of sexual offending. In W.L. Marshall, D.R. Laws and H.E. Barbaree (eds.) *Handbook of sexual assault: issues, theories and treatment of the offender*. New York: Plenum Press, 257–275.

McNay, L. (2000) *Gender and agency: reconfiguring the subject in feminist and social theory*. Cambridge: Polity.

Moore, R. (2012) Capital. In M. Grenfell (ed.) *Bourdieu: key concepts* (2nd ed.). London: Routledge, 98–113.

Parton, N. (1979) The natural history of child abuse: a study in social problem definition. *British Journal of Social Work*, 9(4): 431–451.

Parton, N. (1981) Child abuse, social anxiety and welfare. *British Journal of Social Work*, 11: 391–414.

Parton, N. (1985) *The politics of child abuse*. London: Macmillan Press.

Parton, N. (2006) *Safeguarding childhood: early intervention and surveillance in a late modern society*. Basingstoke: Palgrave Macmillan.

Parton, N. (2014) *The politics of child protection: contemporary developments and future directions*. Basingstoke, Hants.: Palgrave Macmillan.

Plummer, K. (1981) Pedophilia: constructing a sociological baseline. In M. Cook and K. Howells (eds.) *Adult sexual interest in children*. London: Academic Press, 221–250.

Purvis, M. and Ward, T. (2006) The role of culture in understanding child sexual offending: examining feminist perspectives. *Aggression and Violent Behavior*, 11(3): 298–312.

Rush, F. (1980) *The best kept secret: sexual abuse of children*. New York: McGraw-Hill.

Scully, D. (1990) *Understanding sexual violence: a study of convicted rapists*. New York: HarperCollins.

Seymour, A. (1998) Aetiology of the sexual abuse of children: an extended feminist perspective. *Women's Studies International Forum*, 21(4): 415–427.

Smallbone, S.W. and McKillop, N. (2015) Evidence-informed approaches to preventing sexual violence and abuse. In P.D. Donnelly and C.L. Ward (eds.) *Oxford handbook of violence prevention*, 177–181.

Virkkunen, M. (1981) The child as participating victim. In M. Cook and K. Howells (eds.) *Adult sexual interest in children*. London: Academic Press, 121–134.

Ward, T. (2014) The explanation of sexual offending: from single factor theories to integrative pluralism. *Journal of Sexual Aggression*, 20(2): 130–141.

Ward, T. and Beech, A.R. (2006) An integrated theory of sexual offending. *Aggression and Violent Behaviour*, 11(11): 44–63.

Ward, T. and Hudson, S.M. (1998) The construction and development of theory in the sexual offending area: a meta-theoretical framework. *Sexual Abuse: A Journal of Research and Treatment*, 10: 47–63.

Whitehead, S.M. and Barrett, F.J. (2001) (eds.) *The masculinities reader*. Cambridge: Polity Press.

Wortley, R. and Smallbone, S. (2010) (eds.) *Situational prevention of child sexual abuse* (Crime Prevention Studies, vol. 19). London: Lynne Rienner Publishers.

Wyness, M.G. (2000) *Contesting childhood*. London: Falmer Press.

Young, J. (1999) *The exclusive society*. London: Sage.

Young, J. (2009) *The vertigo of late Modernity*. London: Sage.

Chapter 2

An alternative epistemology for approaching childhood sexual abuse

In the previous chapter, I examined current theorizing on sexual offending against children. I argue that theories of sexual offending that work back from the offence to the perpetrator through assumptions of neuropsychological abnormality and deficit are deeply problematic as they fail to provide the conceptual tools to enable *the social* dimension to be properly accounted for, interrogated and theorized. Thus, I have been critical of perspectives that focus on the perpetrator, as a malfunctioning individual, while noting the intent of sex offending theorists to develop broad, inclusive theories that recognize the sociocultural dimension. I also outlined the feminist and sociological critique, as well some shortcomings of these approaches which either fail to theorize social action or else fall back on notions of malfunction and deficit.

Without a clear ontological and epistemological standpoint to underpin research investigations and theory-making in this field, it seems we are left to gather 'surface facts' and 'knit' them together in a rather directionless, hopeful fashion. This is the clear advantage of feminist perspectives on sexual violence. The importance such writers place on a 'warts'n'all', reflexive approach (see Brackenridge, 2001) provides a coherence and a transparency that is mostly absent from other perspectives in the sex offending literature.

In this chapter, I outline a specific alternative epistemology and theoretical framework which forms the foundation for my empirical investigation and subsequent theorization. My intention is to make clear the ontological and epistemological origins of my approach and to introduce the reader to the key concepts I later apply. Chapter 6 puts this approach into practice by applying it to the accounts offered by those subjected to sex within sport settings.

Sex offenders, social agents and social practice

Child sexual abuse is a widespread and historically persistent practice (Jackson, 2000; Jones, 2000; Radbill, 1968). While it is a practice that cuts across class, ethnic *and* gender boundaries (Corby, 1993), as noted by many researchers (Cowburn and Myers, 2015; Smallbone and McKillop, 2015; Wykes and Welsh, 2009), men are overwhelmingly the perpetrators of sexual offences, but not exclusively (e.g. Elliot, 1993). From the evidence available, this also appears to be the case within sport (e.g. Brackenridge, 2001; Leahy *et al.*, 2002; Vertommen *et al.*, 2013). Nevertheless, female perpetrators have been reported and imprisoned (e.g. Claire Lyte in the UK). Therefore, a theory of CSA must first have a clear perspective on how social agents, *generally*, arrive at action. That is, unless behaviour that contravenes social and legal norms is considered somehow fundamentally distinct from all other (sociohistorical) behaviour, or if *men's* sex offending requires a different epistemology than *women's* sex offending, any theory of sexual abuse must first be underpinned by a general theory of action, or practice.

'Deviant' sexual activity is considered principally the intellectual territory of psychology and psychiatry (see Ward *et al.*, 2006), which seems to have had the effect of inhibiting the application of theoretical approaches and concepts at the disposal of *social* science. This problem is part of a much wider theoretical debate about how we account for the individual and his or her action. This disciplinary impasse is recognized by McNay (2000: 19) when she argues that the opposition between 'constructionist' and 'psychoanalytic' perspectives on subjectivity 'needs to be overcome if agency is to be understood both as historically variable and as driven by deep-seated and often opaque motivations'. A coherent conceptualization of the individual or 'social agent' is crucial to be able to approach questions about social action (or 'behaviour'). This is not to suggest that social science has settled this matter – far from it. In her critique of material feminism, McNay (2000: 16) argues that the focus of material feminists on macro sociocultural structures results in a determinist analysis which 'lacks an understanding of how these structural forces are worked through at the level of subject formation and agency'. In other words, what is absent from these accounts is a 'mediatory category such as agency' (16) to enable an understanding of how the structural functions, or plays-out, at the individual level.

It is this lack of an appropriate 'mediatory category' within theorizing the sexual subjection of children that I seek to address here. This is to specifically recall Liddle's (1993: 105) crucial insight that a sociological account of child sexual abuse must centre on 'processes of gendering and embodiment ... [and] allow for a theoretical linkage' between the macro and the micro; and that 'the element of choice is of considerable importance' (Liddle, 1993: 118). Similarly, in this account (and following Cossins, 2000: 88–89), the notion that sexually subjecting a child is a choice that adults make, is central (also Wortley and Smallbone, 2010). However, the notion of 'choice' is one that needs to be carefully constructed within theory.

According to McNay (2000: 22–23) within social theory, there has been an attempt to 'reconfigure agency in terms of the creativity of action' so that individuals are theorized as autonomous agents with the capacity to transcend the material context. However, she cautions that 'any theory of agency must be placed in the context of structural, institutional or inter-subjective constraints' (23). This issue is critical to the development of feminist and pro-feminist perspectives on CSA where gendered power relations, and 'hegemonic masculinity' (Connell, 1995; Connell and Messerschmidt, 2005) in particular, have been central to recent theoretical development and understanding (e.g. Cossins, 2000) drawing attention to the fact that male sexual violence and coercion is not confined to 'sexual deviants' (Kelly, 1988).[1]

However, drawing on the work of Hearn (2004), Cowburn (2005: 228) argues that while 'hegemonic masculinity' was originally intended to be a dynamic and fluid concept, a key weakness 'was that it had potential to become homogenous and of little critical value' and thus to 'distract attention from what men do'. He argues that 'to engage critically with acts of sexual coercion,' attention must now be focused on 'wider issues relating to men and how they exercise and maintain their individual and collective power' (Cowburn, 2005: 229). However, as I have argued, when theorists have gone beyond structuralist perspectives, in an attempt to combat the critique of determinism and a weak conceptualization of agency, the social agent (or 'perpetrator') ultimately appears as a social misfit, an abnormality, or a malfunctioning brain.

In attempting to respond to these issues I consider the work of Pierre Bourdieu, who rejects psychoanalytic and phenomenological theories of the subject and also 'attempt[s] to escape from a determinist or instrumental model of agency by reconstruing subjectification as a generative process' (McNay, 2000: 23). According to Crossley (2001: 81) Bourdieu has developed a theoretical framework which attempts 'to steer a way through some of the key theoretical polarities and problems of contemporary sociological theory'. It appears that these 'theoretical polarities and problems' beset theorizing of sexual offending. In offering an epistemological approach that attempts to overcome such obstacles, Bourdieu allows for the investigation of sexual violence and CSA in a manner that necessitates a focus 'on what men do' as well as how they maintain their collective power.

Thus, as a group, child sex offenders must be constructed as equally capable of the full range of 'normal' social action as any other social group (Parton, 2007; Plummer, 1995). In the last few years this fact has been demonstrated time and again as men (and occasionally women) in high-profile and public positions are convicted of sex crimes against children. The knee-jerk distancing of 'normal men' from 'paedophiles', principally by male commentators, without a comparable interrogation of the masculinist power structures that 'normal' men invest in so heavily (and which appear to house a great deal of child sex offending, e.g. religion, education, politics, gangs and family) renders such accounts partial and myopic. Indeed, as Malcolm Cowburn (2005: 221) argued:

> Forensic discourse relating to sexual coercion serves an ideological function in that it represents the sectional interests of men in that only certain acts of sexual coercion are considered and incorporated into the development of social policy and penal practice in response to the perpetrators of sexually coercive acts. Other acts – the coercive sexual behaviours of a wider (unconvicted) group of men – are excluded and ignored.

Bourdieu's theoretical perspective connects the individual with the wider social universe in a manner that addresses the individual and structural antecedents of social action. In the following section I introduce and discuss Bourdieu's theoretical perspective and the conceptual ideas that I will make particular use of.[2]

Bourdieu's sociology

Pierre Bourdieu (1930–2002) was a French anthropologist turned sociologist. He emerged from relatively humble roots in rural France to become one the world's most well-known social scientists. Through his philosophical training and his critical appreciation of the work of theorists such as Althusser, Bachelard, Durkheim, Heidegger, Husserl, Lévi-Strauss and Marx, Bourdieu developed a conceptual framework which represents an 'effort to escape from structuralist objectivism without relapsing into subjectivism' (Bourdieu, 1990a: 61). That is, he 'seeks to bridge the gap between individualistic and structural theories of human behaviour' (Paradis, 2012: 83).

Bourdieu viewed objectivism and subjectivism as modes of knowledge that 'both offer only one side of an epistemology necessary to understanding the social world' (Grenfell, 2012: 43). According to Loïc Wacquant, a student of and collaborator with Bourdieu (e.g. Bourdieu and Wacquant, 1992; Wacquant, 2004):

> The unsettling character of Bourdieu's enterprise stems from its persistent attempt to straddle some of the deep-seated antinomies that rend social science asunder … In the course of this effort, Bourdieu was led to jettison … dichotomies that recently claimed center stage in the theoretical forum, those of structure and agency on the one hand, and of micro- and macroanalysis on the other, by honing a set of conceptual and methodological devices capable of dissolving these very distinctions.
>
> (Wacquant, 1992: 3)

Bourdieu characterizes his work as 'constructivist structuralism' or 'structuralist constructivism' (1990a: 123): 'constructivist pertaining to the dynamic reproduction of human activity in ever-changing contexts; structuralist to refer to the relations of those involved' (Grenfell and James, 2006: 13). Importantly, for Bourdieu, subjectivity and social action is rooted in history (individual and collective) and sociocultural context. A useful starting point is Bourdieu's construction of the individual:

> ...social agents don't do just anything, that they are not foolish, that they do not act without reason. This does not mean that one must assume that they are rational, that they are right to act as they do, or even, to put it more simply, that they have reasons to act and that reasons are what direct, guide, or orient their actions. Agents may engage in reasonable forms of behaviour without being rational; they may engage in behaviours one can explain ... without their behaviour having reason as its principle...
>
> (Bourdieu, 1998: 75–76)

Conversely, the vast majority of theorizing of child sex offending appears to take the position that because the act is considered to be 'unreasonable' or *beyond* reason, the individual actor must, therefore, be in some way *irrational* or *impaired*. However, as discussed above, recent criminological research has adopted, at least in part, the 'rational actor' perspective (Wortley and Smallbone, 2010) where individuals choose between a range of options based on a rational calculation of the potential outcome (success or failure) of each choice. Bourdieu, however, rejects 'rational actor' theories (see Bourdieu, 1990a: 42–51; Bourdieu and Wacquant, 1992: 132–133) where rational action is defined as having 'no other principle than the intention of rationality and the free, informed calculation of a rational subject' (Bourdieu, 1990a: 50). He claims such perspectives are 'unaware that practices can have other principles than mechanical causes or conscious ends...' (Bourdieu, 1990a: 50). Instead, Bourdieu argues that:

> there is an economy of practices, a reason immanent in practices, whose 'origin' lies neither in the 'decisions' of reason understood as rational calculation nor in the determinations of mechanisms external to and superior to the agents. In other words, if one fails to recognize any form of action other than rational action or mechanical reaction, it is impossible to understand the logic of all the actions that are reasonable without being the product of a reasoned design, still less of rational calculation...
>
> (Bourdieu, 1990a: 50–51)

Action, for Bourdieu, cannot be conceived of as being the result of a *rational* project or plan, yet the *reason* or logic within practice can, nevertheless, be understood. For each social world, or *field*, Bourdieu argues there is an economy of practices which defines and distinguishes that world. However, the difficulty of capturing sufficiently all the constituents of this economy through research cannot be overstated (Bourdieu and Wacquant, 1992). Therefore, Bourdieu considered the sociologist's task was 'to uncover the most profoundly buried structures of the various social worlds which constitute the social universe, as well as the "mechanisms" which tend to ensure their reproduction or their transformation' (Bourdieu and Wacquant, 1992: 7). It is interesting, then, to recall Parton's (1985: 169) argument that 'explanations of child abuse need to establish underlying structures and mechanisms and not just patterned regularities' (such as those found within discussions of incidence and prevalence and profiles of perpetrator/victim characteristics). A point also made by Ward (2014).

One certainty that can be observed in regard to CSA is that, as Jenks (2005b) points out, it is not a new phenomenon (see also Radbill, 1968; Struve, 1990). Thus, it is reasonable to suggest (if pathological arguments are rejected) that human society has persistently reproduced conditions (via its 'various social worlds') that are generative of the practice of adult-child sex and this is, therefore, an activity that many adults (predominantly males) have, and do, engage in (as prevalence studies repeatedly indicate; e.g. Gilbert *et al.*, 2009; Pereda *et al.*, 2009; Stoltenborgh *et al.*, 2011). The sociologist's task then, in problematizing this practice, is to seek out, or uncover, these underlying *structures* and *mechanisms* – both objective and subjective, external and internal – that, it might be argued, ensure the reproduction of this practice. Theory, then, must be able to accommodate *both* dimensions and do so convincingly.

According to Crossley (2001: 83) Bourdieu developed 'a conception of human action or practice that can account for its regularity, coherence, and order without ignoring its negotiated and strategic nature'; for Grenfell and James (1998: 13) within Bourdieu's theoretical scheme 'there is a continual dialectic between objectivity and subjectivity. Social agents are incorporated bodies who possess, indeed, are possessed by structural, generative schemes which operate by orientating social practice'; and for Shilling (2004: 473–474) Bourdieu's sociology emphasizes 'that the embodied actor is indelibly shaped by, but is also an active reproducer of, society'. It is these principles that I employ in order to account for the sexual subjection of children and young people by those in positions of power. I summarize the central aspects of Bourdieu's theoretical framework below.

A conceptual framework for theorizing practice

Bourdieu summarizes the most essential features of his work as follows:

> It is a philosophy of action designated at times as *dispositional* which notes the potentialities inscribed in the body of agents and in the structure of the situations where they act or, more precisely, in the relations between them. This philosophy is condensed in a small number of fundamental concepts – habitus, field, capital – and its cornerstone is the two-way relationship between objective structures (those of social fields) and incorporated structures (those of the habitus).
>
> (1998: vii)

Habitus, *field* and *capital* constitute a conceptual framework to account for action. While they can be explained, as concepts, separately, in practice they must be applied collectively. Thus, 'habitus, capital and field can be defined but only within the theoretical framework they constitute, not in isolation' (Bourdieu and Wacquant, 1992: 96). Therefore, they are most clearly understood in relation to each other and through their application in and to practice. However, in order to introduce Bourdieu's epistemology and following others (e.g. Grenfell, 2012), I offer a brief summary of each concept in turn, beginning with *habitus*.

Habitus

According to Maton (2012: 48) habitus 'is probably the most widely cited of Bourdieu's concepts [but] also one of the most misunderstood, misused and hotly contested'. *Habitus* and *field* are the terms that Bourdieu uses to express the relationship between our internal (or subjective) world and our external (or objective) world. Therefore, 'social reality exists ... twice, in things and in minds, in fields and in habitus, outside and inside agents' (Bourdieu in Wacquant, 1989: 43). 'First and foremost, habitus has the function of overcoming the alternative between consciousness and unconsciousness...' (Bourdieu in Wacquant, 1989: 43). Bourdieu's (1977: 78) classic definition of habitus (not for the feint-hearted) is as follows:

> The durably installed generative principle of regulated improvisations, [which] produces practices which tend to reproduce the regularities immanent in the objective conditions of the production of their generative principle, while adjusting to the demands inscribed as objective potentialities in the situation, as defined by the cognitive and motivating structures making up the habitus.

Bourdieu refers to habitus as a 'structured and structuring structure' (Bourdieu, 2001: 84) and Maton (2012: 50) provides a concise explanation of this (somewhat typical) dense language:

> It is 'structured' by one's past and present circumstances, such as family upbringing and educational experiences. It is 'structuring' in that one's habitus helps to shape one's present and future practice. It is a 'structure' in that it is systematically ordered rather than random or unpatterned. This 'structure' comprises a system of dispositions which generate perceptions, appreciations and practices.

The habitus is, then, an 'acquired system of generative schemes objectively adjusted to the particular conditions in which it is constituted' (Bourdieu, 1977: 95). Crucially, it is a 'kind of practical sense for what is to be done in a given situation – what is called in sport a "feel" for the game' (Bourdieu, 1998: 25); 'a practical sense which reactivates the sense objectified in institutions' (Bourdieu, 1990a: 57). According to Croce (2015: 237) 'it denotes a generative dynamic structure that disposes social agents to move within constrains that are set by the sociohistorical conditions of its own production'. Therefore, for Bourdieu, our sense for how to act, what to do in a given situation is, to some extent, deposited within us as a 'bodily hexis'; thus, 'political mythology [is] realized, *em-bodied*, turned into a permanent disposition, a durable manner of standing, speaking, and thereby of *feeling* and *thinking*' (Bourdieu, 1977: 93).

Thus, to understand action, a Bourdieusian sociology must endeavour to explicitly reveal the *sense* of an institution, while revealing the *sense* of those individuals that constitute it. An understanding of social action lies between the two and is always firmly rooted in history. Thus, Bourdieu refers to Emile Durkheim (1938): '…it is yesterday's man who inevitably predominates in us, since the present amounts to little compared with the long past in the course of which we were formed and from which we result' (in Bourdieu, 1977: 79). Therefore, the habitus is:

> …embodied history, internalized as a second nature and so forgotten as history – [it] is the active presence of the whole past of which it is the product … As such, it is what gives practices their relative autonomy … produces history on the basis of history and so ensures the permanence in change that makes the individual agent a world within the world.
>
> (Bourdieu, 1990a: 56)

To illustrate (by adapting Crossley, 2001: 83) a child raised in a 'hockey town' and a 'hockey family' is likely to 'acquire the dispositions and know-how proper to "true" appreciation and criticism'. This is not so much a conscious and deliberate learning of explicitly taught rules as a gradual sedimentation of beliefs and techniques – what counts as important and what doesn't, what is approved and what is disapproved – within an individual persistently exposed to them. Such an individual will develop the capacity – a feel – for appropriate action which will, therefore, have the appearance of a 'natural' disposition. S/he will then appreciate and criticize in legitimate or approved ways and thus become actively involved in reproducing 'the field' – a 'specialized arena' with 'specific logics' (McCall, 1992: 840). Hence, the habitus is both collective and individual, durable yet dynamic, structured and structuring.

According to McNay (2000: 25–26) 'habitus expresses the idea that bodily identity is not natural, but involves the inscription of dominant social norms or the "cultural arbitrary" upon the body'. For McNay (2000) the strength of this concept is that it refers not simply to embodied norms, but also to the 'moment of praxis' when the individual comes to act *through* these norms. Therefore, there is a 'temporality' within the notion of habitus so that an *active*, or generative, sense of agency is built into the concept. That is, as social agents always act within *fields* – that are semi-autonomous and so shift in relation to the influence of other fields (especially more dominant fields) – the strategies employed by agents (in their acquisition of *capital* which rises and falls in value over time) always require revision and adaptation. Consequently, these adaptations act upon (structure) the field. According to Hardy (2012: 126) 'since change is presupposed in this way, it is often not made explicit in his social analyses' leading to charges of determinism (see below). Yet for McNay (2000: 25) 'habitus is defined, not as a determining principle, but as a generative structure.' Thus:

> The temporalization of the idea of habitus introduces a praxeological element into the idea of embodiment such that the dialectic of freedom and constraint in subjectification permits the emergence of a concept of agency understood through 'regulated liberties'.
>
> (McNay, 2000: 26)

The inscription or inculcation of norms upon the (male) body is fundamental to my account of child sexual abuse and exploitation. However, the key point is that Bourdieu develops a notion of agency as 'inscribed potential' (or 'regulated improvisation'), which has the capacity to overcome macro, determinist arguments and negative constructions of subjectivity, yet without avoiding the centrality of the social space. However, as emphasized earlier, habitus cannot be detached from *field* and *capital*, thus, 'if habitus brings into focus the subjective end of the equation, *field* focuses on the objective' (Grenfell and James, 1998: 16).

Field

Unlike other major social theorists that have been utilized within the study of sport (see Giulianotti, 2004, 2005) Bourdieu wrote specifically on sport (Bourdieu, 1990a: 156–167; Bourdieu, 1993: 117–131) referring to it as a 'relatively autonomous' cultural *field*. For Bourdieu then, 'modern societies are differentiated into interlocking fields … some of these fields coincide with institutions, such as the family or the media … but they can assume sub and trans-institutional forms too' (Crossley, 2001: 86). Therefore, there are fields within fields, so that the health system may constitute a field in its own right but it is also constituted by sub-fields such as paediatrics, ophthalmology and psychiatry. According to Thomson (2012: 65):

> Bourdieu argued that in order to understand interactions between people, or to explain an event or social phenomenon, it was insufficient to look at what was said, or what happened. It was necessary to examine the social space in which interactions, transactions and events occurred.

Immediately, then, it is evident that a great deal of the investigation and theorizing within 'sex offending research' would fall short of this requirement.

Any field, then, 'defines itself by defining specific stakes and interests … irreducible to the stakes and interests specific to other fields' (Bourdieu, 1993: 72). Nevertheless, 'there are general laws of fields', so that while studying one field may result in the discovery of properties 'peculiar to that field', one also furthers understanding of 'the universal mechanisms of fields' (Bourdieu, 1993: 72). However, the crucial point is that investigations of the social world require the examination of 'stakes and interests' or 'logic' of the field as essential for an appreciation of action that occurs within its bounds.

Fields cannot exist on their own but are only brought into being through 'players'. Thus, 'in order for a field to function, there have to be stakes and people prepared to play the game, endowed with the habitus that implies knowledge and recognition of the immanent laws of the field, the stakes, and so on' (Bourdieu, 1993: 72). Structures (fields) within society are, therefore, dependent upon social agents that invest in their specific economies – individuals and groups who understand what is at stake and are prepared to play. A useful way of thinking about this is to consider the reaction of a sports 'fan' (or rather *all* sports fans) to someone who declares 'it's only a game!' Therefore:

> Another property of fields … is that all the agents that are involved in a field share a certain number of fundamental interests, namely

everything that is linked to the very existence of the field. This leads to an objective complicity.

(Bourdieu, 1993: 73)

Thus, agents within a field are conceptualized as possessing, to greater or lesser extent, a 'feel for the game'. This 'feel' can also lead to what Bourdieu refers to as the *illusio*, which he describes as an 'enchanted relation to the game' (Bourdieu, 1998: 77).

McNay (2000: 57) claims '[t]he idea of the *field* potentially yields a differentiated and dynamic model of power relations where each field has its own historicity and logic which may reinforce or conflict with those of other fields'. By these terms then, 'sport' is a complete and fully viable *field*, and can be conceptualized as possessing a 'patterned set of organizing forces and principles imposed on all those entering its parameters' (Shilling, 2004: 475). It is, of course, constituted by many sub-fields of individual sports, which have their own specific historicity and logic while being inseparable from the larger field.

Again, it may be worthwhile recalling that the central task in this work is to examine the relationship between the *field* of organized sport and the (sociocultural) practice of childhood sexual abuse and that 'the purpose of Bourdieu's concept of *field* is to provide the frame for a "relational analysis"' of practice (Postone *et al.*, 1993: 5). Thus, Bourdieu theorizes social action from a position whereby historical social structures 'inhabit' the individual, they are embodied, and it is on this basis that individual action is generated, but not merely determined; it is also generative, as the habitus acts *back* on to the structures that produce it. So for Bourdieu (1989) 'there exists a correspondence between social structures and mental structures' (quoted in Wacquant, 1992: 12). The habitus 'acts within [social agents] as the organizing principle of their action', the 'modus operandi informing all thought and action (including thought of action)' (Bourdieu, 1977: 18). Yet while the habitus is the concept Bourdieu uses to articulate the 'generative principles or schemes which underlie practices':

> ...when individuals act, they always do so in specific social contexts or settings. Hence particular practices or perceptions should be seen, not as the product of the habitus as such, but as the product of the *relation between* the habitus, on the one hand, and the specific social contexts or 'fields' within which individuals act, on the other.
>
> (Thompson, 1991: 14)

The distinct but inseparable concepts of *habitus* and *field* establish social action as simultaneously individual *and* social. Thus, 'to think in terms of field is to *think relationally*' (Bourdieu, 1992: 96): 'field and habitus are locked in a circular relationship. Involvement in a field shapes the habitus that, in turn, shapes the actions that reproduce the field' (Crossley, 2001: 87). Symbolic practices of fields are inherently important for Bourdieu's approach which, in part, occupies similar theoretical territory to symbolic interactionism (Grenfell and James *et al.*, 1998). However, as McNay (2000: 72) argues:

> Bourdieu extends the idea of symbolic inscription by placing it in the context of the material relations of the field. This suggests a complex dynamic between the symbolic and the material, where the logic of the field may reinforce or displace the tendencies of the habitus. It is this tension that is generative of agency.

Thus, as there is a constant dynamic interplay between habitus and field, neither is static. However, habitus is 'durably installed' and the more sustained a social agent's engagement with a field, the greater the complicity between field and habitus. Bourdieu also refers to the notion of *doxa* to describe the apparently 'natural' beliefs, practices and attitudes that fields convey and individual agents embody. Practices that are so fundamental they are beyond question, and, thus go 'unseen': 'pre-reflexive, shared but unquestioned opinions and perceptions conveyed within and by relatively autonomous social entities – fields' (Deer, 2012: 115).

A coherence between habitus and field is more likely in stable social conditions where change is slow and relatively predictable:

> ...so that each individual is 'a fish in water', so to speak, where *habitus* and *field* are well matched ... In other circumstances, and at times of great crisis in particular, habitus must respond to abrupt, sometimes catastrophic, field changes...
>
> (Thomson, 2012: 127)

Such change can result in a disruption to, or mismatch in, the relationship between habitus and field. For example, when new technology is introduced to 'modernise' an industry, those with pre-digital skills and experience may find their working practices suddenly out-of-date and devalued. Bourdieu uses the term *hysteresis* to describe a situation where the habitus no longer corresponds to the field structures. In such circumstances individuals (and groups) may feel out of place and excluded as well as rather helpless to alter their situation. Their loss of influence and status (e.g. cultural and social capital) may well be accompanied by material loss also (economic capital).

Finally, Bourdieu argues:

> The *habitus* is what enables the institution to attain full realization: it is through the capacity for incorporation, which exploits the body's

readiness to take seriously the performative magic of the social, that the king, the banker or the priest are hereditary monarchy, financial capitalism or the Church made flesh. Property appropriates its owner, embodying itself in the form of a structure generating practices perfectly conforming with its logic and its demands.

(Bourdieu, 1990b: 57)

In other words, institutions or fields are, unavoidably, products of history which foster circumstances to enable the regeneration of those practices that will ultimately sustain it because they are, and must be, in accord with the values and principles upon which its enterprise is founded. Therefore, 'we cannot understand the practices of actors in terms of their habituses alone – habitus represents but one part of the equation; the nature of the fields they are active within is equally crucial' (Maton, 2012: 51). Thus, for Bourdieu, the relationship between *field* and *habitus* is central to his theory of human practice. In Webb *et al.*'s (2002: 36) straightforward language, 'this relationship ... does not completely determine people's actions and thoughts, but no practice is explicable without reference to them'.

Capital

According to Crossley (2001: 86):

> The concept of habitus effectively accounts for the dispositions and competence that both generate and shape action. What is added by the concepts of field and capital is an account of the context of action, the resources available to the actor within that context, and the respective role these factors play in the shaping of the action.

Bourdieu conceives the notion of *capital* and its accumulation, as key to understanding the operations of fields and the actions of individuals and groups. While recognizing the central importance of economic capital, *à la* Marx (1867), Bourdieu identifies various forms of capital related to the logic of a field, that is, what is counted, within that field, as valuable and what is not. Therefore, while Bourdieu (1998) emphasizes that the social universe is such that all agents attribute, at least implicitly, a monetary value to their labour or time, *capital* can refer to any number of things (practices, traditions, expertise) that have value within a field that is recognized and valued by the social agents belonging to that field. Therefore, the 'rules of the game' in each, relatively autonomous *field*, determines capital specific to that field. Thus, the unwritten (and sometimes unspoken) rules, evident within many sporting practices may have little or no economic value but simultaneously 'say everything' about them to other members of the field. For example, understanding and obeying – or more accurately 'having a feel for' – etiquette on 'playing through' in golf. Alternatively, understanding the correct attire and appropriate conduct in the club house. Thus, specific capital is 'effective *in relation* to a particular field and ... is only convertible into another kind of capital on certain conditions' (Bourdieu, 1993: 73). Thus, while knowledge of golf etiquette is of little obvious value for success in commercial business dealings, under certain conditions, it may make all the difference between success and failure.

In addition, privilege and status within a field are conveyed according to the value of capital one is able to appropriate and 'those with less valued capital are subordinated or marginalized' (Coles, 2008: 234). Therefore, within popular sports, those with high volumes of symbolic capital are paid to appear on television programmes as 'pundits' while others simply pay to form the 'crowd', to spectate collectively, or perhaps 'call-in' to a dedicated radio programme to briefly explain their view to the experts in the studio who will validate (or otherwise) their opinion.

Furthermore, cultural fields are 'constituted by, or out of, the conflict which is involved when groups or individuals attempt to determine what constitutes capital within that field, and how capital is to be distributed' (Webb *et al.*, 2002: 21–22). For example, the nineteenth century 'split' within rugby football into two distinct 'codes' might be considered a good illustration of such struggle, whereby the 'gentleman's' ethos of amateurism was rejected (by the industrial North) in favour of professionalism (see Collins, 2006). Indeed, this struggle over the 'real' or 'true' form ('code') of rugby continues (in the 'professional era') and the side taken in this struggle can simultaneously say everything, or practically nothing, about the individual, according to the audience.

Crucially, cultural capital exists in three forms: in the *embodied* state (durable cognitive and corporeal dispositions), *objectified* state (e.g. books, equipment) and the *institutionalized* state (e.g. qualifications, titles) (Bourdieu, 1983). All three forms are relevant to this account. Bourdieu (1983: 222–225) states 'cultural capital can be acquired, to a varying extent ... in the absence of any deliberate inculcation, and, therefore, quite unconsciously [however] it always remains marked by its earliest conditions of acquisition'. Therefore, central to any consideration of social practice is the normative logic or cultural capital of a field. This capital exists in an embodied (or inscribed) state, within the social agents of the field, and this process of inscription is most potent for the young. The crucial role that habitus plays in Bourdieu's theory is expressed by Moore (2012: 107–108):

> The formation of embodied cultural capital entails the prolonged exposure to a specialized social *habitus*, such as that of the traditional English public school, the priesthood or the military or ... in the apprenticeship of the artist or, elsewhere, in the cultivation of elite

sporting skills … Cultural capital is acquired in the systematic cultivation of a sensibility in which principles of selection implicit within an environment (a milieu or habitat) translate, through inculcation, into principles of consciousness that translate into physical and cognitive propensities expressed in dispositions to acts of particular kinds.

Bourdieu utilizes the concept of capital in various ways but argues that within each field:

Symbolic capital is any property (any form of capital whether physical, economic, cultural or social) when it is perceived by social agents endowed with categories of perception which cause them to know it and recognize it, to give it value.

(Bourdieu, 1998: 47)

Thus, the acquisition and accumulation of symbolic capital is at the heart of Bourdieu's conceptualization of power relations. It is through 'struggles' within fields that social agents acquire, to varying degrees, symbolic capital and it is this accumulation that affords 'the power to impose upon other minds a vision … Symbolic capital is a credit; it is the power granted to those who have obtained sufficient recognition to be in a position to impose recognition … to consecrate' (Bourdieu, 1989: 21). This situation then lays the ground for what Bourdieu terms 'symbolic violence' where individuals and groups are marginalized, excluded, manipulated or exploited on the basis of their relative lack of capital.

Bourdieu offers a theory of social action whereby actions are only explicable through reference to the social space. The potential for understanding CSA is that it offers us a way of comprehending the relation between the social space, and its constitutive structures, and the behaviour of individuals without recourse to malfunction, mental illness or genetic inheritance. According to McNay (2000: 65) 'by conceptualizing the relation between the material and symbolic as *generative* of variable patterns of autonomy and dependence a more determinate sense of agency emerges' (emphasis added). Through an application of Bourdieu's theoretical perspective, an account becomes possible that locates the origins of abuse both within and without the individual (perpetrator) by establishing a social agent that is both structured and structuring. It also offers the potential of developing a much more 'active' notion of the (sexually subjected) child, without returning to twentieth century notions of the child as a willing accomplice and adult-child sex as harmless (see Kelly, 1988: 55–56). Therefore, through Bourdieu's 'relational' approach to human action, both the micro and the macro can reside in a coherent fashion, within the same account and in a manner which does not sideline crucial features of sexual offending against children, such as gendered power relations.

Critique and development

Despite Bourdieu's claims that his conceptual framework (which I have briefly outlined above) overcome polarities such as structure and agency and objectivism and subjectivism, his work has also been widely critiqued (see Grenfell, 2012). Given one of the key starting points of this discussion around sexual offending against children – namely that *gender* should be central to any theorization of it (Brackenridge, 2001; Cossins, 2000; Liddle, 1993; Rush, 1980) – a consideration of the critique of Bourdieu's work in the field of gender is particularly important. I will briefly outline Bourdieu's perspective on gender relations and masculinity, before considering the feminist critique, and extension, of his work.

Masculine domination

In addition to *habitus*, *field* and *capital*, Bourdieu's notion of *symbolic violence* is key to understanding his work on gender. Wacquant (1992: 13) notes that, for Bourdieu, 'symbolic systems are not simply instruments of knowledge, they are also *instruments of domination*'. For Bourdieu, (as others) language is central to systems of domination and central to the sociological endeavour is to recognize domination inscribed in forms of language that are often misrecognized or go unnoticed because they represent the interests of the dominant and operate to reproduce relations of power. Bourdieu (1992: 142) states 'linguistic relations are always relations of symbolic power through which relations of force between the speakers and their respective groups are actualized in a transfigured form'. As Thompson explains, (developing Mauss, 1954/1990) Bourdieu 'developed the notion of symbolic violence in the context of *gift exchange* in Kabyle [Algerian] society', which he views as 'a mechanism through which power is exercised and simultaneously disguised' whereby 'giving is also a way of possessing' through the obligation of 'indebtedness' created by the giving of a gift that 'cannot be met by a counter-gift of comparable quality' (1991: 23–24). This is a notion I explore further in the context of adult-child relations in sport (Chapter 6). Thus, according to Bourdieu (2001: 42–43) 'symbolic violence is exercised only through an act of knowledge and practical recognition which takes place below the level of the consciousness and will'.

Gender relations are entwined within this process. For Bourdieu (2001: 86) 'the whole of learned culture … makes man the active principle and woman the passive principle'. Thus, symbolic violence is perpetrated through the reproduction of fields that enable glaringly obvious inequities – such as the absence of female sport in the print and broadcast media coupled with the sexualization and infantilization of female sportswomen (e.g. Cooky *et al.*, 2013; Creedon, 1994; Duncan, 1990), and placed alongside, for example, the exclusion (until very recently) of females from many Olympic events – to appear as natural (Hargreaves, 1994).

Indeed, it is the very visible nature of sport practice that makes this naturalization so pervasive and the symbolic violence therein so consuming; the 'belief in the game' (capital embodied) renders such inequality (or symbolic violence) natural and self-evident, so that it 'goes without saying'. Thus, in sport, for example, the contemporary association between the sexualized female 'model' and the sports event (e.g. post-race presentation awards in *Formula 1*, *Tour de France*, *Olympic Games*, and the 'soccerette' in *Sky* TVs long-running UK football programme 'Soccer AM', *etc.*) is considered perfectly normal, natural and self-evident. Therefore, *athletic capital* is far less accessible for females and the capital they possess is undervalued within a masculinist field. These issues are discussed in greater depth in Chapter 4.

Importantly, for Bourdieu, this process also involves a degree of 'misrecognition' on the part of the dominated, where complicity of an agent confronted by an act of symbolic violence implies a disposition to 'understand their veiled social meaning, but without recognizing them consciously as what they are – namely, as words, gestures, movements, and intonations of domination' (Krais, 1993: 172). Therefore, Bourdieu argues 'the dominated apply categories constructed from the point of view of the dominant to the relations of domination, thus making them appear as natural' (2001: 35). This is never more so apparent than in the adult-child relation and the construction of the institution of childhood (James and Prout, 1997). According to Thompson (1991: 24) in modern industrial societies:

> The development of institutions enables different kinds of capital to be accumulated and differently appropriated, while dispensing with the need for individuals to pursue strategies aimed directly at the domination of others: violence is, so to speak, built into the institution itself.

It is worth recalling then Kitzinger's (1997: 185) insight: 'the risk of abuse is built into childhood as an institution itself', thus children's lives are carefully structured and controlled (perhaps increasingly so) and childhood is constructed as a 'becoming' rather than a 'being' where children are constituted in terms of 'lack' rather than 'capacity' (James *et al.*, 1997). Again, childhood is differentiated by gender so that what constitutes symbolic capital in male childhood differs from that in female childhood. Therefore, according to Krais (1993: 170–171):

> The space of the possible – actions, feelings, evaluations, expressive acts, verbal and bodily behaviour – is restricted for every individual. 'Male' aspects/dispositions in the girl are suppressed, and 'female'

dimensions in the boy are suppressed – but they are always related. So, for instance, the phrase 'Boys do not cry', still a familiar phrase, implicitly has to be completed by 'But girls do'.

Thus, in this process of acquiring a gender identity is the 'paradoxical result that both genders, women and men, are restricted in their potential; and it is in this sense that the dominants are themselves dominated by their domination' (Krais, 1993: 171).

Feminist critique

According to Adkins (2004: 208) 'it is widely recognized that Bourdieu's social theory has much more to say about social reproduction than social change'. However, as already noted, sexual violence has a long history and so it might be argued that what needs to be understood for a comprehension of the historical phenomenon of adult-child sexual activity, or sexual violence and abuse, is the seemingly intransient, persistent, durable nature of social practice, particularly where such action is popularly designated as taboo. Thus, in accounting for the sexual exploitation of children, perhaps a theory of social practice that accounts for 'the permanence in change' (Bourdieu, 1990a: 56) is particularly pertinent.

However, Bourdieu's *Masculine Domination* (2001) has been criticized by feminist theorists for 'fail[ing] to bring the destabilizing implications of the concept of the field to bear upon the notion of habitus as he does convincingly elsewhere' (McNay, 2000: 27). For McNay (2000: 54) this has resulted 'in a monolithic account of the reproduction of gender relations' which does not sufficiently account for 'multiple subjectivity' (56). Therefore, McCall (1992: 847) argues that Bourdieu 'must be accused ... of constructing the universal power of gender symbolism too rigidly and deterministically. For women, individual gender identity varies quite dramatically.' The same is true for men (Kimmel and Messner, 2001) although Whitehead and Barrett (2001: 7) note that 'despite the evident multiplicity of masculine expression, traditional masculinities ... still prevail in most cultural settings' (see also Frosh *et al.*, 2003). However, Crossley (2001: 88) responds to some of Bourdieu's critics, arguing:

> Bourdieu's conception of habitus is not centered upon a 'culturally dopey' model of blind adherence to rules, norms, and traditions. The habitus forms the practical-social basis for innovative and improvised action. It consists of forms of competence, skill, and multi-track dispositions, rather than fixed and mechanical blueprints for action.

It is also important to note that the criticisms above are generally perceived as a weakness in Bourdieu's perspective on gender as set down in 'Masculine Domination' rather than being a weakness in his theoretical scheme per se. It is the concept of the *field* that critics claim is neglected here, resulting in a 'hypostatization of relations between men and women' (McNay, 2000: 56). If, however, field *is* considered in conjunction with the habitus, 'a more nuanced view of political agency' can be developed 'in terms of the idea of regulated liberties which escapes from the binary of domination-resistance' (McNay, 2000: 56). The notion of 'regulated liberties' or 'inscribed potentialities' are central to this contextualized account of the sexual subjection of children. Importantly, criticisms regarding determinism:

> ...fail to recognize fully the force of Bourdieu's insistence that habitus is not to be conceived as a principle of determination but as a generative structure. Within certain objective limits (the field), habitus engenders a potentially infinite number of patterns of behaviour, thought and expression that are both 'relatively unpredictable' but also 'limited in their diversity'.
>
> (McNay, 2000: 38)

Moi (1999) usefully suggests that gender, rather than being conceptualized as a distinct field, instead should be thought of in the same way that Bourdieu defined social class – 'as *part of* a field ... that is as dispersed across the social field and deeply structuring of the general social field' (Adkins, 2004: 6). This seems particularly useful in considering the field of sport, which, like other social fields (indeed perhaps more so than most) is 'deeply structured' by gender (it is important to add, however, that this is precisely the point made by Bourdieu (1977; 2001) regarding the gendered nature of social space). As Krais (1993: 159) states 'Bourdieu has used Kabyle [Algerian] society to demonstrate how the division of labor between the genders becomes the foundation of the vision of the world'.

Therefore, despite her criticisms, McNay (2000: 25) claims 'Bourdieu's work on embodiment ... resonates strongly with' but also advances feminist theory. She argues:

> For Bourdieu, the formation of subjectivity within a symbolic system involves subjection to dominant power relations, but also involves the institution of meaning. The instantiation of a subject within dominatory power relations does not negate but rather implies agency.
>
> (McNay, 2000: 47)

This has significant implications for the child as a social agent acting within 'dominatory power relations', indeed, a stronger notion of agency in relation to the sexually exploited child is central to my consideration of CSA (in sport).

McNay (2000: 39) goes on, 'bodily dispositions are not simply inscribed or mechanically learnt but lived as a form of "practical mimesis" as the body believes in what it plays at...' (Bourdieu, 1990b: 73). Again, this notion of embodied action, bodily belief (e.g. Bourdieu, 1990b: 66–79) is central to my approach to child sexual exploitation, and has very clear application to the field of (childhood/youth) sport where the training of the body is an explicit feature. Through such an approach to social action, questions such as: 'what is it exactly that the body is playing at?' and also, 'in doing sport, what exactly is it that the body is trained to believe in?' become accessible.

Recap

The sexual subjection of a child (actual or 'virtual') is a widespread, persistent *social* practice through which social (power) relations are refracted. Nevertheless, it is also an interpersonal relation involving forethought and choice. The habitus provides the conceptual basis for a determinate sense of agency that is inextricably connected to the social space. We act from a sense of our own individual history, particularly influenced by our childhood, but each personal history is inextricably bound to the social space, an historical product, which imposes its own specific limits and culture. Bourdieu provides a theory of practice that allows for the explicit differentiation of social space (*fields* and *capital*), without losing sight of its commonalities and intersections, that defines limits for action according to its constituent logic and within which social agents act (*habitus*), as both structured and structuring individuals. This is important, as sexual abuse occurs across the social space, but also within specific social spaces, such as sports clubs and churches, which constitute particular objectified representations (sub-fields) of the larger fields to which they are affiliated and the symbolic capital specific to that field. Social agents within these spaces represent, to greater or lesser extent, the embodiment of that capital. Therefore, just as Priests and Vicars are the (Christian) Church 'made flesh', so is, for example, a boxing coach the boxing field 'made flesh'.

I have suggested that Bourdieu's approach may offer opportunities for a fuller account of the sexual subjection of children that enables a more appropriate focus on sociocultural factors, not simply traumatic or deeply negative experiences but the underpinning logic of fields, but in a manner that does not lose sight of the individual (*habitus*). I have particularly tried to emphasize the need for any account of this sociosexual practice to engage with a coherent and substantial notion of action as *situated*. But in suggesting a sociological approach to the social problem of

CSA as others have done (e.g. Cossins, 2000; Liddle, 1993; Plummer, 1981) it is then vital to account for the *encounter* between man and boy/girl (or indeed between children and young people) without pathologizing the 'perpetrator' or reducing him (or her) to a ' "culturally dopey" model of blind adherence to rules, norms, and traditions' (Crossley, 2001: 88), or indeed, reducing the child in a similar fashion. Therefore, reference to general 'masculinity' or 'men' in explanations of sexual violence is both necessary but not sufficient. Social agents always act within the social space (*field*) and are structured by, as well as structuring of it, and this notion must be incorporated into theories of 'exploitative male sexuality'.

Theory that does not properly account for sociocultural context will always generate, in theory, a disconnected individual – or perhaps more accurately, a disconnected brain comprised of various systems. Therefore, analysis of sex offending that focuses on sex offenders in isolation (and often in incarceration) may generate 'facts' about offenders that remove them and their action from the social world. A more comprehensive theoretical account of CSA will also incorporate the 'victim' as well as the 'perpetrator'. In other words, it would theorize abuse within a *relation* situated within a social context or *field*. Therefore, I consider social practice not so much the result of a conscious, rational, freely chosen plan of action, nor a mechanistic, unthinking reaction, but rather as an *inscribed potentiality* or a *regulated improvisation*. Here, the potential for action is inscribed in the bodies of agents by the fields in which they act and who actively inscribe that field.

The point of Bourdieu's conceptual framework and the concepts he developed is to put them in to practice, to apply them. This is the focus of subsequent chapters. However, it is first necessary to explore what this means and to address some of the challenges Bourdieu poses for researchers working with his 'theory of practice'.

Theory and method

For Bourdieu, 'research without theory is blind and theory without research is empty' (Bourdieu in Wacquant, 1989: 51). This position is echoed in the work of Celia Brackenridge in relation to sexual exploitation in sport (e.g. Brackenridge, 2001). Furthermore, for Bourdieu (1992: 225), 'the division between "theory" and "methodology" ... must be completely rejected, as ... one cannot return to the concrete by combining two abstractions'. Crucially, Bourdieu's theory is a theory *of* practice (Grenfell, 2012), and he argued that an essential part of comprehending the social world and doing sociology was to do it *in* the world, empirically (and also reflexively). Therefore, his concepts of *habitus*, *capital* and *field* are intended to be put to work, in practice. As noted, while these concepts can be explained, to a degree, separately, they must be deployed together if they are to illuminate social action. His theory then is also a theory of *research* practice that provides 'tools' to think with (Grenfell, 2012) more than a method to follow. Bourdieu's approach is exemplified in his major studies (e.g. Bourdieu, 1986; Bourdieu *et al.*, 1999), and he provides detailed description and discussion of his epistemology and theoretical concepts across a vast body of work (see Grenfell, 2012; Bourdieu and Wacquant, 1992).

However, the manner in which these concepts should be put to work is challenging to discern. Grenfell (2012) identifies a three-stage methodology: (1) the construction of the research object; (2) field analysis; and (3) participant objectivation. Therefore, the first step is to construct the 'research object' and this, he says, is fraught with difficulty because 'its terms – the names of the game – are the product of history' (Grenfell, 2012: 221). A great deal is already pre-configured and may 'silently' shape the construction of the research object. Models and typologies of sex offending seem to illustrate this point, but so too, for example, has the assertion, implicit or explicit, that perpetrators of child sexual abuse are male while victims are female (see Hartill, 2005; Mendel, 1995). Similarly, concepts such as 'abuse', 'paedophilia' and 'grooming' straddle the field – that is, they *structure* it – and, therefore, operate to shape thought and enquiry.

Bourdieu argues that in constructing the research object we must be sensitive to such terms, models and typologies: 'in effect, it is so easy to (mis)take constructs as things *in themselves* rather than as sets of relations' (Grenfell, 2012: 220). So we must be wary of words as they are nothing less than 'socio-cultural time capsule[s] packed with socially derived meaning' (Grenfell *et al.*, 2006: 77). A sensitivity to the pre-constructed, then, is fundamental to Bourdieu's approach, and this is perhaps especially important and challenging within an academic field that is often closely associated with – at times indivisible from – the political and politicized field of 'child protection' as well as one that generates deeply held convictions and, therefore, entrenched positions.

Unlike much research in the study of sex offending which focuses on the various forms of sex offending and often on the motivations of the offender, following Celia Brackenridge, Kari Fasting, Sandra Kirby, Jan Toftegaard Nielsen and others (see Lang and Hartill, 2015), this study delineates the object of analysis in terms of the context or *field* in which it occurs. More precisely, the object of analysis is not the field of sport per se (or one of its sub-fields), but a particular *relation* within that field: the adult – child *relation*; and further delineated by focusing on a specific manifestation of that relation: sexual activity. The object of analysis is, then, best conceptualized as a study of the sexual *relations* between adults and children in sport. The dominant terminology of 'abuse', 'exploitation' and 'violence' obviously imposes something of a cultural judgement upon this relation, and, from a Bourdieusian perspective at least, serves to pre-configure the object. While I ultimately adopt these terms as the most appropriate to reflect the reality of adult-child sexual relations (as the title of this book illustrates), the stories presented here (and elsewhere) also problematize this nomenclature. Thus, I have previously suggested the term 'sexual subjection' – to be subject to sexualized activity – as a means of retaining the power relation at the heart of this issue, while resisting the imposition of terms that construct the nature of that activity (or relation) prior to those that have been subject to it. The importance of constructing adult-child sex as abuse and exploitation cannot be overstated in the development of a political problem with political responses. However, to indicate that self-definition is also important, I also use 'sexual subjection' as a way of creating, symbolically, more space for 'survivors' (not all of whom find this label useful) to construct the *object* – *their* experiences – in *their* terms.

Furthermore, it must be acknowledged that 'sport' is constituted by many different 'sports' that can be considered *sub-fields*, which in themselves are often supranational. It is, therefore, a rather ill-defined social space. Hopefully, research in this field will gradually be able to produce more specific analyses of sub-fields, in their national and international forms.

There are clearly various ways that any relation can be investigated and elucidated. Following Brackenridge (1997), Brackenridge and Fasting (2005) and Fasting *et al.* (2002), my preference has been to work with 'victims'/'survivors' and to investigate the problem of child sexual abuse in sport through data generated from their perspective. Undoubtedly, a more expansive study would benefit from a wider range of perspectives, especially coaches, and a greater capacity to investigate the specific fields in which the relation (the abuse) actually developed. Notwithstanding the considerable difficulty of conducting such research. That said, empirical data from focus groups with officials (coaches, club welfare officers, chairpersons) from within the voluntary sport sector is examined in Chapter 4.

The second stage in Bourdieu's methodology is to conduct a *field ana-lysis*, and this constitutes the approach I have attempted to adopt in this study. However, I certainly do not claim to have performed something akin to an ideal Bourdieusian study, and my appreciation for Bourdieu's ideas has developed gradually and continue to evolve. No doubt there are many weaknesses in my interpretation and application of his theory-method. While Bourdieu rejects the idea that his conceptual framework should map neatly onto a particular method of data collection, he does indicate his methodological sympathies:

I feel a kinship and a solidarity with researchers who 'put their noses to the ground' (particularly symbolic interactionists, and all those who, through participant observation or statistical analysis, work to uncover and to debunk the empirical realities that Grand Theoreticians ignore ...).

(Bourdieu in Bourdieu and Wacquant, 1992: 113)

However, Bourdieu eschews the methodological divisions of social research, instead employing a range of methods of data collection, such as in-depth interviews, large-scale surveys and statistical analysis, frequently associated with opposing theoretical traditions. Indeed, he warns, 'watch out for the methodological watchdogs!' (Bourdieu in Bourdieu and Wacquant, 1992: 227) and 'this scientific monster called "methodology"' (Bourdieu in Bourdieu and Wacquant, 1989: 51). Thus, 'we must try, in every case, to mobilize all the techniques that are relevant and practically usable, given the definition of the object and the practical conditions of data collection' (Bourdieu, 1992: 226). Nevertheless, 'it would be wrong to see Bourdieu as a methodological libertarian' (Grenfell and James, 2006: 178). When questioned by Loïc Wacquant (Bourdieu and Wacquant, 1992: 104–105) Bourdieu outlined a three-stage research process for the analysis of fields. The following is Michael Grenfell's concise summary:

1   Analyse the position of the field vis-à-vis the field of power;
2   Map out the objective structure of relations between positions occupied by agents who compete for the legitimate forms of specific authority of which the field is the site;
3   Analyse the habitus of agents; the systems of dispositions they have acquired by internalizing a deterministic type of social and economic condition.

(Grenfell, 2012: 221)

According to Grenfell (2012), the order in which these are performed is open to interpretation and in his own research (see Grenfell and James, 2006) he reports beginning with stage 3 and this also represents the approach taken here. Specifically, my attempt to reveal a 'system of dispositions' acquired within and through 'sport,' has been informed principally through life history interviews with 'survivors' of child sexual abuse in sport. Bourdieu's (1983: 190) position on the body in relation to divulging habitus, then, is instructive: our 'way of treating it, caring for it, feeding it, maintaining it ... reveals the deepest dispositions of the habitus'. This seems particularly apt for an investigation of the *sexual* exploitation of children in a field centred upon the inculcation of bodily or corporeal habits (or 'skills'). Yet given the object of analysis constitutes both an illegal and taboo act, it is, by definition fiercely and resolutely concealed both by those directly involved, including so-called 'bystanders,' as well as society more widely. Therefore, the 'practical conditions of data collection' are considerable and heavily influence the research design. Nevertheless, the absence of voices other than 'survivors' may be considered a significant limitation. This is countered, partially, through a critical review of the field of sport (Chapter 4) drawing on both past research as well as a critical examination of empirical (previously unpublished) data. This examination of *field* is intended to address stages 1 and 2 in Bourdieu's outline of his approach. However, conducting research with those who experienced, and continue to experience, suffering through the way others treated their bodies seems in keeping with Bourdieu's inclinations (see Bourdieu *et al.*, 1999). Before moving on, however, it is necessary to attend to Bourdieu's third stage, *participant objectivation*.

Participant objectivation, radical doubt and reflexivity

A notion central to contemporary social research is 'reflexivity' and this was given particular priority by Bourdieu who argued that reflexivity should be:

> ...understood as the effort whereby social science, taking itself for its object, uses its own weapons to understand and check itself ... which makes it possible to keep closer watch over the factors capable of biasing research ... a specific form of epistemological vigilance...
>
> (Bourdieu, 2004: 89)

For Bourdieu, as for others (e.g. Brackenridge and Fasting, 2005; Plummer, 2001; Ward, 2014), science and the researcher cannot be conceived of as, somehow, outside the issues they focus on. Thus, the social scientist is not an 'impartial umpire' about the 'truth' of the social world, but it is, nevertheless, her/his 'task to construct a true account of the struggles that take place to impose what is represented as the truth' (Bourdieu, 1990a: 181). Researchers are active participants in the problems and struggles they investigate; that is they construct, and are constructed by, those struggles. This is perhaps especially salient for research on sexual violence, where researchers often adopt the role of researcher-advocate – work that often involves close associations with policymaking organizations and their representatives (Brackenridge, 2013).

As Richardson (1990: 12) argues 'we are always inscribing values in our writing. It is unavoidable' (quoted in Plummer, 2001: 171). Thus, Wellard (2009: 17) points out that in the sociology of sport 'much research has been gathered by men about sports they identify with ... [and] there is often a sense of reverence in the way many men write about sport'. Bourdieu argues that sociologists, while conducting 'objective' research, must simultaneously apply their 'objectivating techniques' to themselves and their own research practice. He argues, then, that researchers have to convert reflexivity into a disposition, 'a *reflexivity reflex*' (Bourdieu, 2004: 89) if they are to avoid simply reproducing the *status quo* and dominant – or 'common sense' – understandings and constructions.

It would be naïve to assume that researchers and the institutions in which they work are unaffected by such narratives. For Bourdieu, 'radical doubt' offers the possibility for researchers to 'objectivate' their own position and so enable them to offer analyses less beleaguered by the 'pre-constructed', 'common sense' or *doxa*. In short, 'science' must question itself (Bourdieu, 1992). Therefore, Bourdieu (in Bourdieu and Wacquant, 1992: 235–236) asks:

> How can the sociologist effect in practice this radical doubting which is indispensable for bracketing all the presuppositions inherent in the fact that she is a social being, that she is therefore socialized and led to feel 'like a fish in water' within that social world whose structures she has internalized? How can she prevent the social world itself from carrying out the construction of the object, in a sense, through her...

He adds, 'the mere fact of being on the alert is important but hardly suffices' (Bourdieu, in Bourdieu and Wacquant, 1992: 238). Bourdieu's notion of 'participant objectivation' is offered as a means by which a researcher may attempt to overcome the problems that arise from the fact that researchers are themselves both agents in, and products of, the problems and worlds they investigate – 'fish in water' as it were. Attempting to 'objectivate' aspects of our unconscious – that may obstruct our understanding of the object under investigation – requires us to acknowledge our own position and interests in the field(s) we are engaged with (Bourdieu, 2004: 92). Reflexivity, then, must be embedded *within* the research activity, indeed within the *researcher*.

Bourdieu (2004: 94) argues 'reflexive analysis must consider successively, position in the social space, position in the field and position in the scholastic universe'. He also warns that this should not prompt a narcissistic reflection (such as an autobiography) 'not only because it is very often limited to a complacent looking back by the researcher on his own experience, but also because it is its own end and leads to no practical effect' (Bourdieu, 2004: 89).[3] This is an especially challenging feature of Bourdieu's epistemology – 'the most difficult but also the most necessary exercise' (Bourdieu in Bourdieu and Wacquant, 1992: 253). In the remainder of the chapter, I attempt to consider my position in the social space, field and scholastic universe.

A participant objectivation

Raised in what is often referred to as a 'rugby league town' situated between Liverpool and Manchester in the north-west of England, childhood ambitions revolved entirely around professional sport, first football, then tennis. At 16, professional tennis felt like an increasingly distant possibility and following an early exit from an international junior tournament, building on my meagre (six GCSEs) school exam results became a more pressing priority. After briefly discussing a new qualification in 'Sport Studies', enrolment at a local college effectively marked the end of elite sporting ambitions. Initially studying 'English Language', 'Psychology' and 'Sport Studies', English was rapidly dropped and replaced by 'Sociology' – one of the few courses with spaces still available.

The problematization of society was a fascinating discovery (particularly Karl Marx and Max Weber and especially the latter's analysis of religion); however, it was the debate between creatures known as 'positivists' and 'interpretivists' that engaged me most of all. No doubt, at least in part, because of the way the debate was framed, I felt much more disposed to those that argued the study of society required different approaches to the study of the natural world. Classroom debate about social problems – which seemed very different to the school experience of learning – coupled with a supportive and warm relationship with a tutor, led to a sense of aptitude for thought and analysis that had not previously presented itself. Coupled with aspects of Sport Studies ('history' and 'social issues'), the seeds of my critical reflections on sport – that slowly appeared to be rejecting me, or at least leaving me behind – were seemingly sown.

'Going to university' began to feature in 'careers advice' in sixth-form college. There was some irony at being offered lower entrance requirements for the renowned 'Loughborough' than at other universities, seemingly based on my acquisition of tennis titles just at the point where I had elected to put my racket down for good. But following my discovery of sociology, the joint honours programme of 'sport and social science' at Birmingham seemed to fit. At the point where my athletic capital had diminished significantly, yet still paying some dividend – not least in securing a university place – the possibility of generating intellectual capital that might open up other 'career options' seemed a rational choice.

In fact, Birmingham housed the radical and influential Centre for Critical Cultural Studies led by, among others, Stuart Hall; but this fact eluded me entirely. Feelings of having made a mistake and of being in the 'wrong place', coupled with some ambivalence towards my courses, sociology most of all, led to a difficult first year. Gradually, my association with the university football team and subsequently a university rugby club – which was in fact more of a social club – enabled me to 'settle in' to university life. I had played rugby league since primary school but was well versed in the ways of rugby union after joining a local club while at college. I was able to engage enthusiastically and with confidence in the various 'tests' that were established for new members, principally involving extensive alcohol consumption and various displays of physicality and risk. I was soon not just playing for the team but firmly 'in the club'.

Difficulties, or rather a lack of ability, with 'natural science' had been established in school and this continued in the sport science aspect of my degree. However, an assignment within a sport sociology module for Charles Jenkins introduced me to John Hargreaves' 'Sport, Power and Culture' and Gramsci's notion of 'hegemony'. Hargreaves' critical approach and use of social theory was illuminating, appealed to my developing interpretation of sport and made a lasting impact. Following an undergraduate thesis on 'new racism and sport' (heavily influenced by Paul Gilroy's (1987) 'There ain't no black in the Union Jack'), I graduated with a 'Second Class, Upper'. A year or so working in bars and restaurants in Canada and another two years in various employment in the UK – most notably 18 months as a full-time customer services representative in the 'water industry' – I elected to return to studying after a recommendation from a university friend who had just completed an 'MA' in 'Sport and Leisure Studies' at the *University of Wales Institute, Cardiff* (UWIC). I applied and was offered a place under the tutelage of sport sociologist Scott Fleming, including a 'teaching assistantship' position.

I elected to further develop my undergraduate interest in racism and was inspired by Fleming's (1995) 'Home and Away' and Grant Jarvie's (1991) 'Sport, Racism and Ethnicity'. The experience of researching a topic in-depth and writing a thesis ('Sport, "race" and higher education') involving several qualitative interviews with black athletes, as well as a national survey (postal questionnaire), introduced more fully the notion of research and academic work. This course also brought me, fleetingly, into contact with Celia Brackenridge and her programme of research, in 1995, when she delivered a seminar at UWIC for a small group of postgraduates. Her research resonated with my own experiences of youth sport and seemed to present possibilities for research that I was keen to pursue. A failed attempt to secure a funded PhD with Professor Brackenridge (I will save myself the ignominy of disclosing my response to a question about 'triangulation') was somewhat balanced with an offer to lecture 'sport studies' in a Further Education College, typically to 16–18-year-old students enrolled on 'technical' or 'vocational' programmes, in the south of England.

Lofty thoughts of contributing to the development of knowledge, that had begun to feel possible during my year at UWIC, were short-lived as the realities of the role of assisting students to acquire FE qualifications set in. An invitation by Professor Fleming to write up my master's thesis for publication seemed a significant opportunity but became an irritating source of guilt as I allowed it to drift by. After a number of unsuccessful attempts to gain a lecturing post within higher education, I attended interview in 2000, for a position lecturing in Sport Studies at Edge Hill College of Higher Education in the north-west of England, during which I declared I was conducting 'research on sexual abuse in sport'. After the preferred candidate declined, I accepted the position and moved 'back up North'.

The distance between 'further' and 'higher' was not as great as I had imagined, neither was there a strong emphasis on research, but the focus on teaching did perhaps afford me greater space and time to develop my own research direction. At this point, I was able to resume my studies of sociology, social theory and the sociology of sport and wrote programmes focused on gender, sexuality, deviance and the body in the context of sport. Foucault and feminist theory were particularly significant influences. In 2001, following a chance meeting with a colleague in a different department, Phil Prescott, an ex-social worker and rugby union player, we began to discuss the possibilities of research into the developing area of child protection in sport.

A speculative phone call to several national governing bodies led to an invitation from the Rugby Football League for us to join their newly convened 'Rugby League Child Protection Advisory Group'. This subsequently met at the JJB Stadium in Wigan in 2001 and the contacts developed enabled us to begin a modest, unfunded programme of research into rugby league and its implementation of child protection policy. This also prompted us to propose a new module – 'Safeguarding and Child Protection in Sport' – which still runs today. This work also led to an invitation, in 2003, from Celia Brackenridge, to join her newly formed 'Child Protection in Sport Research Group', a product of the 'Child Protection in Sport Task Force' that had been established in 1999, in the wake of the Paul Hickson conviction and growing reports of sexual abuse in sport. This subsequently led to the 'Child Protection in Sport Unit' (CPSU) in 2001. Hosting the group at Edge Hill, I presented some of our early work within rugby league (Hartill and Prescott, 2007) and continue to sit on this committee (now chaired by the CPSU).

My doctoral studies had also just begun, and the topic recalled a question I had asked Celia when she spoke to my MA course in Cardiff: 'has there been any research into the abuse of boys in sport?' Seven years later the answer was more or less the same. I was eventually awarded 'PhD' in Sociology, in 2011. The philosophical interests of my supervisors Paul Reynolds and Leon Culbertson (existentialist, Marxist, post-structuralist, Queer) and my reading of Brackenridge as well as Mike Messner, Don Sabo and Jennifer Hargreaves, among many other writers, focused on gender and sport, shaped my interpretation and framing of the problem of child sexual abuse, and continues to do so. My introduction to Foucault, Sartre and later Bourdieu were pivotal moments in my appreciation of the value of theory.

It must also be emphasized that prior to, as well as alongside, my *critical* thinking on sport, I have also been *doing* sport. The former endeavour has been heavily influenced by feminist and pro-feminist sociological thought, whereas the latter has been informed by very different narratives, well-removed from academic thought. In particular, my early adult enthusiasm for rugby union and the 'social life' that came with it took up a considerable amount of my time and energy prior to the age of 30. Indeed, I remain connected to the social networks that were established during this time, seven years or so after I 'retired'.

It is, then, perhaps the case that for a period of 20 years or so, my habitus was closely aligned with that of the field of sport. As a competent youth footballer and an elite youth tennis player, as well as something of an 'all-rounder' at sport-games, I accumulated a significant volume of athletic capital among peers and adults alike. I was a 'sporty boy', captain of football, a rugby player, a cross-country runner, a squash player, a table-tennis player, even occasional golfer. Local press frequently featured my local, regional and national tennis victories (including regional TV news: 'a star in the making'!). I could 'make it', I had 'what it took'! As the realization set in, in late teenage years, that this was in fact not the case, means by which I might reassert or capitalize on the corporeal capacities I had spent many years embodying were evaluated. My tennis capital meant little in the 'world of rugby' – and this was perhaps also an appeal, a fresh start – and I soon identified a level which enabled me to derive at least a little interest from my accumulated sportstock. I became, *again*, enchanted by the game. I knew the stakes and was ready to play, if not 'die for', those stakes: 'no backward steps!' 'Nothing comes through!' 'Show 'em where they are!' Such exhortations mark the masculinist field and are accompanied by a whole objectifying discourse that identifies the group through its opposition to anything or anyone that is *not* the group.

Other groups, especially women and those men that are unable to authentically display allegiance to the norms of the group, are objects of capital, therefore, not without value, but evaluated principally through their value as conquests: teams to 'destroy', individuals to 'nail' in a world where the 'big-hit' could become folklore. My embodiment of such hypermasculinist norms was undoubtedly challenged by feminist and pro-feminist critique, however, this is not to infer – as I read de Beauvoir, Butler, Hargreaves and Lenksyj – a Damascian conversion or anything like it. Rather any 'conversion of gaze' or transfiguration of habitus was gradual and arguably coincided with the dwindling of my final *active* ties with the world, and practice, of sport.

Thus, my *academic habitus* might be thought of as gradually competing with (what I will refer to as) my *athleticist habitus* and doing so on an increasingly level 'playing field'. As my active engagement with the sport *game* has radically diminished, my engagement with the academic *game* has increased exponentially; as my critical reflections on sport and sexual exploitation have developed, so has the requirement to publish academic papers been increasingly linked to career development, as has the need to cultivate, and demonstrate, 'impact'. The 'big-hit' was replaced by the 'REF impact', and it is hard not to observe some similarity in the underpinning logic and collective habitus.

Bourdieu's insistence that researchers apply their objectivating techniques to themselves in order to 'effect in practice this radical doubting' seemed particularly important for my critical consideration of sport and the sexual exploitation of children within it. There is potentially no end to this process and there is much omitted from this brief account. Equally, the extent to which this is in fact a useful exercise rather than 'a narcissistic reflection' is for the reader to decide. Hopefully, it goes some way to providing a fuller elucidation of my trajectory and position in *social space*, *social field* and *scholastic universe* and helps the reader to better situate my position – and *habitus* – in the analysis that follows.

The following chapter focuses on the process of conducting research with 'survivors' of child sexual abuse and exploitation and briefly discusses some of the ethical issues related to this.

Notes

1 Recent events in Germany, where large groups of men used the mass gathering of people for New Year's Eve celebrations to commit numerous sexual assaults on young females illustrates the point explicitly (Connolly, 2016), as does the perpetual use of sexual violence within armed conflict.
2 Fuller critical accounts can be found elsewhere (e.g. Adkins and Skeggs, 2004; Calhoun, 1995; Calhoun *et al.*, 1993; Grenfell, 2012; McCall, 1992).
3 See Bourdieu (2007) for a developed illustration of this.

References

Adkins, L. (2004) Reflexivity: freedom or habit of gender? In L. Adkins and B. Skeggs (eds.) *Feminism after Bourdieu*. Oxford: Blackwell, 191–210.

Adkins, L. and Skeggs, B. (2004) (eds.) *Feminism after Bourdieu*. Oxford: Blackwell.

Bourdieu, P. (1977) *Outline of a theory of practice* [translation R. Nice]. Cambridge: Cambridge University Press.

Bourdieu, P. (1983) The forms of capital [translation R. Nice]. In J.G. Richardson (ed.) *Handbook of theory and research for the sociology of education*. London: Greenwood Press, 241–258.

Bourdieu, P. (1986) *Distinction: a social critique of the judgement of taste* [trans. by R. Nice]. London: Routledge.

Bourdieu, P. (1989) Social space and symbolic power. *Sociological Theory*, 7(1): 14–25.

Bourdieu, P. (1990a) *In other words: essays towards a reflexive sociology*. Cambridge: Polity Press.

Bourdieu, P. (1990b) *The logic of practice*. Cambridge: Polity Press.

Bourdieu, P. (1992) The practice of reflexive sociology ('The Paris Workshop'). In P. Bourdieu and L.D. Wacquant, *An invitation to reflexive sociology*. Cambridge: Polity Press, 218–260.

Bourdieu, P. (1993) *Sociology in question*. London: Sage.

Bourdieu, P. (1998) *Practical reason: on the theory of action*. Cambridge: Polity Press.

Bourdieu, P. (2001) *Masculine domination* [translation by R. Nice]. Cambridge: Polity Press.

Bourdieu, P. (2004) *Science of science and reflexivity* [translation by R. Nice]. Cambridge: Polity Press.

Bourdieu, P. (2007) *Sketch for a self-analysis* [translation by R. Nice]. Cambridge: Polity Press.

Bourdieu, P. and Wacquant, L.D. (1992) *An invitation to reflexive sociology*. Cambridge: Polity Press.

Bourdieu, P. and Accardo, A., Balazs, G., Beaud, S., Bonvin, F., Bourdieu, E., Bourgois, P., Broccolichi, S., Champagne, P., Christin, R., Faguer, J-P., Garcia, S., Lenoir, R., Œuvrard, F., Pialoux, M., Pinto, L., Podalydès, D., Sayad, A., Soulié, C. and Wacquant, L.J.D. (1999) *The weight of the world: social suffering in contemporary society*. Stanford: Stanford University Press.

Brackenridge, C.H. (1997) 'He owned me basically': women's experience of sexual abuse in sport. *International Review for the Sociology of Sport*, 32(2): 115–130.

Brackenridge, C.H. (2001) *Spoilsports: understanding and preventing sexual exploitation in sport*. London: Routledge.

Brackenridge, C.H. (2013) Dancing with the devil: the politics of working with sport organisations. *Researching and enhancing athlete welfare: Proceedings of the Second International Symposium of the Brunel International Research Network for Athlete Welfare* (BIRNAW), 18–21. Available at: http://bura.brunel.ac.uk/handle/2483/8243.

Brackenridge, C.H. and Fasting, K. (2005) The grooming process in sport: narratives of sexual harassment and abuse. *Auto/Biography*, 13: 33–52.

Calhoun, C. (1995) *Critical social theory*. Oxford: Blackwell.

Calhoun, C., LiPuma, E. and Postone, M. (1993) *Bourdieu: critical perspectives*. Cambridge: Polity.

Coles, T. (2008) Finding space in the field of masculinity: lived experiences of men's masculinities. *Journal of Sociology*, 44(3): 233–248. DOI:10.1177/1440783308092882.

Collins, T. (2006) *Rugby League in twentieth century Britain: a social and cultural history*. London: Routledge.

Connell, R.W. (1995) *Masculinities*. Cambridge: Polity.

Connell, R.W. and Messerschmidt, J.W. (2005) Hegemonic masculinity: rethinking the concept. *Gender and Society*, 19(6): 829–859.

Connolly, K. (2016) 'I've never experienced anything like that': Cologne in deep shock over attacks. *The Guardian*. 8 January. Accessed at: https://www. theguardian.com/world/2016/jan/08/ive-never-experienced-anything-like-that-cologne-in-deep-shock-over-attacks [12 January 2016].

Cooky, C., Messner, M.A. and Hextrum, R.H. (2013) Women play sport, but not on TV: a longitudinal study of televised news media. *Communication and Sport*, 1(3): 203–230.

Corby, B. (1993) *Child abuse: towards a knowledge base* (1st ed.) Buckingham: Open University Press.

Creedon, P. (1994) *Women, media and sport: challenging gender values*. Thousand Oaks, CA: Sage.

Cossins, A. (2000) *Masculinities, sexualities and child sexual abuse*. The Hague: Kluwer Law International.

Cowburn, M. (2005) Hegemony and discourse: reconstruing the male sex offender and sexual coercion by men. *Sexualities, Evolution & Gender*, 7(3): 215–231.

Cowburn, M. and Myers, S. (2015) Sex offenders. In J. Wright (editor-in-chief) *International Encyclopedia of the Social and Behavioural Sciences* (2nd ed.). London: Elsevier, 672–677.

Croce, M. (2015) The *habitus* and the critique of the present: a Wittgensteinian reading of Bourdieu's social theory. *Sociological Theory*, 33(4): 327–346.

Crossley, N. (2001) The phenomenological habitus and its construction. *Theory and Society*, 30: 81–120.

Deer, C. (2012) Reflexivity. In M. Grenfell (ed.) *Pierre Bourdieu: key concepts* (2nd ed.). Durham: Acumen, 195–210.

Duncan, M.C. (1990) Sports photographs and sexual difference: images of women and men in the 1984 and 1988 Olympic Games. *Sociology of Sport Journal*, 7: 22–43.

Elliott, M. (1993) (ed.) *Female sexual abuse of children: the ultimate taboo*. Chichester: John Wiley and Sons Ltd.

Fasting, K., Brackenridge, C.H. and Walseth, K. (2002) Coping with sexual harassment in sport: experiences of elite female athletes. *The Journal of Sexual Aggression*, 8(2): 16–36.

Fleming, S. (1995) *Home and away: sport and South Asian male youth*. Aldershot: Avebury.

Frosh, S., Phoenix, A. and Pattman, R. (2003) *Young masculinities: understanding boys in contemporary society*. Basingstoke: Palgrave Macmillan.

Gilbert, R., Spatz Widom, C., Browne, K., Fergusson, D., Webb, E. and Janson, S. (2009) Child maltreatment 1: burden and consequences of child maltreatment in high-income countries. *The Lancet*; Jan 3-Jan 9, 373 (9657): 68–81.

Grenfell, M. (2012) (ed.) *Bourdieu: key concepts* (2nd ed.). London: Routledge.

Grenfell, M. and James, D. with P. Hodkinson, D. Reay and D. Robbins (1998) *Bourdieu and education: acts of practical theory*. London: Taylor & Francis.

Grenfell, M. and James, D. with P. Hodkinson, D. Reay and D. Robbins (2006) *Bourdieu and education: acts of practical theory*. London: Taylor & Francis e-library (Mobipocket.com).

Gilroy, P. (1987) *There ain't no black in the Union Jack: the cultural politics of race and nation*. London: Routledge.

Giulianotti, R. (2004) (ed.) *Sport and modern social theorists*. London: Palgrave Macmillan.

Giulianotti, R. (2005) *Sport: a critical sociology*. Cambridge: Polity.

Hardy, C. (2012) Hysteresis. In M. Grenfell (ed.) *Pierre Bourdieu: key concepts* (2nd ed.). Durham: Acumen, 126–148.

Hargreaves, J.A. (1994) *Sporting females: critical issues in the history and sociology of women's sports*. London: Routledge.

Hartill, M. (2005) Sport and the sexually abused male child. *Sport, Education and Society*, 10(3): 287–304.

Hartill, M. and Prescott, P. (2007) Serious business or 'any other business'? Safeguarding and child protection policy in British Rugby League. *Child Abuse Review*, 16 (4): 237–251. DOI: 10.1002/car.990.

Hearn, J. (2004) From hegemonic masculinity to the hegemony of men. *Feminist Theory*, 5: 49–72.

Jackson, L.A. (2000) *Child sexual abuse in Victorian England*. London: Routledge/ Taylor & Francis.

James, A. and Prout, A. (1997) (eds.) *Constructing and reconstructing childhood: contemporary issues in the sociological study of childhood* (2nd ed.). London: RoutledgeFalmer.

Jarvie, G. (1991) *Sport, racism and ethnicity*. London: Routledge.

Jenks, C. (2005b) *Childhood* (2nd ed.). London: Routledge.

Jones, I.H. (2000) Cultural and historical aspects of male sexual assault. In G.C. Mezey and M.B. King (eds.) *Male victims of sexual assault* (2nd ed.). Oxford: Oxford University Press, 113–124.

Kelly, L. (1988) *Surviving sexual violence*. Cambridge: Polity.

Kimmel, M.S. and Messner, M.A. (2001) *Men's lives* (2nd. ed.). New York: Macmillan.

Kitzinger, J. (1997) Who are you kidding? Children, power and the struggle against sexual abuse. In A. James and A. Prout (eds.) *Constructing and reconstructing childhood: contemporary issues in the sociological study of childhood*. London: Falmer Press, 165–189.

Krais, B. (1993) Gender and symbolic violence: female oppression in the light of Pierre Bourdieu's theory of social practice. In C. Calhoun, E. LiPuma and M. Postone (eds.) *Bourdieu: critical perspectives*. Cambridge: Polity, 156–177.

Lang, M. and Hartill, M. (2015) (eds.) *Safeguarding, child protection and abuse in sport: international perspectives on research, policy and practice*. London: Routledge.

Leahy, T., Pretty, G. and Tenenbaum, G. (2002) Prevalence of sexual abuse in organized competitive sport in Australia. *The Journal of Sexual Aggression*, 8(2): 16–36.

Liddle, A.M. (1993) Gender, desire and child sexual abuse: accounting for the male majority. *Theory, Culture, and Society*, 10: 103–126.

Marx, K. (1867/1976) *Capital: a critique of political economy, Vol. 1*. Middlesex: Penguin.

Maton, K. (2012) Habitus. In M. Grenfell (2012) (ed.) *Bourdieu: key concepts* (2nd ed.). Durham: Acumen, 48–64.

Mauss, M. (1954/1990) *The gift: the form and reason for exchange in archaic societies*. London: Routledge.

McCall, L. (1992) Does gender *fit*? Bourdieu, feminism, and conceptions of social order. *Theory & Society*, 21: 837–867.

McNay, L. (2000) *Gender and agency: reconfiguring the subject in feminist and social theory*. Cambridge: Polity.

Mendel, M.P. (1995) *The male survivor: the impact of sexual abuse*. London: Sage.

Moi, T. (1999) *What is a woman?* Oxford: Oxford University Press.

Moore, R. (2012) Capital. In M. Grenfell (2012) (ed.) Bourdieu: key concepts (2nd ed.). Durham: Acumen, 98–113.

Paradis, E. (2012) Boxers, briefs or bras? Bodies, gender and change in the boxing gym. *Body & Society*, 18(2): 82–109.

Parton, N. (1985) *The politics of child abuse*. London: Macmillan Press.

Parton, N. (2007) Book review. *Child Abuse Review*, 16: 132–133.

Pereda, N., Guilera, G., Forns, M. and Gomez-Benito, J. (2009). The international epidemiology of child sexual abuse: a continuation of Finkelhor (1994). *Child Abuse & Neglect*, 33: 331–342. DOI:10.1016/j.chiabu.2008.07.007.

Plummer, K. (1995) *Telling sexual stories: power, change and social worlds*. London: Routledge.

Plummer, K. (2001) *Documents of life 2: an invitation to critical humanism*. London: Sage.

Postone, M., LiPuma, E. and Calhoun, C. (1993) Introduction: Bourdieu and social theory. In C. Calhoun, E. LiPuma and M. Postone (1993) *Bourdieu: critical perspectives*. Cambridge: Polity, 1–13.

Radbill, S.X. (1968) A history of child abuse and infanticide. In R.E. Helfer and C.H. Kempe (eds.) *The battered child*. London: University of Chicago Press, 3–16.

Rush, F. (1980) *The best kept secret: sexual abuse of children*. New York: McGraw-Hill.

Shilling, C. (2004) Physical capital and situated action: a new direction for corporeal sociology. *British Journal of Sociology of Education*, 25(4): 473–487.

Smallbone, S.W. and McKillop, N. (2015) Evidence-informed approaches to preventing sexual violence and abuse. In P.D. Donnelly and C.L. Ward (eds.) *Oxford Handbook of Violence Prevention*, 177–181.

Stoltenborgh, M., van Ijzendoom, M.H., Euser, E.M. and Bakermans-Kraneburg, M.J. (2011) A global perspective on child sexual abuse: meta-analysis of prevalence around the world. *Child Maltreatment*, 16(2): 79–101.

Struve, J. (1990) Dancing with the patriarchy: the politics of sexual abuse. In M. Hunter (ed.) *The sexually abused male, vol. 1: prevalence, impact and treatment*. Lexington, Massachusetts: Lexington Books, 3–46.

Thomson, P. (2012) Field. In M. Grenfell (ed.) *Pierre Bourdieu: key concepts* (2nd ed.). Durham: Acumen, 65–82.

Thompson, B. (1991) Editor's introduction. In P. Bourdieu, *Language and symbolic power*. Cambridge: Polity Press, 1–31.

Vertommen, T., Schipper-van Veldhoven, N.H.M.J., Hartill, M. and Van Den Eede, F. (2015) Sexual harassment and abuse in sport: The NOC*NSF helpline. *International Review for the Sociology of Sport*, 50(7): 782–839. DOI: 10.1177/1012690213498079.

Wacquant, L.D. (1989) Towards a reflexive sociology: a workshop with Pierre Bourdieu. *Sociological Theory*, 7(1): 26–63.

Wacquant, L.D. (1992) Toward a social praxeology: the structure and logic of Bourdieu's sociology. In P. Bourdieu and L.D. *Wacquant: an invitation to reflexive sociology*. Cambridge: Polity Press, 1–47.

Wacquant, L.D. (2004) *Body and soul: notebooks of an apprentice boxer*. New York: Oxford University Press.

Ward, T. (2014) The explanation of sexual offending: from single factor theories to integrative pluralism. *Journal of Sexual Aggression*, 20(2): 130–141.

Ward, T., Polaschek, D.L.L. and Beech, A.R. (2006) *Theories of sexual offending*. Chichester: John Wiley and Sons, Ltd.

Wellard, I. (2009) *Sport, masculinities and the body*. London: Routledge.

Whitehead, S.M. and Barrett, F.J. (2001) (eds.) *The masculinities reader*. Cambridge: Polity Press.

Wortley, R. and Smallbone, S. (2010) (eds.) *Situational prevention of child sexual abuse* (Crime Prevention Studies, volume 19). London: Lynne Rienner Publishers.

Wykes, M. and Welsh, K. (2009) *Violence, gender and justice*. London: Sage.

Chapter 3

Research with 'survivors' of child sexual abuse in sport

The previous chapter has set out the epistemological perspective that underpins this investigation. In this chapter, I briefly discuss some other important issues related to the undertaking of research with those who have experienced childhood sexual abuse.

Many investigations into CSA have utilized a qualitative interview or narrative approach to uncover the reality of the experience from the perspective of either the victim or perpetrator (e.g. Brackenridge, 2001; Colton and Vanstone, 1996; Etherington, 1995; Hunter, 2009; Lisak, 1994). Indeed, Brackenridge (2001: 239–240) argues 'avenues for further research ... include ... life history analysis through athlete survivor and coach perpetrator narratives ... and multidimensional analyses of coach-athlete interactions'. According to Cole and Knowles (2001: 20) 'both narrative and life history research rely on and depict the storied nature of lives; both are concerned with honouring the individuality and complexity of individuals' experiences'. For Lawler (2002), the significance and value of the narrative approach is its ability to link the past to the present, and the individual to the social.

While Bourdieu approaches data collection from his own particular epistemological perspective, it is clear that narrative approaches to data collection – or rather data *generation* – offer the means by which *habitus*, *capital* and *field* can be explored and elucidated. Indeed, this approach is adopted within a number of his works, including *The Weight of the World* (Bourdieu *et al.*, 1999). However, given the sensitivity of the research topic, there are many ethical concerns to consider and the choice of method is also central to the management of these concerns.

Ethical dilemmas and considerations

Following the (re)discovery of child sex abuse in the latter part of the twentieth century, (feminist) researchers have determined that, in opposition to the silence that surrounds CSA and sexual violence generally, research must include the 'voices' of victims who have previously gone unacknowledged or been silenced. As Griffin (1971: 27) observed on the issue of rape, 'the subject is so rarely discussed by that unofficial staff of male intellectuals ... that one begins to suspect a conspiracy of silence'. Her insight still has considerable resonance today, despite national inquiries in some countries (e.g. Australia, New Zealand, UK). Three decades later, Plummer (2001: 252) argued, 'as many writers have long known, the telling of stories – and especially life stories – goes to the heart of the moral life of a culture'. However, according to Israel and Hay (2006: 3):

> Social scientists do not have an inalienable right to conduct research involving other people. That we continue to have the freedom to conduct such work is, in large part, the product of individual and social goodwill and depends on us acting in ways that are not harmful and are just.

In research on childhood sexual abuse, where participants are 'victims' or 'survivors', this imperative is accentuated by the fact that the individual has already been exploited and very possibly been harmed as a result. In such cases, *non-malfeasance* or ensuring that the research process does not contribute further harm or exploitation must obviously be the central and overriding consideration, within the research design and subsequent stages of the research process. Central to the principle of non-malfeasance is the choice of method used to gather data. According to Holloway and Freshwater (2007: 709):

> Vulnerable people are sometimes at risk of being exploited in questionnaires or semi-structured interviews because their voices are not predominant, their thoughts are disrupted, as are their identities. The narrative method carries with it the potential to empower individuals to see beyond the boundaries of their vulnerability and – to some extent, regain their normal self by enabling them to take control.

Therefore, ethical conduct and choice of method are not separate categories but closely related ones. Træen and Sørensen (2008: 378) argue for a similar approach in their research with female 'survivors':

> The in-depth interview makes it possible to present the ways in which the women understand themselves, interpret what happens to them and create meaning from it. It explores stages of the informants' life, which makes it possible to generate new theory about the relationship between the individual and her social structures and culture.

This closely resembles the approach taken here (and discussed further). A key feature of my approach was to allow, or enable, the participants to tell their stories, in their own words using their own language, rather than to demand they answer my questions, generated from *my* categories and *my* (mis-)conceptions of their experiences. Hence, for Byrne (2004: 182) the in-depth interview 'has been particularly attractive to researchers who want to explore voices and experiences which they believe have been ignored, misrepresented or suppressed in the past.'

Given the risks involved for the participant being asked to divulge potentially highly distressing information for the purposes of research, it was essential that participants were self-identifying based on as full an understanding as possible of the research project, the criteria for inclusion and the potential impact and outcomes of the study. Following other research in this area (e.g. Brackenridge, 2001; Etherington, 1995; Fasting *et al.*, 2002), the decision to seek the testimony of *adult* 'survivors' was taken very early in the design of the research.

As a *potentially* vulnerable population, studies with adult 'survivors' typically emphasize the necessity for anonymity, confidentiality, right to withdraw, sources of professional support and informed consent (e.g. Brackenridge, 2001; Træen and Sørensen, 2008). These issues were all attended to in this study (see Appendix 1), and the research that underpins this work has been approved, on two separate occasions, following scrutiny from an institutional Research Ethics Committee.

Method

To assist with recruitment some information and contact details were placed on an institutional website and several individuals contacted me via this method, one of whom was interviewed. The remainder were contacted by email following public disclosures or else contact was facilitated by a victim-support organization. Following initial contact, usually by email, all the participants were provided with written and verbal information. Anonymity was discussed and agreed. Each participant confirmed their consent to participate in writing. Each interview began, prior to recording, with discussion about the participant's willingness to proceed. The 'face-to-face' interviews were conducted in one 'sitting' while the telephone interviews were conducted over two or more (up to five) 'sittings'. The spoken interviews were recorded via a digital voice recorder. Two interviews were conducted in person at the participants' homes, one via Skype, two via email correspondence and two via telephone. The recordings were transferred to a personal computer secured by my institution. Transcription was completed by me or an assistant employed by my institution. All data was anonymized at this point and stored securely. Interviewees were sent copies of the full transcription.

An interview schedule was drawn up but not applied within the interview. Broadly, participants were invited to tell their story with the understanding that I would then ask questions on the issues they referred to and ask for more detail or to explain more fully. However, typically, the conversation would begin with a focus on early childhood and family life and took in childhood experiences and contexts (often school and sport) gradually leading to when the sexual abuse began. Therefore, following initial broad questions, such as, 'can you tell me about your early family life?' and 'how did sport begin for you?', a conversational-style allowed the participants to lead the conversation with occasional prompts for further detail related to their line of thought. Bourdieu *et al.* (1999: 609) refer to this as 'active and methodical listening': a style employed in order to 'reduce as much as possible the symbolic violence exerted through that relationship'; whereby the researcher 'engages in conversation and brings the speaker to engage in it' (Bourdieu *et al.*, 1999: 619). For example:

> *Can you tell me how the sports stuff started? How you got into it?*
> Well I don't know. When I was a child, I played constantly even by myself. I invented basketball games. I even organised softball teams in my neighbourhood and a football team. This is even before I got involved in organised sports. So I took like coffee cans and nailed them to the doorways in my house. I don't know how my parents permitted it. So I just kept looking for the opportunity to enter sports...

Bourdieu *et al.* (1999: 621) argue that the 'craft' of sociological research 'disposes one to improvise ... strategies of ... encouragement and opportune questions, *etc.*, so as to help respondents deliver up their truth'. One strategy I employed was to make notes on areas of the participant's story that appeared interesting or significant then used these as prompts for further questions. I explained beforehand that I would be making occasional notes to reduce the extent to which this was distracting. However, the approach of active and methodical listening was itself by far the most important means of creating an authentic encounter within the synthetic environment of the research interview. My questions were also informed by Bourdieu's framework for social action – *habitus*, *capital* and *field*. I was interested then, not only in their experiences of abuse and their individual dispositions towards that experience (the 'impact'), but also in enabling them to evoke the situated or context-specific character of that abuse; in other words, *field*.

It was anticipated that this approach would facilitate a 'richer' conversation and one in which the participant felt comfortable and able to speak freely, without feeling overtly pressured within the research process to conform to expectations about their experiences that may be conveyed through more rigid questionnaire-style data collection. However, Bourdieu *et al.* (1999: 610) argue 'social proximity and familiarity provide two of the conditions of "nonviolent" communication'. He continues, where 'the interviewee is perfectly well aware of sharing with the interviewer the core of what the questions induce the other to divulge, and of sharing, by the same token, the risks of that exposure' 'even the most brutally objectifying questions have no reason to appear threatening or aggressive' (Bourdieu *et al.*, 1999: 611). This should not be overstated, but common experience perhaps enabled conditions for a less threatening, more authentic exchange. This is perhaps especially important given the power imbalance potentially at play when the research discourse is structured around such differentiated positions as 'academic' and 'victim'/'survivor'. However, it is also important to record that all seven participants are mature, 'successful', articulate individuals who appeared very self-assured and confident in their exposition and not in the least intimidated by the process.

Confidentiality, anonymity and guilty knowledge

Anonymity for participants is a key concern in social research, especially where the research population may be considered vulnerable or the topic sensitive. This certainly applies to the issue of childhood sexual abuse; therefore, the identities of all participants remain confidential via processes of anonymization. However, an issue related to confidentiality and anonymity is 'guilty knowledge' (Brackenridge, 1999). In research of this nature, it is possible that participants will pass on information that could be used by authorities to prevent harm to a child. In such a situation, a researcher holds knowledge that could potentially protect other children from harm.

However, there are a whole host of outcomes from official disclosure that may have negative and serious consequences for the research participant. Thus, researchers should be wary of assuming that a disclosure to the authorities will result in a positive outcome for all where, for example, an abuser is convicted and the participant experiences the process and outcome as a positive one. Propelling research participants towards an official disclosure may seem to be in their best interests, but the research will have unalterably affected the life of the participant and not necessarily for the better. Hunter's (1990: 118) cautionary point, should be carefully considered by researcher and participant: '...since telling your story publicly is such a powerful experience, it also carries the possibility of harming you. As a sexual abuse victim you already know about loss of control ... you don't need another lesson in it'.

Prior to interviewing, participants were informed that specific details (i.e. names) may be passed on to authorities if disclosed, but it was emphasized that this was not the objective of the study and such details would not be sought. This strategy potentially creates a space for the participant to decide for themselves, in advance, whether to include incriminating details of perpetrators within the interview process in the full knowledge that this information would be passed on and may become the subject of a judicial inquiry. This also allows for discussion of the potential outcomes and impact of such action. However, in all but one case, perpetrators were either already known to the authorities or deceased. In the one exception, no identifying details were supplied.

Non-malfeasance and the research relationship

While the principle of non-malfeasance, or 'doing no harm', must be central to all research, it must be acknowledged that the potential for doing harm clearly exists within research of this nature, and this is impossible to fully eradicate. As Plummer (2001: 224) warns:

> Telling their stories could literally destroy them – bring them to suicidal edges, murderous thoughts, danger. More modestly, they may be severely traumatized. The telling of the story of a life is a deeply problematic and ethical process in which researchers are fully implicated ... in practice life story research always means you are playing with another person's life: so you had better be careful. Very careful indeed.

Harm may be caused by the exercise of talking to those who have experienced CSA (even by the act of contacting them); harm may be caused by falsely interpreting their stories; and harm may be caused by the mere action of putting into concrete text (written word) an expression of their experiences that had previously remained (forcibly) hidden and unspoken (see Brackenridge, 1999). The nature of this harm is potentially multiple and diverse and is not confined purely to the individual participant. There are perhaps ways to mitigate this harm as suggested here, but no certain way of preventing it. *All* strategies are of the order of intention and hope rather than certitude. The argument from potential harm versus potential benefit should also not be overstated; whatever wider benefits may accrue from research of this kind may well be immaterial for the individual who is damaged as a result of the research experience.

Arrangements were made for participants to be provided with access to appropriate support materials, including contact details of supportive agencies. In offering and providing advice, the comments of Brackenridge (2001: 153) were taken very seriously:

> No researcher should overstep the limits of her professional training or skills by giving counselling or advice which lies outside her competence. I worked with a qualified social worker before commencing my first set of interviews ... It is good practice to prepare in this way before embarking on potentially dangerous work where distress may be caused to the researcher and harm to the participants.

Therefore, I adopted Brackenridge's method of securing access to a qualified and experienced social worker prior to starting the interview process. While the interviews were often 'emotional' experiences for both researcher and participant, ultimately, there has been no indication that any of the participants experienced adverse effects from the process, and most made explicit references to the therapeutic and positive nature of the experience. However, it should be noted that all these adults declared themselves *ready* to tell their story based on years of reflection, sometimes based on professional support. For example:

> JACK: I did finally seek out professional help ... I have dealt with the pain, anger, guilt and loss, so I am at a point in my life that talking about this with people, who have reason to hear this, doesn't get me down or disturbed. I willingly shared this with you because I am able to and because I now wear a badge that reads 'SURVIVOR'. I believe that others will benefit through your work and I hope that my small contribution could add just a little more weight to create an even larger impact that may just save another child.

Bourdieu likens the role of the interviewer to that of the midwife, in the sense that the interviewer assists in the *delivery* of the participant's story. The analogy is especially apt for research with 'survivors' of abuse – the interviewer can aid and assist, yet the difficulty, indeed pain, belongs to the individual being asked to *deliver* their truth. The analogy is also appropriate based on the degree of intimacy and personal intrusion required in the act of 'delivery' and, as a consequence, the degree to which the individual must trust the researcher is exceptionally high. Therefore, establishing such a relationship holds inherent difficulties and dangers. According to Kirsch (1999):

> As researchers and participants get acquainted, establish trust and friendship, they become vulnerable to misunderstanding, disappointment and invaded privacy. It can lead amongst other things to false intimacies, fraudulent friendships, a deceptiveness over equal relationships, and a masking of power.
>
> (Quoted in Plummer, 2001: 212)

This seemed to be one of the greatest dangers of the research, thus care was taken, upon initial contact, to discuss what the likely and potential (including unlikely) outcomes of the research might be and the possibility of publication. One advantage of communicating entirely by email (as with Jack) is that these early context-setting, informal exchanges are also documented and reveal something of the relationship-forming process.

In each case then, to varying degrees, participants were interested in why *I* was interested – in other words, 'what was my angle?' For example, following some initial discussion and disclosure, Jack asked:

> If I may be so bold to ask and here are my questions – why your interest in this? The reason, one of three things come to mind – being a survivor always leaves one a bit suspicious and curious so forgive me, here goes: 1. I can only think that something happened to you or somebody close to you that compelled you to this; 2. you were assigned this for a grant or educational requirements from a superior, or 3. you (and if I am over stepping and offending, sorry but I am going to ask) derive some sexual gratification from accounts like this.

As Plummer puts it, motivations must be considered carefully, 'yours and your subjects ... at the outset it is necessary to come fairly clean with the subject, who will very likely sense a whiff of exploitation unless you do' (2001: 136). Following my response to Jack's question, he replied:

> Thank you for filling in the blanks for me, not taking offense to my questions, and also for your honesty on all levels with an opening to ask personal questions, which I more than likely will not ask routinely ... Murky, blurry lines can impact the outcomes of a study and no need to explain the roles of researcher and participant ... I concur, it is best for the outcome to remain clear and distinct within the respective and appropriate roles. Interestingly enough, and this brought a smile to me ... I digress and moving along here, I am fine and feel reassured with your response to my previous email. Shoot, ask away, and I will do my best to fill in the blanks.

Plummer (2001) suggests there is a 'continuum of involvement' for the researcher that characterizes the varying levels of involvement a researcher might have with their research participants. These are the 'Stranger Role', the 'Acquaintance Role' and the 'Friendship Role' (he also adds a 'controversial' fourth – the 'Lover' role). It seemed clear to me that for the process of gathering information to be successful for *all* involved, it would be inappropriate to simply conduct an interview and then automatically terminate the relationship on the grounds that the research was concluded – or that I had what I wanted. In my submission to my institution's Research Ethics Committee, I wrote:

> ... it is my intention to develop a genuine relationship with those who agree to participate, therefore, multiple meetings/interviews will be requested and the research will be terminated through a process of

mutual consent. This seems essential if the research is to attempt to develop from an ethically sound position. That is to say, to contact individuals who had experienced CSA and request of them details of the most intimate and disturbing nature, only to 'dismiss' them when I had what I wanted (to achieve my own ends) would be morally vacuous and resemble the original abuse.

I gave considerable thought to the research relationship. I was particularly concerned that the familiarity and related feelings and emotions that might be fostered by the experience of the research should negatively affect the participant. In actual fact, possibly because of the maturity of my participants and the fact that they had all had considerable time to 'work through' their abuse, including with professional therapists and counsellors, this does not appear to have been the case. However, the potential for a relationship to continue beyond the term of the study was anticipated. Indeed, in my submission I stated:

> It is anticipated that if a genuine relationship develops, albeit originally based upon the *ostensibly* instrumental objective of eliciting information, then this will be to the benefit of both the research(er) and the participant; it is also anticipated that if these relationships were to continue beyond the duration of the study, this would be entirely correct and to that extent should not be discouraged (if, at the same time, not actively sought).

However, Plummer (2001: 210) warns that intimate friendship between the researcher and a participant 'can create an enormous tension between the professional role of the researcher and the personal commitments of friendship.' Therefore, I sought to maintain an appropriate and respectful distance with my participants, while maintaining contact on the progress of the study where possible. In some instances this contact has petered out, but I maintain contact with several of my participants.

Analysis

As always, Bourdieu's demands are, indeed, demanding. He states:

> ...the analyst will be able to make the most unavoidable intrusions acceptable only through a rewriting that reconciles two doubly contradictory goals. On the one hand, the discussion must provide all the elements necessary to analyse the interviewees' positions objectively and to understand their points of view, and it must accomplish this without setting up the objectivizing distance that reduces the individual to a specimen in a display case. On the other

hand, it must adopt a perspective as close as possible to the individual's own without ... turning into the subject of this worldview.

(Bourdieu in Bourdieu *et al.*, 1999: 2)

The reader must be the judge of the degree to which the following analysis
(Chapter 5 and 6) achieves this finely balanced goal. Hopefully, there are
at least moments when this is the case, albeit plenty where I fall consider-
ably short. Again, however, this reiterates Bourdieu's point regarding the
central task of construction within research. The interview 'data' could be
interpreted in different ways and put to different uses. Different theoretical
models and conceptual instruments produce differing interpretations – different constructions of reality. Certainly, my intent has not been to extract
risk factors and suchlike but rather to allow the stories, as far as possible
within space limits, to speak for themselves and, hopefully, speak directly
to the reader. The intention of the participant objectivation in the previous
chapter, and the description of the research process and management of
ethical concerns above is intended to make the operations behind the construction more visible – indeed, to make the researcher more visible and,
therefore, at least a little more vulnerable. Given the power to construct,
conveyed in the privileged position of 'researcher', this seems important.

Nevertheless, while my participants consented to giving their accounts
and the use of them for research purposes, the process of delivering these
stories of extreme personal suffering is not done without some anxiety.
The stories presented in Chapter 5 constitute the first element of my analysis of *habitus* in relation to sexual subjection in sport. While they are the
words spoken within interviews (with only minor revisions and adjust-
ments to assist coherence), they are clearly reformulations of their
accounts. While in some instances these narratives have been seen by the
participants, with very minor additions or clarifications offered, in some
instances this was not possible. Ultimately, decisions have been taken
about the elements that remained and the elements that were removed.
Beyond the veracity of the interview encounter itself, this introduces a
further moment of analysis and interpretation, and these narratives should
be understood both as the products of a specific encounter (between
researcher and participant) as well as constructions generated, or at least
significantly influenced by, the *habitus* of the researcher. This is also obviously the case for the subsequent analysis offered.

The aim is to treat, or analyse, these stories in a substantive and serious
fashion, but also to subject them to robust 'scientific' investigation according to the epistemology I have outlined. I can offer no guarantees that my
participants would agree with either aspects of my reconstruction of their
life stories. Therefore, I asked my participants not just to *give up* their life
stories, to deliver them, but also, in a sense, to give them away. To allow
them to be 'adopted'. The feelings of anxiety this has generated were

largely unanticipated, and I hope that I have treated these 'gifts' with the care and respect they warrant. Nevertheless, anonymity is then crucial, therefore, details of the stories have been both withheld and altered to protect the identities of the participants and others.

References

Bourdieu, P. Bourdieu, P. and Accardo, A., Balazs, G., Beaud, S., Bonvin, F., Bourdieu, E., Bourgois, P., Broccolichi, S., Champagne, P., Christin, R., Faguer, J-P., Garcia, S., Lenoir, R., Œuvrard, F., Pialoux, M., Pinto, L., Podalydès, D., Sayad, A., Soulié, C., Wacquant, L.J.D. (1999) *The weight of the world: social suffering in contemporary society*. Stanford: Stanford University Press.

Brackenridge, C.H. (1999) Managing myself: investigator survival in sensitive research. *International Review for the Sociology of Sport*, 34(4): 399–410.

Brackenridge, C.H. (2001) *Spoilsports: understanding and preventing sexual exploitation in sport*. London: Routledge.

Byrne, B. (2004) Qualitative interviewing. In C. Seale (ed.) *Researching society and culture*. London: Sage, 179–182.

Cole, A.L. and Knowles, J.G. (2001) *Lives in context: the art of life history research*. New York: Altamira Press.

Colton, M. and Vanstone, M. (1996) *Betrayal of trust: sexual abuse by men who work with children – in their own words*. London: Free Association Books.

Etherington, K. (1995) *Adult male survivors of childhood sexual abuse*. Brighton: Pavilion Publishing.

Fasting, K., Brackenridge, C.H. and Walseth, K. (2002) Coping with sexual harassment in sport: experiences of elite female athletes. *The Journal of Sexual Aggression*, 8(2): 16–36.

Griffin, S. (1971) Rape: the all-American crime. *Ramparts*. September: 26–35.

Holloway, I. and Freshwater, D. (2007) Vulnerable story telling: narrative research in nursing. *Journal of Research in Nursing*, 12(6): 703–711.

Hunter, M. (1990) *Abused boys: the neglected victims of sexual abuse*. New York: Fawcett Columbine.

Hunter, S.V. (2009) Beyond surviving: gender differences in response to early sexual experiences with adults. *Journal of Family Issues*, 30(3): 391–412.

Israel, M. and Hay, I. (2006) *Research ethics for social scientists*. London: Sage.

Lawler, S. (2002) Narrative in social research. In T. May (ed.) *Qualitative research in action*. London: Sage, 242–258.

Lisak, D. (1994) The psychological impact of sexual abuse: content analysis of interviews with male survivors. *Journal of Traumatic Stress*, 7(4): 525–548.

Plummer, K. (2001) *Documents of life 2: an invitation to critical humanism*. London: Sage.

Træen, B., and Sørensen, D. (2008) A qualitative study of how survivors of sexual, psychological and physical abuse manage sexuality and desire. *Sexual and Relationship Therapy*, 23(4): 377–391. DOI: 10.1080/14681990802385699.

Chapter 4

A sketch of the field

Children are integral to the practice of contemporary sport, and the child's participation in sport is overwhelmingly considered to be a virtue. Therefore, children are explicitly encouraged, recruited, from a young age, to participate in sport and conspicuously rewarded for doing so. Sport is, then, integral to many children's lives and to how we construct, globally, a 'good' childhood. If, then, as Kitzinger (1997) argues, the risk of child maltreatment is built-in to the 'institution' of childhood – it is important to consider the role that the institution, or rather *field*, of sport plays in constructing the child, childhood and adult-child relations.

Contextualized historical understanding is crucial in Bourdieu's sociology. Thus, he states, 'through the practical knowledge of the principles of the game that is tacitly required of new entrants, the whole history of the game, the whole past of the game, is present in each act of the game' (Bourdieu, 1993: 74). He adds, 'the history of sport is a relatively autonomous history which, even when marked by the major events of economic and social history, has its own tempo, its own evolutionary laws, its own crises, in short, its specific chronology' (Bourdieu, 1993: 118). Indeed, according to Brackenridge (2001), it is precisely this autonomy that has frequently enabled sport to remain resistant to external scrutiny and impervious to criticism from forces outside the sports 'universe'.

In Bourdieu's theory of social practice, agents actively determine their lives, but they 'don't do just anything'; the *field*, and the structure of *capital* therein, is central to any understanding of social practice. Fields are semi-autonomous and have their own history and logic and social action is related to the context in which it occurs. In developing a Bourdieusian-informed account of the sexual subjection of children in sport, it is, then, crucial to interrogate the nature of the social space that the institution of sport constructs for girls and boys. In the following chapters, I explore this space specifically through the experiences of individuals that were subjected to sexual abuse in sport. However, in this chapter and following Bourdieu (e.g. 1998a, 2004), analyzing social action in any *field* necessitates an analysis or 'sketch' of the field to which that action pertains. Bourdieu (1990: 160) states:

> Rather than remaining content with knowing really well a small sector of reality ... one must, then, in the manner of academic architects who used to present a charcoal sketch of the building as a whole within which one could find the individual part worked out in detail, *endeavour to construct a summary description of the whole of the space considered* (emphasis added).

This is instructive for researchers examining abuse in sport. Findings, whether quantitative or qualitative (to slip back into traditional and divisive nomenclature) must be situated within an understanding or interpretation of context. Bourdieu clarifies this specifically in regard to sport: 'it is impossible to analyse a particular sport independently of the set of sporting practices; one has to imagine the space of sporting practices as a system from which every element derives its distinctive value' (Bourdieu, 1990: 156). Therefore, in this chapter, I offer a 'sketch' of the 'space of sporting practices' as a contextual frame through which further empirical data can be considered. The purpose of this chapter, then, is to introduce the reader to a critical and empirically informed reading of the cultural context at stake: the *field* of organized sport, and its relation to the child. This 'sketching' exercise, albeit partial, will constitute the backdrop against which the narratives of athletes sexually abused in sport, during childhood, will be presented.

The child, education and the cult of athleticism

The origins of contemporary 'sport' are generally acknowledged to lie predominantly in nineteenth century England (Huizinga, 1966; Guttmann, 2004) and particularly the Victorian public school, which drew on classical notions of the importance of training mind *and* body (Holt, 1989). Populated by the sons of the dominant classes, public school 'games' were used to 'develop a form of character, broadly understood as an amalgam of self-reliance, loyalty, endurance, teamwork and self-sacrifice' (Schirato, 2007: 48) in order to equip them for future leadership. Therefore, adherence to the (middle-class) ethos or spirit of 'the game' was crucial, 'to the extent that by the end of the Victorian period, sport and the notion of fair play was (almost universally) synonymous with British national character' (Schirato, 2007: 51).

However, games, particularly the early form of football and rugby, were marked by brutal physical engagement, aggression and bullying (Dunning and Sheard, 2005). The particular brand of education offered in the English public school developed out of seventeenth and eighteenth century

Enlightenment thinking on the nature of childhood. According to Cunningham (1995), the work of John Locke (1632–1704) and Jean-Jacques Rousseau (1712–1778) offered a new focus on 'the child' but from competing perspectives. Locke (1693) was primarily concerned with shaping the child, through education (including use of corporal punishment if necessary) to become a successful, moral adult. Rousseau (1762) on the other hand, conceptualized the child as having arrived fresh from God (as opposed to Puritan ideas of arriving in original sin) and being close to nature; crucially, he claimed that childhood was the best part of life (Cunningham, 1995). But Rousseau's romantic ideas of the child, while revolutionizing thinking about childhood, were considered difficult to implement (Cunningham, 1995). Locke's ideas of discipline were much more appealing to those focused on the perceived need to educate unruly young males in the rules of 'manliness' and 'gentlemanly conduct'.

Thus, Thomas Arnold, one of the key protagonists of 'muscular Christianity' and headmaster at *Rugby School* (1828–1841) for boys aimed to create an enlightened ruling class of educated men based on 'loyalty … [and] self-sacrifice' (Hargreaves, 1987: 39). The largely secular 'cult of athleticism' – that grew out of Arnold's approach – led to the organization of sport in the forms that we know them today. This cult of athleticism can be seen to have resonated (or been put to work) in three important ways:

> It fed into the growing concern for national defence; it met the growing demand among dominant groups for a form of leisure activity which was complementary to work; and above all it was a way of disciplining or 'normalizing' the male youth of the dominant classes to enable them to take their places in the modern social order.
>
> (Hargreaves, 1987: 41)

As Whitehead and Barrett (2001: 8) point out 'the crisis of masculinity thesis goes back a long way' and informed the character of English public school system, as well as movements such as 'the Boy Scouts of America … and dominant definitions of race, class and nationhood'. Drawing on the ideas of Michel Foucault (1977), John Hargreaves sums up the rationalist origins of English public schools and the sports to which they gave rise:

> In the public schools a new disciplinary technology was discovered and developed, which was deployed for the first time on the sons of the dominant classes themselves. Like the workhouses, asylums, hospitals, prisons, barracks and factories of the era, these schools closed off the individual from society, subjecting him to the uninterrupted gaze of authority.
>
> (Hargreaves, 1987: 42)

Therefore, athleticist discourse and practice constituted a 'new disciplinary strategy' which enabled the state to extend its disciplinary gaze into leisure as well as work. Thus, 'the body was made uninterruptedly visible and control was thereby extended over the "soul" of the individual' (Hargreaves, 1987: 42).

Through the education system, this new 'athleticism' – underpinned by a discourse of control, discipline and surveillance – is constructed as 'the means of correct training' (Foucault, 1977). That is, a means to instil those values/characteristics in the male children of the dominant classes thought to be central to maintaining their position in the social system. It is evident then that the origins of sport were organized around the maintenance of power relations, both those based on class (emphasized by Hargreaves, 1987) and 'race' (Hoberman, 1997), but more importantly for this discussion, those based on gender. As Hargreaves (1987: 56) notes, 'wherever we look ... sports culture seems overwhelmingly a masculine culture'. Indeed, this was true, generally speaking, regardless of which social class or ethnic group might have been engaged in sport. As Hargreaves (1987) points out, the male working-class (including black and minority ethnic communities) were co-opted into this athleticist discourse early on in the mass organization of sport (for example, through the *Working Men's Club and Institute Union*, 1863).

Athletic masculinity

Cunningham (1995) argues that while in the 1830s the notion of the *un-gendered, neutral* child was popular, towards the end of the century this was no longer the case. The emergence of sport in its organized form, at a time when women were agitating for suffrage, was instrumental in naturalizing the division of the sexes from childhood into adulthood (Burstyn, 1999). Utilizing the enthusiasm for games, instilled within upper and middle-class boys, Arnold and many who followed him, melded Lockean notions of disciplining the boy into a 'gentleman' through the use of corporeal means. As Roberta J. Park states:

> Whereas earlier callisthenics, gymnastics or simple out-of-door pursuits provided the means by which the body – and morals – were to be developed, by the last decades of the [nineteenth] century it was in the crucible of athletic competition that the male character was to be forged.
>
> (In Mangan and Vertinsky, 2009: 46)

Thus, according to Kimmel (2005) a new form of masculinity – 'Marketplace Man' – arose in the west in the 1830s that pushed aside previous models of manhood – the 'Genteel Patriarch' and the 'Heroic Artisan':

> Marketplace Man derived his identity entirely from his success in the capitalist marketplace … an increasingly homosocial environment … [it] was a manhood that required … the acquisition of tangible goods as evidence of success. It reconstituted itself by the exclusion of 'others' – women, non-white men, non-native-born men, homosexual men … Marketplace masculinity describes his characteristics – aggression, competition, anxiety…
>
> (Kimmel, 2005: 29)

Therefore, this new model of masculinity emerges during the Victorian period alongside the codification and organization of sports as we know them today. Indeed, more than that, it was those very men, most vehemently and meticulously schooled (at Eton, Harrow, Rugby, etc.) to dominate in the 'marketplace', that were central figures in this process. Modern sport can be seen as a manifestation of 'Marketplace Man'. Thus, in the mid-twentieth century, Goffman (1963) writes that, aside from other crucial characteristics (e.g. white, heterosexual), it is 'a recent record in sports' that signifies the dominant male (cited in Kimmel, 2005: 30).

For Bourdieu (1993: 72), 'there are general laws of fields' as well as 'specific properties … but we know that in every field we shall find a struggle' and 'a dominant agent who will try to defend the monopoly and keep out competition' (Bourdieu, 1993: 72). The origins of contemporary sport lie, in part, within British/western nineteenth century male fears over the feminizing effects of industrialization on male children (Burstyn, 1999). While fathers had played a central role in parenting in the seventeenth and eighteenth centuries, particularly in regard to their moral development, their increased absence from the home due to the changing nature of work (agricultural to industrial) as capitalism developed, meant that nineteenth century childhood was characterized by an 'over-present' mother and an absent father (Burstyn, 1999). Burstyn (1999: 52) argues that this absence 'created an emotional and pedagogical need for extra-familial social fatherhood to prepare boys for the competitive, public world of men.' According to Messner (1997: 9), physical activities were seen as 'masculine returns to nature', which would fulfil this function and provide rites of passage into manhood. If the British were to meet the tasks of industrialization and empire, the socialization of the future leaders could not be left to the vagaries of the family, especially a female-headed one: 'instead, the professions, armies, and bureaucracies emerged, organized on principles of utilitarian affiliation, exclusively male and profoundly gendered' (Burstyn, 1999: 52). For Burstyn, a 'masculinity market' developed and 'sport responded to and fed the attraction and power of hypermasculine symbols, ideals, and fields of endeavour and thus led to the valuing of excessive instrumentality and aggressive physicality' (Burstyn, 1999: 54).

In other words, vigorous, aggressive and competitive games were seen as essential to healthy masculinity, and this is undoubtedly a relation that has endured. This relation was (and is) often facilitated (or legitimized) through the notion that physical activity had strong educational benefits, hence the popular idiom, *mens sana in corpore sano* ('a healthy mind in a healthy body'). While boys can now play netball and girls can play football (at least in some countries), the education system continues to distinguish the sexes through *Physical Education* and *School-Sport* (e.g. male and female sports, male and female competitions) thereby naturalizing difference through systems and narratives that serve the patriarchal endeavour and its essentialist discourse (Renold, 1997). As Bourdieu states, 'the most important effect of the rite is the one which attracts the least attention: by treating men and women differently, the rite *consecrates* the difference, institutes it' (1991: 118). The institution of difference and inequality between males and females through the rite (or practice) of sports continues to be a key effect of children's 'physical education' and 'school sport'. Indeed, in the UK, even as women's participation in higher education begins to exceed their male peers, the gender imbalance in sport-based courses (e.g. *Sport Science*) remains (UCAS, 2015). In the following section, I consider the historical trajectory of the athleticist field in terms of the current distribution of capital that generates field positions. Again, the focus is on gender relations.

Field positions: gender relations, science and sport

It can be argued that the association between sport, education and science has had a durable impact on gender relations. Thus, according to Jennifer Hargreaves (1994: 44):

> By the second half of the nineteenth century science ... provided a supposedly 'factual' or 'objective', but in effect conservative, legitimation of patriarchal relations or male domination, and scientific method was viewed as a rational replacement for previously held emotional and uncritical theories about the role of women.

Patriarchal forces utilized science as an instrument, perhaps the ideal naturalizing instrument, for placing the patriarchal organization of social relations beyond doubt. Therefore, while in ancient Greece women were barred from entering the Olympic arena on pain of death because it would insult the gods, in the contemporary version, established in 1896 and inspired by the English public school system, women were barred from many events because, for example, it would damage their ability to conceive, and this was no less than a scientific fact.

Organized sport, then, provides a powerful expression of the 'natural' superiority of males over females. The emphasis on performance in 'Sport and Exercise Science' arguably operates to maintain and reproduce difference through its emphasis on the hierarchical ordering of the species. Thus, the explicit *scientific* measuring of all aspects of physical performance can be seen as an effective tool to perpetuate gender difference through the unassailable guise of 'objective', 'scientific' assessment. This gendered ranking is then abundantly and explicitly mediated and meticulously recorded through the powerful collaboration between organized sport and multinational corporations that control print and audio-visual media (see Wenner, 2002).

Thus, with the exponential growth in sport *science* (especially within western systems of higher education), it may be observed that *Marketplace Man* continues to anxiously and voraciously monitor, measure and enhance, with ever-increasing precision, the performances of his fraternal brothers. The growth in performance enhancement in sport *science* within higher education (and within elite sport) might be considered more critically through a gendered analysis of those who benefit most from this field of science and technology.

It is perhaps unnecessary to make *too* much of the fact that – in 2015–16, 14 of the 15 positions of the *Journal of Sport Sciences* (the journal of *BASES: The British Association of Sport and Exercise Sciences*) editorial board are currently filled by men; or that of the journal's 10 Advisory Boards only 15 per cent of positions are held by women; or that eight of the ten positions of the BASES board are filled by men (including the chair) while four of the five management divisions are chaired by men, with only 20 per cent of these committee positions filled by women – but the fact remains nevertheless.[1] Similarly, the editor and the assistant editors for the *Journal of Human Kinetics* and the *Journal of Human Sport and Exercise* are all male.

In this way, patriarchal forces can be seen to generate, organize and appropriate science as a (particularly) powerful instrument to maintain male domination (as indeed it has been used to legitimize class and particularly 'racial' oppression; see Edwards, 1984; Hoberman, 1997). Therefore, the influence of 'science' on sport should not be seen as coincidental or arbitrary, nor indeed should the proliferation and dominance of *Sport and Exercise Science* in the academic study of sport – an intellectual enterprise inherently *un*critical of its social context – be seen as unrelated to (or disinterested in) the patriarchal endeavour and its discourse.

The influence of science – the *Academy* – is also evident within the practice of organized sport and exemplified in elite, professional sport where athletes and teams surround themselves with individuals (the 'entourage', the 'medical' team) whose expertise derives from the disciplines of biology, chemistry and physics, as well as psychology, in order to give them the vital 'edge' that engaging with the latest (*scientific*) developments can potentially offer them (the exemplar case *perhaps* being genetic modification).

However, this appeal to science is not confined to elite adult sport as Hoberman (1992: 32) notes reports from the US that (two decades ago) 'some American parents began asking paediatricians to administer human growth hormone (hGH) to their children to make them into more imposing athletes'. Therefore, in the sport-project of turning 'children' into 'athletes', the rigorous methods of 'science' are frequently and increasingly employed as a key mechanism of this patriarchal (masculinist) endeavour.

Media and participation

One outcome of the internet is that newspapers now put their content online and this format, to enable readers to more efficiently navigate to the desired content, has led them to be quite explicit about the categories of sport they cover. Typically, a category-menu provides a list of the key sports that are covered, while other, less popular sports are not identified explicitly. Taking the UK as an example, football – arguably the 'national sport' (if not national obsession) in the UK – is positioned at the far left or top of these menus in at least five of the leading national newspapers. Therefore, within such menus there is an implicit ranking system (horizontally: left to right; or vertically: top to bottom); see Table 4.1. This indexing is presumably devised according to the paper's understanding (or perception) of the popularity of each sport within its readership.

If the rankings for each sport per publication in Table 4.1 are used to produce an overall mean score, where the lowest mean score equals the most dominant sport (e.g. Football: $(1 \times 5) = 5/1 = 1$; Formula 1: (2×2) (4×2) $(5 \times 1) = 17/5 = 3.2$) then the picture in Table 4.2 emerges.

This will hardly come as a surprise to readers – indeed it will probably seem very natural – nor is it difficult to observe how this agenda is reinforced further, perhaps with even more vigour, through live coverage of events on television and radio and the long-standing institutions therein (see Cooky *et al.*, 2013). In the UK, for example, very few people would ask which sport 'Match of the Day' referred to, nor would they query whether TV or radio broadcasting references to a forthcoming 'Six Nations' tournament or the 'Test Match' from *Lord's* related to the men's or women's 'game'.

Gender relations are also similarly evident in the construction of 'sport' through the public celebration and commemoration of sporting achievement. For example, in the UK, the annual BBC *Sports Personality of the Year* awards receive a great deal of media coverage. From 62 winners, only 13 (20 per cent) have been female (including Jane Torville *with* Christopher Dean) and there have been only three female winners in the last 20 years, between 2002 and 2006 (BBC, 2015). A similar pattern emerges in relation to how we commemorate sporting achievement (see Appendix 3). During the period 1 March 2014–29 December 2015 the English national

Table 4.1 Listing of sports in British newspapers online 'sport menu' (June 2015)

Newspaper	Listing position in sport menu (left-to-right or top-to-bottom)									
	1	2.	3	4	5	6	7	8	9	10
Daily Mail	Football	F1	Boxing	UFC	Tennis	Golf	Cricket	Rugby Union	Rugby League	Racing
Guardian	Football	Cricket	Rugby Union	F1	Tennis	Golf	Cycling	Boxing	Racing	Rugby League
Sunday Express	Football	Boxing	Cricket	F1	Rugby Union	Tennis	Golf	Racing	Other	–
Mirror	Football	F1	Boxing	Cricket	Racing	Football	Rugby Union	–	–	–
Telegraph	Football	Rugby Union	Cricket	Golf	F1	Racing	Tennis	Cycling	–	–

Table 4.2 Sports ranked by position and frequency of listing in online newspaper sport menus in five national newspapers (*Daily Mail, Guardian, Sunday Express, Mirror, Telegraph*) in June 2015.

Sport	Rank	Score	Mean
Football	1	5	1
Formula 1	2=	17	3.2
Cricket	2=	17	3.2
Boxing	4	26	5.1
Rugby Union	5	25	5
Golf	6=	33	6.3
Tennis	6=	33	6.3
Horse Racing	8	38	7.3
Ultimate Fighting Championship (UFC)	9	44	8.4
Cycling	10	45	9
Rugby League	11	49	9.4

Note
n.b. non-appearance in a menu awarded score of 10.

daily newspaper *The Telegraph* (online) published 144 obituaries under the category 'sport'. Only 14 of these related to females (9.7 per cent). Presumably this represents an increase from coverage in previous decades. Of the sports covered within the total sample, four reached double-figures: cricket ($n = 23$); horse racing ($n = 22$); football ($n = 17$); and motorsport ($n = 10$). In the 72 obituaries associated with these four dominant sports, only *two* related to females – both in horse racing: one of whom one was a successful 'owner' (Midge Burridge), the other a renowned 'trainer' (Lady Herries of Terregles).

Thus, we can see how the preferences expressed by those in the *field of power* (such as national newspapers and broadcasters, including commercial entities that purchase their 'space') reflect and reinforce a deeply gendered sporting cultural space. Such analysis can also be supplemented by an examination of the positions (or *field*) of power within the governance of these sports. At time of writing, all of the sports listed in Table 4.2, with the exception of tennis, have both male CEOs and male Chairmen/Presidents. The British *Lawn Tennis Association* has a female president, Cathie Sabin (appointed in 2014), in addition to a male CEO and a male chairman.

Likewise, in the governance of international high-performance sport, there are 129 members of the *International Olympic Committee* (IOC) (including honorary members) yet only 24 (18.6 per cent) are female. Similarly, there are currently 206 National Olympic Committees affiliated to the IOC. These are divided geographically into five areas (Africa, the Americas, Asia, Europe and Oceania) and each is led by a president, all of whom are male. The *British Olympic Association* board consists of 21 members (including honorary members and observers): five (24 per cent) are female, including the president HRH Princess Margaret.

The implications of such conditions within this symbolic cultural space become more evident if one then examines data on participation in sport. Within England such data has been gathered, since 2005, by the British government through its quasi-autonomous agency with responsibility for the governance of sport, *Sport England* (via the 'Active People Survey'). For example, examining one of the major 'national' sports, cricket, in 2012/13, 0.63 per cent of the 16+ male population participated in cricket but only 0.06 per cent of the female population; in 2013/14, the sample size for females was 'insufficient' to enable recording. Similarly, in 2013/14, 8.47 per cent of the 16+ male population played football but only 0.54 per cent of the female population (marking a steady decline for female participation). In tennis and boxing, the difference is less marked (1.47 per cent vs 0.74 per cent and 0.51 per cent vs 0.16 per cent respectively) but still considerable. Even in one of the most popular sports, cycling, the difference between male and female participation (7.2 per cent versus 2.4 per cent) is substantial (Sport England, 2015).

While these are just general examples, it is possible then, through relatively simple observation to empirically construct the gender configuration of the field of sport and to sketch a picture of the relative objective positions within that field. The symbolic dominance of men over women in organized sport is, then, considerable. Sport is a masculine, and masculinist, social space. It has been and continues to be the site of gender-related 'struggle' (Hargreaves, 1986, 2000; Lenskyj, 1986), however, the historic ability of (white, middle-class) males to determine what constitutes capital (in any field, but certainly masculinist fields) and how it should be distributed, provides a clear example of how the relationship between agents and capital operates to constitute a field; a field in this case which has been for some time dubbed 'a male preserve' (Hall, 1985; Hargreaves, 1994; Messner, 1988). Thus, Sabo and Panepinto (1990: 116–117) describe 'American' football:

> ...football is a social theatre with an all-male, intergenerational cast. The older-coach/younger-player relationship develops over many years and, at least in part, is defined as a testing ground for adult manhood.... If women are present, they are usually in subservient positions vis-à-vis men ... football is also hierarchically structured ... Authority is concentrated almost totally in the coach, and players are expected to obey the rules.

The imprint of patriarchy is evident, then, both in sports practice and its governance. Therefore, Brackenridge (2002: 256) states 'sport is a sex segregated social institution. The separation of sports into male and female on biological grounds is reinforced by powerful ideological and political mechanisms.' Before presenting some of my own empirical research in the field of organized sport, I will make some brief but important comments on terminology.

Masculinity and masculinism

Patriarchy and masculinity have been prioritized by feminist and gendered accounts of childhood sexual abuse (e.g. Rush, 1980; Cossins, 2000) including within the critical analysis of sport (Brackenridge, 2001). The work of R.W. Connell has been particularly influential within the sociology of gender (and sport), especially her concept of 'hegemonic masculinity': 'the configuration of gender practice which ... guarantees (or is taken to guarantee) the dominant position of men and the subordination of women' (Connell, 2001: 38–39). According to this perspective, sport is an exemplar of this configuration of gender practice. However, according to Brittan (2001: 53) it is important to distinguish between three concepts that are often confused: 'masculinity, masculinism and patriarchy.' Brittan (2001: 53) argues that masculinity 'refers to those aspects of men's behaviour that fluctuate over time', thus:

> Those people who speak of masculinity as an essence ... are confusing masculinity with masculinism, the masculine ideology. Masculinism is the ideology that justifies and naturalizes male domination. As such, it is the ideology of patriarchy. Masculinism takes it for granted that there is a fundamental difference between men and women, it assumes that heterosexuality is normal, it accepts without question the sexual division of labour, and it sanctions the political and dominant role of men in the public and private spheres. [It] is not subject to the vagaries of fashion – it tends to be relatively resistant to change.

Brittan's conceptualization of masculinism as 'relatively resistant to change' resembles Bourdieu's description of habitus as 'embodied history', 'durably installed' (see Chapter 2) and depicts a dominant form of masculine identity which is widely accepted without being permanent or beyond challenge. Young (2003: 4) observes:

> ...a model of masculinity assumed by much feminist theory as self-consciously dominative ... [where] masculine men wish to master women sexually for the sake of their own gratification and to have the pleasures of domination ... an image [which] corresponds to much about male-dominated institutions and the behaviour of many men within them.

This notion of masculinity certainly underpins much writing in the feminist and sociological consideration of sexual violence and appears to accurately reflect the actions of men where sexual violence against women and children is not an aberration but in fact commonplace (Jones, 2012). However, Young (2003: 4) observes an alternative, chivalrous image of masculinity where 'the role of this courageous, responsible, and virtuous man is that of a protector'. However, 'central to the logic of masculinist protection is the subordinate relation of those in the protected position' (Young, 2003: 4). Therefore, 'the logic of masculinist protection works to elevate the protector to a position of superior authority and to demote the rest of us to a position of grateful dependency' (Young, 2003: 13). Thus, regardless of which position is perceived to be most valid or most evident in practice – 'master' or 'protector' – the principle of masculinism (the ideology of patriarchy) is the subordination of the other.

Observations on field conditions

It can be argued that a key struggle within contemporary sport is between a traditionalist, masculinist discourse, based on the reproduction and maintenance of what can be termed a 'discourse of control', against more recent attempts to introduce a 'discourse of welfare' (Hendrick, 2003) or a greater 'ethic of care' in sport (Kirby *et al.*, 2000). In the UK at least, the introduction of 'child protection in sport' (Boocock, 2002) (more recently 'safeguarding') has been at the centre of this struggle through its advocacy of a welfare discourse and (perhaps more tacitly) a children's rights perspective. The data below are from an unpublished 2005 study that used focus groups of male and female coaches, referees, and youth development officers ($n = 38$), all working within a traditional male-team sport environment, to investigate how the sports community was managing the introduction of child protection. However, this approach facilitated wide ranging discussion of children's sport as well as the changes that 'child protection' heralded and provides interesting data through which to consider some of the themes highlighted above:

> *Focus Group 1*
> PARTICIPANT (B) (MALE): ...I've been down here twenty years ... and it's completely different now. Twenty years ago, you could get a whack at back o' head, d'you know what I mean? Which obviously, you know, is not acceptable, and you know ... [interrupted]
> PARTICIPANT (A) (MALE): Can I just say that it's a shame, sometimes, that it's not accepted.
> PARTICIPANTS (C) (FEMALE) & (D) (FEMALE): Yeah.
> PARTICIPANT (B) (MALE): Oh you're right, you're right...

The tension within (masculinist) sport over the best way to teach, or socialize, children (especially boys) through sport is evident here. Maintaining discipline through physical punishment (including punitive 'drilling') as well as preparing children for the physicality (and brutality) of the game is at the core of the (historically generated) logic or symbolic order of the field manifest as a hierarchy based on physical domination; being able to 'handle yourself' is central. Thus, disciplinary maxims such as 'no pain, no gain' are characteristic, yet also at odds with the new discourse of welfare and 'rights' where children are afforded the right to protection from violence and abuse, as well as a voice in decision-making (David, 2005). The following extract reveals not only the tension between these positions but also the fundamental nature of the characteristics that 'child protection' and 'safeguarding' seek to challenge and change:

Focus Group 6

PARTICIPANT (D) (MALE): You're never gonna rule [sport] anyway are you, there's always going to be – if you lose the swearing, if you lose the referee abuse, if you lose the aggressiveness from parents and coaches and everybody, then you might as well pack [sport] up and call it a day cos it's, it's a physical and aggressive sport isn't it.

Within the focus groups there was a great deal of anecdotal evidence to support this characterization (see following extracts). Therefore, alongside the *discourse of control*, it also seems necessary to speak of a *discourse of aggression* within youth sport. This is illustrated through the recollections of the participants, who nevertheless, appear to demonstrate a more critical stance in relation to the more obvious manifestations of this discourse:

Focus Group 1

PARTICIPANT (A) (FEMALE): ...the attitude you get to that [confronting violence on the pitch during children's matches] though is 'toughen up' and this is a man's game.

PARTICIPANT (B) (MALE REFEREE): ...and at the end of the day, the abuse, I'm not saying it were [team name], I'm not saying it were the opposition, I'm saying the whole area, you can go to any game, and it's just – verbal abuse!... the parent actually went onto the pitch to stop two children actually physically beating each other up, because the referee couldn't control it, and when this parent went onto the park, one of the parents from the opposition went on and hit this parent.

Focus Group 3

PARTICIPANT (C) (MALE): There's some clubs they must coach it [aggression and violence] into their players, they must coach it into them!

PARTICIPANT (D) (MALE): ...they're shouting and swearing, not just at their kids but at your kids, and I've actually seen parents fighting at an under 8s game.

Focus Group 4
PARTICIPANT (B) (MALE): I must admit though, through refereeing ... when those teams come over here their coaches absolutely amaze me, cos they do, like he says, eff and blind at the kids – 'you can't be doing that on touchline' – 'I'm the fucking coach, I'll do what I want' ... some of it's horrendous...

Focus Group 6
PARTICIPANT (B) (FEMALE): Same with me ... disgusting. Some of the things he was saying to get his kids going you know, it was vile, and I was like 'I've got to go round the other side, I can't deal with this'. But really I suppose he should be reported for his behaviour.

Given these (illustrative) examples of what *actually* happens at young children's sport competitions, it is worthwhile noting Don Sabo's reflections of his youth experiences of football ('Grid Iron') in the USA:

> I learned to be an animal. Coaches took notice of animals. Animals made first team ... The coaches taught me to 'punish the other man', and to secretly see my opponents' broken bones as little victories within the bigger struggle.
>
> (Messner and Sabo, 1994: 84)

The *athleticist field* is replete with such sentiments and reflections. Masculinist sport in late modernity means caring about winning and the means by which victory is secured, but not caring about anyone else, at least anyone who might adversely affect the possibility of winning, and least of all pain (one's own or that of others). In this regard, Sabo was indeed, the 'field made flesh', the embodiment of the field and this is exactly what his coaches desired.

What this research also reveals is that this *field* (or sport), and doubtless many other sports of a similar ilk – which constitute the vast majority of youth sports participation in 'western' societies – is an environment, cultivated specifically to attract children and adolescents (especially males), that requires physical aggression (and pain) between children (Sabo and Panepinto, 1990) and in which the abusive treatment of children by (male) adults is widespread:

Focus Group 5
PARTICIPANT (A) (MALE): ...we had to, you know, refer to the child protection policy, but it weren't really a child protection thing if you know what I mean. It didn't warrant any further action you

know, we did it internally as a club, which we got sorted, you know, *when a father hit his lad on the pitch* – nevertheless, it *was* a child protection thing so we had to do it.

It might be observed, then, that children, from a young age develop a 'feel for the game', an installed instinct for appropriate action, agreeable to the field – in this case a deeply masculinist field characterized as 'hard' and 'aggressive'. For the following participant, the observation that children and adults engage in violent conduct at competitions/matches is only unusual because the children are *so* young:

Focus Group 6
PARTICIPANT (A) (FEMALE): I mean unfortunately there's been a few incidents with some of the other clubs where we've had under 8s actually brawling, and parents brawling at under 8s [matches] and I've thought well 'this is getting really serious stuff' you know, usually you could expect that at 14s, 15s, 16s upwards, but not at an under 8s...

Where a field is promoted as somewhat crucial to a child's health and physical, if not moral, development it seems legitimate and important to indicate where children's interests are subordinate to those of adult interests. In the discussion below, the chief concern (in relation to child protection policy) is seemingly for what the *adults* have 'lost', or had taken away from them:

Focus Group 4
PARTICIPANT (E) (MALE): The thing for me is, before all the child protection [policy] came out I were a very – I liked to be with the kids and I liked to get with the kids and I liked to be able to sit with them and put my arm round them, you know, there are kids that want a cuddle and there are kids...
PARTICIPANT (B) (MALE): Course there is...
PARTICIPANT (E) (MALE): ...that want to sit on your knee, *and that's been taken away from me*, and I feel...
PARTICIPANT (G) (MALE): It's a shame...
PARTICIPANT (E) (MALE): I mean, I've had one on each knee, just talking and having a laugh, and I feel that, that I'm being ... I'm being put in a position, that, you know, I can't do that, because other people are going to...
PARTICIPANT (B) (MALE): Say something, yeah...
PARTICIPANT (E) (MALE): ...about paedophiles – it's those people that they should look at and really, when they're found out, should do something against them. I'm being victimised for other people, and it's something that does – it's something that really gets to me that.

PARTICIPANT (C) (MALE): I mean, I've seen coaches change how they are, like you've just said there, from being, when they're training kids, physically, you've got to hit this bag, and literally picking them up and dumping them into the bags, whereas now, they'll just stand there and say 'you've gotta do that' they won't physically get involved with the kids as they would have done, 2 or 3 years ago.

PARTICIPANT (E) (MALE): Everybody is getting tarred with the same brush and everybody is to fall into that line.

PARTICIPANT (B) (MALE): End of day we're here for the kids...

PARTICIPANT (A) (MALE): Yeah, that's the tricky thing...

PARTICIPANT (B) (MALE): End of day, we're here for't'kids, that's all we're here for, *and this* [Child Protection Policy] is starting to take it away from us.

The notion that adult involvement in children's sport could be about the accruement of capital (symbolic, cultural, economic) based on the pursuit of adult-designated (masculinist) ranking has to be thoroughly and persistently denied. Otherwise the deception is exposed, recognized as such, and the illusion rendered fraudulent. Hence the persistent refrain 'it's all for the kids' (Messner, 2009). In this way, the athleticist field can also be seen to draw moral authority from the persistent involvement of children, in that the child's participation serves as a purifying element against the evident brutality and aggression inherent to the field.

In the following section, I will discuss the logic of the field in relation to the construction of childhood and the adult-child relation that emerges from this data.

The logic of the field: children, sport and the spirit of capitalism

By identifying the Enlightenment philosophy of science, coupled with a rigidly patriarchal society, as fundamental to the origins and development of sport, arguably, a particular form of logic or reason lies at the heart of this cultural practice. The purpose of competitive sport is singular: to conquer the opposition, to win; a draw is of little interest. This tendency is not open to dilution, despite frequent calls to recognize that it's the 'taking part that counts'. Indeed, such rationalizations of a practice that revolves around the principle of corporeal domination – pitting child against child – clearly operate in service to that principle. Bourdieu (1998: 21) makes a similar point in the field of education and the school institution, where 'a high-pressure, competitive atmosphere, inspires submissiveness and presents a conspicuous analogue to the business world'. Thus, the tautological phrase of 'competitive sport' is repeatedly rolled-out by politicians as a remedy to enable our children – frequently perceived as weak, lazy and unhealthy – to develop into adults that will be able to compete in the global marketplace. According to British Prime Minister David Cameron:

> If we want to have a great sporting legacy for our children – and I do – we have got to have an answer that brings the whole of society together to crack this, more competition, more competitiveness, more getting rid of the idea all must win prizes and you can't have competitive [school] Sports Days. We need a big cultural change – a cultural change in favour of competitive sports. That's what I think really matters.
>
> (Cordon, 2012)

According to Maguire *et al.* (2002: 12) 'sport is arguably one of the most powerful transfer mechanisms for culture and structure ever known to humankind'. Perhaps unsurprisingly then, it is also tightly bound to contemporary 'childhood'. Indeed, according to Bourdieu (1993: 126) sport was conceived as an:

> ...extremely economical means of mobilizing, occupying and controlling adolescents [and] was predisposed to become an instrument and a stake in struggles between all the institutions totally or partly organized with a view to the mobilization and symbolic conquest of the masses and therefore competing for the symbolic conquest of youth ... sport is an object of political struggle.

Bakan (2004) and Giroux (2000) illustrate how corporations now aggressively market to children through schools in an attempt to make them lifelong consumers who perceive few choices in what and how they consume.[2] Similarly, the disciplinary work carried out by the athleticist field, through the discourse of discipline (obedience), dedication, commitment, drive, achievement and single-mindedness – aimed specifically at children and young people as essential requirements for 'success'[3] – can be seen to be highly effective in promoting and naturalizing the interests of many powerful multinational corporations. In his discussion of first wave Critical Theory, How (2003: 92) observes:

> The calculative, instrumental qualities required by the spirit of capitalism produce a depersonalised form of interaction and a human (male) subject capable of rigid self-discipline, of acting independently of others, in effect treating himself as an instrument for achieving goals.

As the discussion so far demonstrates, the qualities required by the 'spirit of capitalism' are also integral to the discourse of athleticism developed in nineteenth century England. Instrumental reason is one of the central concepts of

Habermas (1984) who maintained that within capitalist society, *reason* was increasingly reduced merely to its instrumental function. This refers to, 'an outlook where the world is made up of *mere* objects, and reason's task is only to show subjects how best to manipulate these objects, be they natural or human objects' (How, 2003: 177). Similarly, for Chomsky (2004: 174):

> The goal for corporations is to maximize profit and market share. ... They have to ... drive out of people's heads natural sentiments like care about others, or sympathy ... The ideal is to have individuals who are totally disassociated from one another, who don't care about anyone else.

For Critical Theory, the demands of capitalism on modern industrial societies have led to the widespread adoption of instrumental reason which emphasizes domination and control and 'squeezes other aspects of life to the margins' (How, 2003: 177). Reflecting 'on sport at the beginning of a new century', Digel (2005: 4) argues that societies are increasingly organized on the basis of:

> ...an input/output calculation ... The 'economization' of our lives goes hand in hand with this rationalization of our basic motives for acting ... Personal benefit and maximization of personal advantage become a rule of human action. ... Life is completely capitalized and marketed.

In addition, the strategy of capitalizing *everything* is not a neutral process. A field structured on patriarchal interests must necessarily endeavour to capitalize those same interests. Therefore, Bourdieu (1993) argues that orthodoxy within any field is defended and conserved by those who monopolize the specific capital that characterizes a field. Hence, Brackenridge (2002: 265) notes 'most of the major sport organizations are run by self-selecting (male) oligarchies who are reluctant to give up their power'. The current FIFA scandal surrounding Sepp Blatter and other officials are simply the most high-profile illustration and the data presented clearly support Brackenridge's observation. Thus, according to Connell (2000: 35):

> ...the market operates through forms of rationality that are historically masculine and involve a sharp split between instrumental reason on the one hand, emotion and human responsibility on the other ... modern masculinity is deeply connected with industrial capitalism.

Bourdieu's perspective observes that each field has its own economy, or market, not reducible to financial capital, but heavily influenced by it.

Given gains made by feminism, real and imagined (such gains are often wildly exaggerated within masculinist popular opinion) patriarchal forces are perhaps compelled to capitalize their interests more aggressively and comprehensively, although perhaps more surreptitiously, than previously. Therefore, feminist writers draw attention to a 'backlash' against feminism (Brackenridge, 2002; McRobbie, 2009) with calls for a return to a masculinist nature (e.g. Bly, 1990; see Messner, 1997). Organized male-sport, with its instrumentalist logic (win-lose) and deeply gendered, masculinist, cultural symbolism, can be seen as central to this endeavour. Therefore, Burstyn (1999: 23) argues:

> The actions that the dominant sport forms practise and celebrate are 'higher, faster, stronger', in the succinct words of the Olympic motto. This is at once an industrial and a masculinist motto, for it condenses within its ideal bodies and activities the technomorphism of industrial capitalism (the ideal of the machine) and the biomorphism of maleness (the muscular superiority of males). It is, in this sense, a hypermasculinist slogan.

Thus, the practice of sport, with all its 'virtuous potential', as Morgan (1994: 138) puts it, is subject to the 'instrumental rational calculus' of the athleticist field. This instrumental rationalization is not only confined to professional or elite sport but also encompasses the practice of sport at lower levels: 'because professional sports generally set the moral tone for the rest of the sports world, their narcissistic manner has, alas, rubbed off on sports at all levels' (Morgan, 2002: 281). Morgan includes U.S. collegiate and high school sport, as well as the *Olympic Games*, as examples of sporting practice where we might reasonably expect to find resistance to instrumentalism but instead find that 'they let money rather than morals do their bidding' (Morgan, 2002: 281). However, given the origins of organized sport, Morgan's lament for the demise of 'virtuous' sport seems somewhat romantic; the athleticist field has continued to regenerate itself, but always in a manner that enables it to maintain the course charted within its historical inception, alongside those masculinist institutions it serves and complements.

It is only a nostalgic, ahistorical construction of sport that ignores its origins as a product of and symbol for the dominance of western patriarchal forces and the dominant groups within that system, whatever it may mean for individual participants or spectators. In a (late-) capitalist system, the end (profit) always justifies the means (exploitation of labour); in the practice of sport, maxims that extol this very perspective – such as, 'winning isn't everything, it's the only thing' (the late Vince Lombardi,[4] iconic US football coach); 'football isn't a matter of life and death, it's more important than that' (the late Bill Shankly, iconic Scottish football manager) – are commonplace and central to the ethical logic of the field

(Pronger, 1999). Similarly, according to Chomsky, the corporation of late-capitalism is an amoral one that, by necessity, treats people like 'tools':

> If you had to worry about whether the tool was going to be happy it would be inefficient. If the tool can be treated just like a piece of metal you use it if you want, you throw it away if you don't want it ... So if you can get human beings to become tools ... it's more efficient by some measure of efficiency.
>
> (Chomsky, 2004: 179–180)

In many ways, this description is also appropriate for the contemporary field of organized sport, increasingly dominated by large capitalist corporations, where children become objects of value (as well as surveillance and examination, see Lang, 2010) determined through their ability to efficiently produce a specific outcome prescribed and evaluated by 'legitimate' adults. If they are unable to satisfactorily generate this product, consistently and under specific conditions, they are discarded or 'not required'.

Thus, the recruitment of primary school (10 years and under) children to professional football clubs is now common practice in the UK (see Barlow, 2009) whereby thousands of children, and their parents, each year respond to invitations to attend 'trials' and 'training camps' during which a handful are selected to attend 'centres of excellence' and progress to the next level where greater expertise and specialized resources are available. This is also common practice well beyond football. The child 'under surveillance' or 'on trial' is an institutionalized element of organized sport. Certainly the application of Foucault's (1977) articulation on the modern use of the 'examination' to both normalize and individualize children and young athletes as a technique of disciplinary power is highly relevant here (Markula and Pringle, 2006; Shogan, 1999).

Similarly, the sponsorship and promotion of sport by corporate marketing aimed specifically at children, more obviously objectifies the child. Where, for example, *McDonald's* sponsors youth football (through national governing bodies) and employs football 'stars' to promote their brand (see McDonald's, 2015), the commodification of children through sport is more blatant – children are reduced to the (dehumanized) role of consumers, or rather conduits-to-consumers, valued for their parent's spending power. According to Giroux (2000: 14), 'childhood is being reinvented, in part through the interests of corporate capital' and the role of sport in this reinvention is a significant one. Indeed, it might be suggested that it is only in a field of practice (a symbolic economy) where winning (at all/any cost) is the ultimate objective and overriding ethos, that rationalizations and (child-friendly) counter-maxims are particularly necessary. Hence, school-children are told of the 'character building' properties of sport, and that 'it doesn't matter who wins' by an adult community who persistently demonstrate that this is not the case to children who easily comprehend it as a falsehood. Seeing convicted rapists or homophobes who compete for boxing world titles, or footballers who physically assault opponents as well as female acquaintances, subsequently rewarded with 'fame-and-fortune', simply confirms the obvious.

For Morgan, then, 'the crucial question is not that high-performance sport has transformed our human identity – this is, it is safe to say, a given – but rather what we are to make of its transformation of our humanness' (Morgan, 1992: 105). Masculinist sport – more precisely, the *athleticist field* – seems to represent a context that exaggerates the instrumental nature of late-modern life, perhaps more than most but certainly in parallel with the 'the Corporation' (Bakan, 2004). Conquest is valued far above any other considerations, although rationalization and euphemism abound, especially where children are concerned. In the athleticist field, as in the corporation, the child becomes a commodity, to be used in pursuit of an arbitrary goal. An instrumentalist approach to life, where everything, including human beings, is commodified, works to install in the habitus the notion that other people, including children, are means-to-ends, tools, available to be exploited in the individualist, culturally legitimized pursuit of personal and organizational desires. Given the centrality of males to a field dominated by the quest for (physical, bodily) domination, it is little surprise that the individual male habitus frequently and persistently embodies the essence of this symbolically powerful realm; a realm which, in late modernity, is ever more closely associated with the global corporation – itself a '*psychopathic*' manifestation (Bakan, 2004).

Summary

The above discussion has attempted, in summary fashion, to articulate the *field* of organized sport. I utilize the notion of the *athleticist field* to express an historical essence that I see as fundamental to the dominant configurations of global sports practice, while not a totalizing description of everything that falls within 'sport'. The athleticist field, fundamentally underpinned by masculinism (the ideology of patriarchy) attaches the highest form of *cultural capital* to corporeal domination within a binary game. In this regard, it may be possible to reasonably articulate the dominant habitus (as a collective notion) that constitutes, and is constituted by, this field and I utilize the term 'athleticist habitus' in this fashion. Through the dispositions inherent to masculinism, I suggest that the distribution of *capital* within this field is generative of an adult-child relation that may be best expressed through the positions (or relation) of master-and-servant.

To recall, then, the habitus expresses a determinate notion of agency characterized by 'inscribed potentialities' where individuals are constituted with a freedom of choice albeit embedded in culture and the logic of fields.

These fields are durable yet dynamic – structured, structuring structures – as is the habitus. The former expresses the objective (external) and the latter the subjective (internal), but action, or practice, is 'the product of the *relation between* the habitus, on the one hand, and the specific social contexts or "fields" within which individuals act, on the other' (Thompson, 1991: 14). A key element of Bourdieu's account of social action is that it is 'relational' and agents act in relation to each other based on positioning in the field (volume and configuration of capital). Thus, McNay (2000: 38) argues 'within certain objective limits (the field) habitus engenders a potentially infinite number of patterns of behaviour, thought and expression that are both 'relatively unpredictable' but also 'limited in their diversity'. Furthermore, any serious consideration of CSA cannot confine itself to the motivations and actions of the perpetrator but must also consider the position of the child/youth. Both positions must be constructed, empirically, in relation to the context or field. In the following chapter, seven narratives of sexual subjection in sport are presented and discussed.

Notes

1 By contrast, of the 36 members of the international editorial board (including editor and associate editors) of the Journal of Applied Sport Psychology 17 (47 per cent) members are female; and of the 52 strong editorial board (including editor and corresponding editors) of the International Review for the Sociology of Sport (IRSS, the journal of the International Sociology of Sport Association, ISSA), 50 per cent ($n=26$) are female.

2 Many schools in the USA are now run by private companies that work with other corporate sponsors, whose primary business is, for example, fast-food, clothing and cars (see Bakan, 2004; Giroux, 2000 for more extensive discussion) to finance children's education. Schools in England now regularly utilize commercial organizations to deliver sport.

3 For example, the Rugby Football Union's 'Core Values project' identified the following principles that lie at the heart of rugby in England: Teamwork; Respect; Enjoyment; Discipline; Sportsmanship (see ESPN, 2009).

4 Also: 'Football is like life – it requires perseverance, self-denial, hard work, sacrifice, dedication and respect for authority' (Vince Lombardi).

References

Bakan, J. (2004) *The corporation: the pathological pursuit of profit and power.* London: Constable and Robinson.

Barlow, M. (2009) Secrets of Arsene's football nursery. *Daily Mail,* 18 December 2009.

BBC (2015) Sports personality. *Sport.* Accessed at: www.bbc.co.uk/sport/sports-personality/19587151 [21 December 2015].

Boocock, S. (2002) The child protection in sport unit. *The Journal of Sexual Aggression,* 8(2): 99–106.

Bourdieu, P. (1990) *In other words: essays towards a reflexive sociology.* Cambridge: Polity Press.

Bourdieu, P. (1991) *Language and symbolic power*. Cambridge: Polity Press.

Bourdieu, P. (1993) *Sociology in question*. London: Sage.

Bourdieu, P. (1998a) *Practical reason: on the theory of action*. ,Cambridge: Polity Press.

Bourdieu, P. (1998b) *On television* [translation by P.P. Ferguson]. New York: The New Press.

Brackenridge, C.H. (2001) *Spoilsports: understanding and preventing sexual exploitation in sport*. London: Routledge.

Brackenridge, C.H. (2002) Men loving men hating women: the crisis of masculinity and violence to women in sport. In S. Scraton and A. Flintoff (eds.) *Gender and sport: a reader*. London: Routledge, 255–270.

Brittan, A. (2001) Masculinities and masculinism. In S.M. Whitehead and F.J. Barrett (eds.) *The masculinities reader*. Cambridge: Polity, 51–55.

Burstyn, V. (1999) *The rites of men: manhood, culture and the politics of sport*. London: University of Toronto Press.

Chomsky, N. (2004) Interview with Noam Chomsky, October 24, 2000. In J. Bakan, *The corporation: the pathological pursuit of profit and power*. London: Constable and Robinson, 169–196.

Connell, R.W. (2000) *The men and the boys*. Cambridge, Polity.

Connell, R.W. (2001) The social organization of masculinity. In S.M. Whitehead and F.J. Barrett (eds.) *The masculinities reader*. Cambridge: Polity, 30–50.

Cooky, C., Messner, M.A. and Hextrum, R.H. (2013) Women play sport, but not on TV: a longitudinal study of televised news media. *Communication and Sport*, 1(3): 203–230.

Cordon, G. (2012) David Cameron urges change in sports ethos. *The Independent* (online). 8 August. Accessed at: www.independent.co.uk/news/uk/politics/david-cameron-urges-change-in-sports-ethos-8022032.html [17 June 2015].

Cossins, A. (2000) *Masculinities, sexualities and child sexual abuse*. The Hague: Kluwer Law International.

Cunningham, H. (1995) *Children and childhood in western society since 1500*. London: Longman.

David, P. (2005) *Human rights in youth sport: a critical review of children's rights in competitive sports*. London: Routledge.

Digel, H. (2005) Brief reflections on sport at the beginning of a new century: a German perspective. *Sport in Society*, 8(1): 1–10.

Dunning, E. and Sheard, K. (2005) *Barbarians, gentlemen and players: a sociological study of the development of Rugby Football*. London: Routledge.

Foucault, M. (1977/1995) *Discipline and punish: the birth of the prison* [translation by A. Sheridan]. New York: Vintage.

Giroux, H.A. (2000) *Stealing innocence: youth, corporate power and the politics of culture*. Basingstoke: Palgrave.

Goffman (1963) *Stigma*. Englewood Cliffs, NJ: Prentice Hall.

Guttmann (2004) *From ritual to record: the nature of modern sports*. New York: University of Columbia Press.

Habermas, J. (1984) *The theory of communicative action, Volume 1: reason and the rationalization of society*. Heinemann.

Hall, M.A. (1985) How should we theorise sport in a capitalist patriarchy? *International Review for the Sociology of Sport*, 1: 109–113.

Hargreaves, J.A. (1986) Where's the virtue? Where's the grace? A discussion of the social production of gender relations in and through sport. *Theory, Culture & Society*, 3(1): 109–121.

Hargreaves, J.A. (1994) *Sporting females: critical issues in the history and sociology of women's sports*. London: Routledge.

Hargreaves, J.A. (2000) *Heroines of sport: the politics of difference and identity*. London: Routledge.

Hargreaves, John (1987) *Sport, power and culture*. Cambridge: Polity.

Hendrick, H. (2003) *Child welfare: historical dimensions, contemporary debate*. Bristol: Policy Press.

Hoberman, J. (1992) *Mortal engines: the science of performance and the dehumanization of sport*. New Jersey, USA: The Blackburn Press.

Hoberman, J. (1997) *Darwin's athletes: how sport has damaged 'Black America' and preserved the myth of race*. Orlando: Houghton Mifflin Company.

Holt, R. (1989) *Sport and the British: a modern history*. Oxford: Clarendon.

How, A. (2003) *Critical theory*. Hampshire: Palgrave Macmillan.

Huizinga, J. (1966) *Homo ludens*. Boston: Beacon Press.

Jones, H. (2012) On sociological perspectives. In J.M. Brown and S.L. Walklate, (eds.) *Handbook on sexual violence*. Oxon: Routledge, 181–202.

Kimmel, M. (2005) *The gender of desire: essays on male sexuality*. Albany, New York: State University of New York Press.

Kirby, S.L., Greaves, L. and Hankivsky, O. (2000) *The dome of silence: sexual harassment and abuse in sport*. London: Zed Books.

Kitzinger, J. (1997) Who are you kidding? Children, power and the struggle against sexual abuse. In A. James and A. Prout (eds.) *Constructing and reconstructing childhood: contemporary issues in the sociological study of childhood*. London: Falmer Press, 165–189.

Lang, M. (2010) Surveillance and conformity in competitive youth swimming. *Sport, Education and Society*, 15: 19–37.

Lenskyj, H.J. (1986) *Out of bounds: women, sport and sexuality*. Toronto: The Women's Press.

Locke, J. (1693) *Some thoughts concerning education*. London: A & J Churchill.

Maguire, J., Bradley, J., Jarvie, G. and Mansfield, L. (2002) *Sport worlds: a sociological perspective*. Leeds: Human Kinetics.

Mangan, J.A. and Vertinsky, P. (2009) (eds.) *Gender, sport, science: selected writings of Roberta J. Park*. Abingdon: Routledge.

Markula, P. and Pringle, R. (2006) *Foucault, sport and exercise: power, knowledge and transforming the self*. London: Routledge.

McDonald's (2015) *Football*. Accessed at: www.mcdonalds.co.uk/ukhome/Sport/Football.html [23 November 2015].

McNay, L. (2000) *Gender and agency: reconfiguring the subject in feminist and social theory*. Cambridge: Polity.

McRobbie, A. (2009) *The aftermath of feminism: gender, culture and social change*. London: Sage.

Messner, M.A. (1988) Sports and male domination: the female athlete as contested ideological terrain. *Sociology of Sport Journal*, 5: 197–211.

Messner, M.A. (1997) *Politics of masculinities: men in movements*. Thousand Oaks, CA: Sage.

Messner, M.A. (2009) *It's all for the kids: gender, families and youth sports.* University of California Press.

Messner, M.A. and Sabo, D. (1994) *Sex, violence and power in sports: rethinking masculinity.* CA: The Crossing Press.

Morgan, W.J. (1992) Review essay: mortal engines: the science of performance and the dehumanization of sport by John Hoberman, New York: The Free Press, 1992. *Journal of the Philosophy of Sport*, XIX: 101–106.

Morgan, W.J. (1994) *Leftist theories of sport: a critique and reconstruction.* Chicago: University of Illinois Press.

Morgan, W.J. (2002) Social criticism as moral criticism: Habermasian take on sports. *Journal of Sport and Social Issues*, 26(3): 281–299.

Pronger, B. (1999) Outta my endzone: sport and the territorial Anus. *Journal of Sport & Social Issues*, 23(4): 373–389. DOI:10.1177/0193723599234002.

Renold, E. (1997) 'All they've got on their brains is football': sport, masculinity and the gendered practices of playground relations. *Sport, Education and Society* 2(1):5–23.

Rousseau, J-J. (1762/1911) *Emile, or Treatise on Education.* London: D. Appleton.

Rush, F. (1980) *The best kept secret: sexual abuse of children.* New York: McGraw-Hill.

Sabo, D. and Panepinto, J. (1990) Football ritual and the social reproduction of masculinity. In M. Messner and D. Sabo (eds.) *Sport, men and the gender order: critical feminist perspectives.* Illinois: Human Kinetics, 115–126.

Schirato, T. (2007) *Understanding sports culture.* London: Sage.

Shogan, D. (1999) *The making of high-performance athletes: discipline, diversity and ethics.* Toronto: University of Toronto Press.

Sport England (2015) Who plays sport? *Research.* Available at: www.sportengland.org/research/who-plays-sport/ [Accessed 12 September 2015].

Thompson, B. (1991) Editor's introduction. In P. Bourdieu, *Language and symbolic power.* Cambridge: Polity Press, 1–31.

Webb, J., Schirato, T. and Danaher, G. (2002) *Understanding Bourdieu.* London: Sage.

Wenner, L. (2002) (ed.) *Mediasport.* London: Routledge.

Young, I.M. (2003) The logic of masculinist protection: reflections on the current security state. *Signs*, 29(1): 1–25.

Chapter 5

Narratives of sexual subjection in sport

In this chapter, I present the stories of seven individuals – five men and two women – who were subjected to sex with an adult who occupied a position of trust within their sporting life. These are their stories in their words, reconstructed from interview data so they can be read as a more or less coherent whole. Following these reconstructed stories, I then offer a second construction through the application of Bourdieu's conceptual framework to the individual accounts provided by these 'survivors'. As Grenfell notes:

> Biographical data are not enough on their own. They also need to be analysed with respect to field positions, structures, and their under-lying logic of practice; and most importantly the *relationship* between field and habitus – not just the one and/or the other.
>
> (Grenfell, 2012: 223)

Therefore, my approach has been to present the stories, told within interviews, in as much detail as space will permit, and then to subject these stories to a further analysis, with respect to the relationship between *field* and *habitus*. This is to take seriously both the stories as told by the participants – their experiences and the impact upon them – as well as Bourdieu's view that all is not immediately evident from empirical observation, as 'interactions ... mask the structures that are realized in them' (Bourdieu, 1989: 16). It is an attempt, then, to reveal the sociocultural antecedents and mechanisms of sexual abuse in sport while retaining the lived experience of sexual violence at the centre of analysis. The final chapter builds on the themes identified through the 'survivor' stories and offers a more general analysis and theorization of child sexual abuse and the athleticist field.

Simon

We were a prosperous middle-class family. My father was from immigrant parents, *extremely* hard working, extremely driven. He had a huge work ethic. So we didn't want for anything and we had a big detached house. But there was no sense of family there at all. We never ever – I mean never *ever* sat down as a family to eat, except maybe at Christmas and maybe when there were guests. There was never a great feeling around my dad – he was an obnoxious, very uncomfortable, edgy guy. At weekends he'd get up even earlier than on weekdays to go to the golf club and after that he'd come back and sleep – so there was very little interaction.

My mother was always doing room service. She served dinner or lunch to my father separately, she'd feed my sister and I separately, and feed herself separately, and so I thought life was a hotel. But that's just the way it was. I'd say that family life was prosperous, but dysfunctional. My father was always shipping me off to school as soon as he could. I always felt he just wanted us out of the house so he could get better room service from my mother. I went to primary school when I was four and one day, which is a little early really, for full-time school. Then when I was seven I was sent to Prep School. I didn't mind at first because I would come home after school and it was close by.

But when I was eight there was a defining moment. They said that because my sister, who was four years older, was going to go to boarding school, there couldn't be one rule for her and another rule for me. I didn't see why that was the case because she was so much older than me. But I was shipped to this *concentration camp* which absolutely traumatised and horrified me. I came home for half-term – I could have *walked* home every day – but at half-term they were going to leave me at the school. I literally begged them not to. I said 'I just don't want to go back there, it's not right, it's horrible, horrible!' My mother broke down, but my father just said 'no, he's got to stay', and that was it. I think that something turned in me then. I thought 'well they just absolutely don't want me at home', so I became a bit disposable, in my own mind.

I was extremely bright when I was six or seven but I just kind of stopped working. There was no motivation for anything really. And I think that, looking back, there was very much a sense of that ingredient – of a lost child, disconnected from his family – that the predatory paedophile instinctively picks up on. Because if there is no clearly defined communication path between kids and parents, it's very unlikely that the kids can shop the paedophile. And they don't. Once you're groomed, you're groomed.

I didn't do any sport at all before I got there, but sport was the thing – you're not a hero at that kind of school for being clever, in fact you're a swot. But if you're in the first team, you're one of God's creatures, you're the elite of the elite. Everyone had to do it. You did sport five days a week. Various sports, but everybody had to do rugby and out of the melting pot of each year they'd choose the best players. There's something nice about being in the winning team whether you're three or thirty-three. I guess that's a kind of given about sport, I guess that's why people like it. I was just good at rugby, for whatever reason, I could just do it. I got kudos. I was in all the first teams at all the age groups – and that's where I met my abuser. He was the rugby teacher.

He was a sexual predator who was also able to attract the most attractive of the mothers. I'm not sure how many teachers were abusing kids. I was abused by three teachers. I know a significant number of the other teachers used to seduce the mothers of the pupils. I used to get the reports about which teacher was having sex with which boy's mother, from my abuser. We'd have sex and then he'd say 'well you know this one's having sex with that one and the other one'. Maybe the boys never knew that their mother was also having sex with the same person they were having sex with. I don't know whether my mother ever had sex with any of the teachers, she could have done. So it was like some kind of weird sexual soap opera. You couldn't make it up really!

So he put himself into the situation – well he created a situation – where he felt he was beyond the law. He was all-powerful and he could do whatever he liked. And they liked sporty boys. When you're sexually abused at that kind of age – you don't *know*, you just accept. I was absolutely terrified of this guy. He was big, he must have been 6'2", overweight – this *huge* guy. I was absolutely terrified of him. He abused me every day. I used to go and wake him up in the morning and have sex with him in the morning. I still wake up with terrible forebodings.

I was never sodomised by him, generally he'd put me on my stomach and put his penis between my legs and he'd have sex with me that way, and lots of 'French kissing'. Sometimes he had oral sex with my friend – but he never gave me oral sex and that made me upset. So my values were disastrously and completely destroyed – 'cos I'm thinking, you know, 'he's not giving me oral sex, what's wrong with me?' Sometimes he'd come and get me from home in the school holidays and it was almost like he didn't want sex, he just wanted someone to touch his bits. It's about control. If you could get the truth out of these guys you'd find that really what they're about is control. Sex is not that important, it's not about sex itself, it's more about control, absolute control. He put me in a situation where I knew I was doing something profoundly wrong, that didn't escape me, but I was *helpless*. So I pretended that everything was okay.

There was also that whole thing of mindlessly complying. You don't argue when you're that young. But you do have a sense of inner rebellion. This came out with the other boys – that came out a lot. It's pretty serious stuff really when you are confined with same-sex kids. You start to act out sexually with them. It's kind of a genital-based world. That's the cut and thrust of everyday life at school. That's what happened. And unfortunately, the younger ones, sort of 10 and 11 year olds – they were a sexual *Smorgasbord*.

I couldn't go back to my parents because they didn't want anything to do with me. But one side of me was quite happy. I had good status at the

school – I was in the *first fifteen*. But what was really, *really* depressing
was that my parents – and parents of other boys who were being systematically abused by the same couple of teachers – used to show up at every
bloody rugby match! And wander up and down the touchline clapping the
children. I'm going 'what are they doing here, what are they doing here,
they sent me to this place, they threw me to the Lions, I'm being devoured
by the Lions, and here they are *watching* me! Why don't they just f-off and
leave me alone!' I had the feeling of: 'this does not compute in such a big
way that I can hardly stay standing up!' *So* confusing.

   I coped with it by literally splitting myself. I've done that all my life and
I think that's because there's no way I could express any of this. I couldn't
go up to my mother and father when we're playing the big fixture of the
year and stand in front of them and say 'Look! This one here is abusing
this boy, this one is abusing me, he's abusing this one, this one and this
one, *and why are you here clapping*? What is going on? *Are you mad or
what*?' That's what I would have liked to have said – and then called the
police! But I felt abandoned by my parents – I had nowhere to turn. Where
am I going to turn? Expressing my hurt! That's not an option is it? We
can't tell our parents about the abuse that we've suffered. My childish
brain goes 'well they sent me here so they must have wanted it to happen'.
So I made friends with other little boys, to have a bit of comfort with
them, because that's what happened to me. So I'd do the normal stuff but
actually, I've got a secret world, which was fantasy and masturbation, and
having sex with other boys and being abusive to other boys, and starting
to be a perpetrator. I was very cruel to the other boys – I was the dominant
partner. I would completely cut them dead in the normal cut and thrust of
school life, but when I wanted sex I'd do anything to get it from them.

   I believe there was a lot of sexual content going on in the training, and I
believe that a lot of us tried to excel in the sport, and in the training, and
in the coaching – in the whole thing – to be more and more attractive to
our abusers. I think there was that feeling of – you know it was almost a
sexual experience when you did something good, a good tackle or something, they would give you a smile or pat you on the back – it would be
like, 'oh my god' that's just like, *that thing*. He was an *extravagant* man.
He used to get the stars of the day – you know, the rugby internationals –
to come to our Sevens competitions and things like that. He was always
doing things in larger than life, grandiose sort of way. What could be
better than being a rugby hero? It's literally a *Faustian Pact*. But you have
to sign you know, it's not a choice, you have to sign, you're consigning
yourself to this really, *really*, powerfully destructive relationship – that you
probably never escape.

   You never escape the psychological consequences of it. I'm sure I never
felt more frightened in my life than when I first had sex with this guy.
Because this became an everyday thing I had to sublimate it, I had to put it

away. And the cruel thing about abuse is that it's this sort of perversion, or subversion, of the natural drives we have. I mean we're all sexual, and so to be stimulated sexually is entrancing, it's beyond good or bad it's just entrancing, it takes you over; being sexually stimulated by a big and powerful man is really a compelling experience. I'm sure that was extended on to the rugby field, and I'm sure that, just as I was compliant in bed, I was compliant on the rugby field, and that probably actually made us better rugby players. Because, you know – we were little tarts basically. I'm not sure how many kids he abused simultaneously but I would say it was probably up to ten at any one time. For me one of the big shocks was that – I thought I was kind of special. But a close friend of mine said 'no he has sex with everyone, he's had sex with me'. So, then, I felt the special-ness of being chosen to be a sexual partner of this heroic rugby teacher was suddenly totally devalued.

He was caught one night by the matron. She knew that this guy was having sex with the boys – for years. *Everybody knew.* I mean that's the other thing – there is this culture of compliance. No one will blow the whistle. I guess its hierarchies, authority. 'If I blow the whistle now, will they say "well why didn't you blow the whistle four years ago when all this was happening?"' There's all this guilt and shame and shit that goes on.

But this was such a public event that the parents had to be called in. All this is happening without my knowledge. So I'm called in to the head-masters study, and I'm going 'what have I done wrong now?' Because that's how I'd started to think. You always think you're doing something wrong, because once you've been abused you go 'well why have *I* been abused? Because I've done something bad'. Anyway, I walk into the study and my dad's there and I go 'oh my god what's going on here?' And my dad, not being the most communicative and comforting sort of person, said 'oh I need to talk to you'. So we walked out onto the school driveway and he was sort of coughing embarrassedly and he said, 'so did he ever interfere with you?' And without really much of a second thought I said 'no, he never touched me'. So something had gone so wrong with my brain that I was prepared to defend the abuser against my own flesh and blood. And that makes no logical sense to anybody who hasn't been abused, but everybody who's been abused goes 'yeah I absolutely understand that'.

As a victim of child abuse you're in a situation where, through no fault of your own, you have the seeds of serious mental illness – neurosis, psy-chosis – planted in your brain. Because coping with reality after significant serious abuse is very, very difficult. It doesn't happen to everybody, I'm sure some people get over it. Some people say, 'well, it didn't do me any harm'. I was just angry, I destroyed a lot of photographs as well. I kind of wished I'd kept them now, because they would say a lot about what was going on. This guy was putting little boys on pedestals so that he could have sex with them. It's just completely beyond, *beyond the beyond.*

And you can't blow the whistle. Because within the atmosphere of these places there's the view that no one's going to listen anyway. So it's absolutely written in that, as young kids, we're disposable. And if we're good at sport we can be abused – trained to within an inch of our lives to perform – and that's entirely the 'right-and-proper' thing to do to young kids! It's a culture that actually creates a machine where kids are abused and they go on to abuse, and this is what happens. Why we would be surprised is anyone's guess. But we do this feigned 'oh, how disgusting, how awful', but actually it's intrinsic to the system. If it's part of the furniture of our society, the removal man should come and move it.

And then the follow on from that is – why historic abuse is so difficult, is that most people won't come forward with a confession or look for any kind of redemptive action at all, is – until their parents are dead. Because somehow there's this connection – it's a love-hate thing – you hate your parents for putting you in the situation but you don't want to devastate them by telling them 'actually what you did resulted in this'. If I was to give anybody any advice I'd say 'blow the whistle'. Doesn't matter about your parents, they should know.

These men were totally obsessed with having sex with as many boys as they could. An obsession – an *addiction* – moves you into an amoral universe. Because nothing is more important than getting your drug. So nothing would override their proclivity. There's nothing – no law, no duty of care – that would override it. It's an illness that builds up over time to a point where they have no control over it. What is the formula? Is he evil or crazy – I'm prepared to say that he's crazy, not evil. That's where I go with it. It's easier for me to do that.

Analysis

Simon's parents were affluent and able to afford fee-paying private schools for their children. The family unit was firmly established on a patriarchal model with clear demarcation of roles: his mother was responsible for the home and children and his father was responsible for financial security. Simon's relationship with his father is clearly very distant and difficult, and from a young age Simon felt abandoned by his parents, recalling explicitly the feeling of rejection and disconnection when he was forced to return to boarding school – a 'concentration camp' – during the holidays.

Simon's interest in sport emerged directly from the culture of the school. His father played golf regularly and seems to have been happy, as his son got older, to watch him representing the school team. But it is at school that Simon first discovers his athletic ability and how development of this ability could benefit him socially. As he explains, all the pupil's had to do sport, every day, and so 'if you're in the first team, you're one of God's creatures, the elite of the elite'. This is, then, an institution firmly and explicitly built around the notion of *mens sana in corpore sano* and which believed in preparing boys for life, not just through lessons taught in the classroom, but also through those learned on the playing field.

Achievement in sport was conveyed as a fundamental element of the school's identity – it's cultural and social capital – and those that were most able to contribute to the maintenance of this identity were afforded highest status. Indeed, both the boys that attained a place on the sports teams, *and* the teachers that coached these teams, occupied dominant positions within the school.

The collective habitus of the school community was shaped according to athleticist principles of loyalty, obedience and self-sacrifice in the pursuit of athletic domination and the associated social capital that accompanied sporting success within the education *field*. Therefore, sports were central to the structure and distribution of capital – field positions – within this school. As Simon says, 'I got kudos. I was in all the first teams.' The boys, especially those that struggled with the academic work, quickly learned that sport was a way for them to succeed, to gain status. In other words, sporting success was an extremely powerful form of cultural capital and those that were most able to embody the principles of the athleticist field were richly rewarded.

Entry to the rugby team was part of the process by which boys were systematically and collectively recruited and acculturated into a sexual environment. Recruitment to the rugby team was, in effect, also recruitment to sexual activity with the rugby master-coach and other teachers. Training, and the violent disciplinary regime surrounding entry to the team – which the boys had to successfully navigate, persistently, to maintain their position – was clearly a culturally legitimate practice of symbolic domination. Quite contrary to the overt narrative of empowerment, it facilitates a *symbolic violence* which renders them dominated, 'disciplined', compliant and ultimately 'willing' in their sexual subjection. That is, Simon, subjected to sex on a daily basis, is forced to make a virtue out of the necessity to *give* himself to the rugby master. The fields of *rugby* and *intimacy* become indistinguishable: 'just as I was compliant in bed, I was compliant on the rugby field'.

There is, then, a clear and explicit economy of symbolic goods within this school and proficient sports participation offers Simon access to this economy and the cultural capital it contains. Just as their skill in sport renders them complicit in their own subordination, reduced to objects or commodities in the struggle for domination in the education field (via inter-school sports), equally they acquire access to the most privileged spaces and individuals. However, the symbolic goods within this field are valued so highly because of their rarity – only a small number of boys can be selected. Thus, within this *field* (represented in its objectified, material form as an actual 'institution') the boys struggled, literally *fought*, to be recognized, to acquire status (capital) – to stay in the team. The 'rugby master' is perhaps the most potent formulation of the field in human form, the *field made flesh*, ordained to distribute or withhold *gifts* accordingly. Therefore, Simon and his peers struggled for the (sexual) attention of their masters.

Subjected to daily sexual assaults and selected for the highest honours in the school, Simon unsurprisingly developed a 'feel for the game'. Isolated, feeling abandoned by his parents, he plays the 'game' that he has embodied and which offers guaranteed 'reward' – domination and subordination. He is dominant on the rugby pitch and utilizes his accumulated physical and social capital to subject other boys to sexual activity. His developing habitus is forged within this field of exploitation, a 'game' imposed upon him, with its own economy, its own forms of capital and its own *doxa*. To succeed in this field means being favoured by those that are dominant within it and, thus, struggling – *labouring* – for this favour.

Simon expresses this in vivid terms. He experiences feelings of jealousy because other boys received more attention or more intimate sexual activity. Rugby practice was an opportunity to gain favour in the eyes of their abusers and this 'heroic rugby teacher'. Conspicuous conformity to – or *investment* in – the values and principles of the culture, established by the rugby master, was a necessary feature of maintaining favour among the coaches and a position in the team. Therefore, being singled-out for what felt like special attention, was immediately desirable for Simon. He was, in fact, trying to be *more* 'attractive' to his abuser, not less. Thus, recognition from those that held the power of selection and de-selection was paramount in the boys' minds and so they competed, fiercely, for this. Being in the team allowed them access to substantial symbolic capital, widely valued throughout the school.

For Simon, the experience itself was 'beyond good or bad, it's just entrancing, it takes you over; being sexually stimulated by a big and powerful man is really a compelling experience'. Given the size of the investment he had made in this field and the meaning it held for him – his *habitus* – this should not be viewed with surprise. There is sheer belief – *illusio* – in the game and especially its dominant agents. Therefore, his habitus, appears perfectly aligned with – *entranced* by – the field (and those dominant within it) on which he relied heavily for his social status, and all that flowed from that: 'What could be better than being a rugby hero? It's literally a Faustian Pact. But you have to sign you know, it's not a choice, you have to sign.'

Of course, he would, and did, 'sign'. He had been systematically trained to appreciate the stakes of the game and to value all that it represented – and in the act of doing so, his complicity, is secured, as is his silence. Simon's description offers a compelling evocation of both agency, constraint and reproduction, or in Bourdieu's terms, the *illusio*. Simon did not only believe in the game, he *became* the game – 'the field made flesh' – dominated and dominating. Thus, to reveal his abuser is to reveal himself. To name 'abuse' with its corollary 'perversion' is to name himself. It is not difficult to appreciate how debilitating this would be and it is (perhaps) not difficult to understand why, despite the explicit opportunity, indeed, encouragement, to tell, he declines.

In conclusion, then, it is also crucial to note that, many years later, Simon did tell.

Paul

My parents didn't have education beyond school. My father was given a scholarship but he went to work at a steel forge instead – and then he went to war. My mother was offered a scholarship too but she didn't take it. She studied Latin and wanted her children to be educated. She was an interesting, complex person, held back and frustrated by having so many kids and a husband who didn't want her to work. My parents could be very affectionate but also fought violently, usually about family and religion. When my father came back from the war he worked at the forge again, but then got a couple of years at college and went into sales. He sold toilet supplies for a pretty long time and then took a job selling construction material. He worked well into his seventies, selling and also loading bricks. We were pretty poor but they would never acknowledge that. They were very proud.

I didn't regard myself as unhappy or poor. I had neighbourhood friends but I was pretty solitary. My dream was to pursue sports: football and basketball. So I did that every chance I got. I played constantly. I invented basketball games and I organised softball teams in my neighbourhood. I just kept looking for the opportunity to enter sports, but my father wanted me to work. As a child his parents made him work. They baked bread in the house and he delivered it. So he made me work, until finally I stood up to him and said I was going to play football and basketball, and he kind of let it happen and eventually he became a big fan.

He didn't play organised sports but he was a powerful man. He was like a 5ft 11' 215lb Marine. So he should have certainly played football but he was also a wonderful ice-skater. And he played the guitar and could sing beautifully – often for the whole family. So there were times of great family unity and joy. But there was also violence. He never put any of us in the hospital. He wouldn't punch you, he'd open his hand at the last second. But he could rough you up, if he got mad enough.

Sport was a big deal at my school. They had won several football championships. Clarke was like this legendary basketball coach. I guess I might have made the team in 7th Grade but my father wouldn't let me play. Then in 8th Grade I played and that was when I came under Clarke's influence.

He spent long hours coaching me. After practice I would go home for dinner and then go back to the gym, and he would have several of us there working out. Eventually other guys dropped out and I was the only one there. So he spent a lot of time developing me. I played for hours a day, every day. I played all the time. Sometimes I would go home and do my homework and he would pick me up at 11 at night and take me to the gym and we would work out until 1 or 2 in the morning. I got pretty good.

He would take you in the back room off the gym, the storage room, and he would grab you by the balls and spank you. It was kind of a Litmus Test: if you can put up with that you can go to the next level. The thing is you want to play basketball for the best team in the City and go on to have a career. So you put up with it. The longer the grooming process went on the more intimately I was involved with him. Then there was the threat of pulling it away from me, so I let it continue. He was also a physical thera-pist. I'd figured it out by the time he was giving me a hand-job in order to improve the muscle tension in my groin! That was part of his seduction, you know, go to work on your thigh, or your back or something – then the next thing he had your penis between his legs.

One of the guys in my class tried to warn me. He was dropped when I was picked up as the main guy and he kept saying 'he'll ruin you, he'll ruin you'. I didn't understand. Yet it was kind of understood that whichever boy was in his car at practice was the boy he was sleeping with. And that was right in front of your face, everybody knew it, but nobody said anything.

But 'sleeping with men'! None of us knew what that meant. We knew *something*, but we didn't know *what*. Even when it was happening to you, you didn't know what was happening! He took four of us on an away-trip – we were all 13 – and he just took us, one after the other, out of our motel room. And none of us said a word. Each of us got fucked and none of us said a word to each other – what was there to *say*? By the time I figured it out it was too late, I was too deep in, there was too much at stake. In any case nobody would believe me.

I was drinking by the time I was 13 or 14. He started bringing me to his house and he would say that it was better for me to get experience of alcohol 'here with me where it's safe'. And so I drank, and then we would go to bed. By that time I was loosened up. I would even sneak to his house, say for an away-game. He would be upstairs working and drinking and I would take a flask and fill it and take it with me on away games on the bus. Nobody noticed, except my older sister. But she always was suspi-cious of him – and jealous – because we were a poor family and this guy was buying me clothes and taking me out to dinner.

But he always told me that I really had no talent and he would say that I was a B-intellect; I was never going to be an A-intellect. As an athlete he would undermine my confidence and tell me that I was never going to make it. Besides undermining my confidence he would portray it as though I was a member of an elite club involved in this 'Platonic' relationship that the rest of society would not understand. One of his favourite historical stories was Hadrian and his love of Antinous. So you were exposed to stories in which homosexuality, or special sexual relationships, were ok: 'the Greeks were that way, the Romans were that way'.

There was this one guy who asked me once whether Clarke did any 'weird things' with me and I said 'no'. But his *younger* brother once said to me, 'I go to Clarke for a blow-job once in a while, so what!' It was just weird – walking the line between knowing and denying. I think my parents suspected something. They never said anything about it. It was incomprehensible – sex between a man and boy – I don't think it was in their psychosocial world. They couldn't comprehend it. No one could! But at one point, they told me they didn't want me to see him – and that's when he hired my mother and started to get my father work. That ended that. He was a very powerful man in the city. He was very respected professionally, within education, and he was involved in local government. My mother was a receptionist and she eventually became his assistant. She was really uncomfortable working for him and eventually she took a job somewhere else. She said when the 'shit hit the fan' it all came down on her. She was suspicious of him, but she didn't speak about it. We never spoke about it.

By the time I was 15 I'd really made it in the team, but the following year was a disaster. There was an assistant coach that didn't like me and saw through Clarke and hated him and it led to some real problems for me getting playing time. But Clarke was always there. Before every game I would go and see him and have sex with him and drink, and then he would drive me to the game. I *wanted* to see him. He was my path to success. He had convinced me that without him I couldn't play or compete. He influenced my choice of university too. I really wanted to go to a bigger university but he suggested that I stay closer to home, and so I did. I led the team in scoring for most of my second year. I did that without him, but he would travel over to watch the games. He was supportive … but by then I had discovered a lot of things. I mean it wasn't just me he was molesting, it was probably a handful of guys at a time. I may have been his favourite for a while. When I was 18 or so he took me and another guy down to the Caribbean for two-weeks. I ran into some homosexual men who were there with younger boys and that's when … I really figured it out, but by that point it didn't matter.

I quit the university basketball team for any number of reasons, but one was to say, 'fuck you' to him, 'I'm not going to be your basketball star. I'm not going to fulfil that dream for you'. I drove home to tell him to his face that I was quitting. He tried to sleep with me. I said that I wasn't having sex, I was quitting. He said I'd regret it for the rest of my life. I went back to university and the next day I quit.

My younger brother was in his team. When I quit, my brother quit the week after. Because he was being molested as well – Clarke did the same thing to him. He talked about getting out of the car, having Vaseline all over him, feeling like everybody knew. I don't know how much he lines up the troubles in his life to that. We've spoken about it since. Clarke would use the same strategy. He would ridicule him and try to use that same kind of yo-yo: 'Look you've succeeded' and then 'you're no good!' So this back and forth was part of the grooming. He did it to me and did it to my brother as well. There were 5 guys in my class alone that he abused, so, I don't know – over 20 years or more? There were a couple of guys who played for him after me who killed themselves. There were plenty of guys he did work on as a therapist, and even their parents, but nothing ever came of it. So for everybody that he abused there were tonnes of people he hadn't. He was a pretty sophisticated manipulator.

I enjoyed competing, but there was a lot of anxiety for me. Before games I would sit on the toilet and was just sick to my stomach, afraid of failure. That continued even into college. There were other times when I was very successful and I exploited it, particularly in college. During those basketball days, I was quite notorious. I was still ambivalent about everything, but I enjoyed the game – I *loved* the game.

I would come back to the gym and play even after I quit the college team. He didn't throw me out. It didn't matter what I had done, he would always try and sleep with me. So then it didn't matter that I had quit. But I loved the game and I still played every day and loved to play.

This guy was tremendously manipulative – he got deep into guys' lives, he even picked their wives for them. I married, at 19, under pressure from him. I didn't want to marry and we soon got divorced. I was so immature sexually. I'd fucked Clarke a thousand times but I hadn't been with women. I broke up with my wife but then he brought her back home and gave her a job – and then he offed *me* a job, teaching. And I took it. And there I was, back there. After the divorce there were times when I refused to have sex with him and we fought about it, physically.

Then my mum died and I got out of town for good. He would always tell me that I would come back, but I said 'No, I'm not'. He would get me jobs; summer jobs and things like that and then still try and get me to sleep with him, but I wouldn't. Except once; he wanted me to have anal sex with him and I said 'I can't do it!' I tried, but I intentionally didn't get hard. I kept myself from getting hard so that he could see that I couldn't do it and that was probably the last occurrence. I was in my mid-20s. I tried to make him say that he loved me, but he wouldn't do that.

When I left, I decided to study. I also did a lot of drugs in my 20s and 30s, but I turned it around, met my wife and had a family. I was in denial into my 40s. I would tell people openly that I had had sex with my basketball coach for years. Some people wouldn't respond at all, some people were kind of shocked. When I was with a friend, somehow it came up and I told him that I had slept with my coach and he asked how old I had been and I told him that I was 13 when it had started. He said that I hadn't had a sexual relationship with my coach – I had been raped. I told my wife and she said 'yeah, that's what happened to you'. I started to face it then.

I guess I had never really portrayed it to myself as something that – I wasn't involved in. I felt that I was the guilty party and he was, in a sense, innocent. And that lingers with you and I guess that was part of the shame of the act. The position is somehow reversed, but I never really regarded him as guilty of anything except denying his own homosexuality. So it took a long time for me turn that around. It needs a real change in your attitude – suddenly you have to understand yourself as a victim. And people, even people close to you, don't want to see you as a victim.

I heard from other people whose marriages broke up after the man began to admit that he had been sexually molested. It does put a lot of pressure on because suddenly my wife was having to confront that I was a sexually abused victim, but in many ways didn't want to perceive me in that way. You know – *she had met this guy* – 'how is it possible that you let this man do this to you?' And so what happens? When the person who you perceive as your lover or your masculine protector…? I don't mean to be anachronistic – but that was an adjustment.

When I started to confront it and to talk to counsellors, who were unequivocally pointing out to me that I had been victimised – *you* were the victim – that took time; and the completion of a few years of writing – hundreds of pages – and reviewing it, before I could see that I was manipulated. And then I read books about abuse and saw the correlations between what happened to me and the grooming process.

But even to this day if I talk to someone who has been abused, I probably have a much more tolerant response, about what happened to me than what happened to them. And if I say 'I loved him', people cannot *stand* to hear that, but that's what happened. I was so psychologically dependent, and sexually dependent and *materially* dependent. So that took time, and my daughter was becoming a teenager so there were things that had to be … it was delicate, and my marriage was threatened by it. There were some difficult times, I mean this is something that I decided to take on and deal with, but my wife has to deal with this every day too.

One thing that abuse victims do is, in the act of abuse, they take on another personality and they let that personality be abused, or have the sex, and they separate the self. I *did that*. I used the personality of a female. So that was really subversive, and coming off that in order then to try and find my sexual identity – it never ended completely, but I managed to understand it and let it be a part of my fantasy life and learn to accept it. I don't act it out, at least not now. I did back in my late 20s a few times, with a female sexual partner. But that's something that was indelible and for a couple of decades, pretty disconcerting, pretty devastating. I didn't understand who I was. If you do that a thousand times – and I probably did have sex with him a thousand times – and if you do that in your form-ative sexual years, how do you get that out of you? Well you don't. It was just something I had to hide – in a small, industrial town. I didn't have anywhere to go to talk about that. I mean even homosexuality was com-pletely under the radar let alone *that*, so I was just confused. There was nobody to talk to about it.

I kind of solved the identity issues in my late 20s. I *look* heterosexual and I became very promiscuous and that's pretty much how I identified myself. In many ways it really helped me identify myself as a heterosexual. So in that way I solved it. Later I started seeing psychological counsellors. Some didn't want to deal with it but one guy worked hard with me and gave me books to read and made me understand that I was a child and that I was raped. I continue to see someone and he's helped.

You don't want to let yourself be victimised or perceive yourself as a victim in every situation; as though somebody's out to get you or taking issues personally, which I guess I have a tendency to do. I have to try to avoid that, I think it's a bad aspect of my personality, which keeps me from moving forward. Not that moving forward is the greatest thing in the world either. Living your life every day and getting your work done and loving the people that need your love and doing the work that you need to do. It's important to have those things and a lot of men who have been abused don't have those things; they don't have someone who loves them and that they love and they don't have work because their lives have been ruined – and then what are the alternatives? Well there's drugs, alcohol certainly, which I have used all my life. I've always been a drinker. I suppose I use it to kill consciousness and to deal with a lot of things that I feel bad about – the way you've failed to succeed – I think it's a way of anaesthetising yourself. It's been a crutch for me. I would even say that it's helped me in ways – whatever gets you through the night. But you have to become aware of that and stop it.

I guess I don't identify with the labels 'victim' or 'survivor'. I mean I'm willing to accept the fact that I was victimised, but you can't live on as a victim. So once you accept the fact that you were a victim you have to let it go, even though there are tremendous repercussions psychologically for anybody who has been abused. I know for me – lots of things – it com-pletely destroyed my confidence; it made me unable to take credit for my accomplishments; it made me indecisive in situations for years. Those are things that subconsciously you have to get yourself out of – the shadows of your victimisation.

But neither do I think of, or see myself as, a 'survivor'. Why does some-body survive and somebody not? The number who have committed suicide ... there was a guy in my class who is semi-homeless – his life was destroyed. I think the fact I managed to keep my life together in some way, did not kill myself – and you could describe my life in my twenties and early thirties as almost suicidal. But I stayed productive and went to school and I held down jobs and I moved forward – and developed my sexuality. I don't know how responsible I am for that because there's so many other people that failed. So why does somebody survive and another not? I don't know, but I don't think you take credit for it. I think *surviving* has that connotation. I don't know how much heroism is involved – I don't see my survival as heroic. But I'm willing to try and help other people get through it and I try to tell my story … I understand that I was victimised but I don't see myself as a *victim* or a *survivor* because of the connotations.

When the story broke it created a little bit of a flurry but most people turned on us. A letter was published in the local press signed by 50 or so people exonerating him and calling him a 'great man' and explicitly calling us liars, accusing us of trying to make money. A few of the other men who came out were either in jail or drug addicts and a number of those that signed the letter were guys that I knew had been abused, because I'd been in the house when they were coming out of the bedroom. Several of them had told the local newspaper that they had been molested, but then they backed off. Some who were abused have never spoken out.

He resigned, but within a year he just picked up where he left off. He's still pretty influential in the town. There are people everywhere for whom he has gotten jobs. We tried to sue him but the statute of limitations is very short for this kind of crime. You practically have to be a child being molested at the time to go to court! With any organisation or institution or group, say religious groups, there's always an underbelly, there's *always* an underbelly. I think it's the same thing as going along with the whole coaching thing – discipline and loyalty and becoming a success – all those things can be used against you.

Just before my father died I was at his house – unfortunately it was the last time that I ever saw him – he was dying – and the newspaper was calling me because they were working on an exposé on Clarke. And he *knew* – he said 'are you talking about Clarke?' and I said 'yeah', and he said, 'because he had sex with boys?' And I said, 'yeah – your boys', and he wept.

Analysis

Paul's parents worked in semi-skilled and manual jobs with few opportunities for progression. Paul describes his childhood as happy, but says his parents 'fought violently'. There were also episodes of aggression towards the children that sometimes included physical abuse. There was clearly a strong work ethic but Paul describes his mother's life as thwarted by her husband's traditional views on the division of labour in the household and the limitations placed on her by the demands of raising children. However, she displayed a positive disposition towards education and classical subjects and was determined that her children would have the education that she did not.

Paul's inclination towards sports emerged in early childhood. His family appear ambivalent rather than clearly supportive. Certainly Paul was not pushed into sport but identified it as an activity that gave him pleasure and that he could succeed in. As he grew, so did his father's opposition to his pursuit of sport beyond play and games. However, Paul's resistance and success within school and college teams appears to have eventually won his father's approval. Certainly it seems he was supported sufficiently to allow him to attend daily practice and at unusual hours.

Paul's determination to succeed in sport distinguished him and his commitment to becoming a basketball player motivated him to practice hard and learn quickly. The school environment he had entered was clearly heavily disposed towards sports. He found himself with an enthusiasm for, and growing ability in, a culturally venerated activity that provided him with status among peers and the adult community alike. His personal ambition for sporting success was matched, if not surpassed, by that of the institution. Thus, his young habitus is increasingly shaped by his desire to improve his position within a highly institutionalized field of practice (sports, basketball). In these circumstances, 'potential' or 'talent', coupled with an evident 'drive' to achieve is a valuable institutional commodity. Similarly, a man who dedicates knowledge, experience, time and effort to supporting this proclivity is a substantive asset. In this case, the coach's proven ability to deliver success – his 'legendary status' – positions him as both an expert in the field and a valued part of the local community culture and history.

The disparity in cultural capital, between the coach and the boy, could not be more pronounced. This man occupied a high-status position across a number of fields. He displayed significant levels of all forms of capital: *cultural capital*, particularly in an embodied form, through his athletic abilities and sports achievements for the local community; *social capital*, through his professional, commercial and political networks; both of which he was able to efficiently transform into *economic capital*, illustrated through his significant material wealth. The recognition of his qualities within the field of sports and education (or 'physical education') extended this man a volume of symbolic capital that ordained him with the power 'to impose [his vision] upon other minds' (Bourdieu, 1989: 21). But this was not a vision created from nothing, rather it was closely aligned with that of the institution. Thus, the objectification – or perhaps more accurately *consecration* – of boys bodies in the pursuit of 'success' and the enhancement of the institution's reputation was 'taken for granted' and 'went without saying'.

Rigorous training of bodies and minds, where ends justified means, was ingrained in the logic of the field and embodied by its most dominant agents. The symbolic power accumulated by this man situated him in the field of power, allowing him to foreclose on challenges to his position (and practice) well before the voicing of any 'difficult' questions. This is emphasized in stark terms when Paul's parents tell him to stop seeing the coach. At this point the coach exerts his influence over the whole family by providing employment opportunities for his parent's. It is not possible to know the extent to which Paul's parents suspected the true nature of their son's relationship with Clarke, or the extent to which they understood the implications of setting aside their apparent concern in light of the opportunity to advance the family's economic position (and all that comes with that). However, it seems reasonable to assert that they allowed this opportunity for intervention to pass; as Paul says, 'we never spoke about it'. It is, perhaps, the knowledge of this that Paul's father is tragically forced to confront shortly before his death as he learns that more than one of his son's had been abused by this man.

Paul's account makes clear the *coercive interpersonal strategies* he was subjected to. The relationship is physicalized and sexualized through therapeutic massage and more overtly sexual 'trials' – 'the Litmus Test' – to gauge whether the boy would either 'tell' or implicitly endorse the sex through silence. Alcohol is also used by the coach, which Paul perceives as a means to 'loosen him up' for the sexual activity. This is no doubt the case, however, this is also best understood as part of a strategy to draw him further into an illicit relationship which presumes an immediate understanding that secrets had to be kept from 'outsiders'. Thus, alcohol, as an activity both approved by adults (socially acceptable) but also prohibited by them (inappropriate for children) provides a powerful enticement. Certainly the use of alcohol to facilitate sex is not evident in all the accounts of other victims, but for a boy from a working-class family in an industrial town, alcohol consumption is part of the transition to manhood and carries cultural prestige. Being able to 'drink' ('hold your liquor') is a symbol of masculinity, especially within the culture of traditional team sports where many post-game celebrations and rituals revolve around tests of an individual's capacity to consume alcohol. Therefore, alcohol consumption is a culturally approved, indeed, symbolically powerful activity within the field of masculinist sport. Within a heteronormative, homophobic environment, such symbols of traditional masculinity may seem especially appealing when faced with the prospect of being subjected to sex with a dominant male.

The coach also employs erratic emotional swings, from mentor and supportive confidante to aggressor, aiming personal verbal/psychological attacks at the boy in order to degrade his confidence and keep him 'off-balance'. Yet this 'yo-yo' strategy is also an expression of the significance of Paul's position in relation to this coach. In fact, it has the effect of situating Paul at or close to the centre of the coach's world – a 'privileged' position for a young boy. This 'centring' marks him out, affording him status and increasing his cultural capital while offering a glimpse of much greater 'riches'. Thus, in some way, it establishes Paul as a lead protagonist in the coach's 'game'. He is transformed from pupil to protégé, the lead role in the coach's sporting ambitions. In this sense, for a time, he perhaps appears to hold the 'hopes and dreams' of this powerful man, quite literally, in his hand. Thus, his basketball endeavours are simultaneously the source of his power and his sexual subjection.

Therefore, maintaining equilibrium – keeping the coach 'happy' – becomes something that he is made to feel responsible for. The coach strategically and erratically abrogates the role of benefactor and mentor, switching to detractor and tormentor. He ridicules the boy, but also in some way infantilizes himself as it suits, devolving the adult role and conferring responsibility upon the young boy: 'I felt that I was the guilty party and he was, in a sense, innocent.... The position is somehow reversed'. In addition, the coach (also an academic) draws upon and establishes a classical narrative of Platonic Man-Boy Love. Thus, the strategy of coercion is manifold, complex and prepared. The boy is subjected to a range of tactics that construct the relationship as normal, situated within a context where the boy is compelled to view the adult as the trustworthy and essential gatekeeper of his future.

A further factor is Paul's appreciation for the *stakes* of the game. Aside from the simple imbalance of power, the boy's aspirations are clearly the emotional leverage which the coach is able to apply for his own ends. Paul's home-life is relatively impoverished and he has seen his parent's work hard to maintain a basic standard of living for the family, yet the coach is evidently wealthy and considered an important figure in the community and the 'city'. Unsurprisingly, Paul identified an opportunity to enhance his position and committed himself to it fully. Indeed, he had fought for the right to 'play' rather than 'work'. Thus, Paul's childhood habitus is revealed by what he was prepared to endure: 'The thing is you want to play basketball for the best team in the City and go on to have a career. So you put up with it.' The *field* demands subservience and acquiescence. This is the symbolic violence of the athleticist field. The child, to become part of the field, must recognize the stakes of the game – what counts and what has value – and must reproduce those stakes, successfully and persistently or face expulsion. In other words, the game dictated that Paul must capitalize on those stakes or withdraw.

This is euphemized as having 'what it takes' to 'make it', and all manner of metaphor and allegory is employed to convey to the child what is required; frequently captured in concise idioms such as 'no pain, no gain' and 'there's no "I" in "team"'. In such a context, there are few more potent questions than 'Do *you* have what it takes?' Indeed this question is embedded within each game, if not each practice, and is thus transfigured into embodied dispositions. This can be seen in young athletes who commonly state that they 'eat, sleep, breathe' their sport and coach's, managers, etc. who applaud such commitment, if not insist upon it. Those designated with the authority to determine whether in fact the child does possess the necessary, illusive combination of 'qualities' to achieve '*it*' are those who have themselves demonstrated their *doxic* relation to the field. That is, their habitus is structured towards the transmission of the field's structures and principles and, as such, is what the child has to believe in, therefore, comes to believe in, to invest in, 'body and soul'. Within this wholesale investment and belief – an *illusio* – is the root of the boy's powerlessness, explicitly recognized by Paul: 'going along with the whole coaching thing – discipline and loyalty and becoming a success – all those things can be used against you'.

Paul's view of the relationship clearly alters over a period of time. His decision to quit the team is evidently a key moment in his life that indicates a shift in his habitus so that he begins to perceive his life in different terms. The promise of a basketball career gradually fades through his late teenage years, and while he experiences a growing realization of the limits of his athletic capacities, the grip of the *illusio* that had bound him to this man is simultaneously weakened by degrees. He becomes increasingly disinvested in the field, and the nature of the 'game' this coach had manufactured slowly becomes more evident. That is, he is increasingly able to see it for what it is: not a game of basketball, but a game of exploitation.

Nevertheless, given the volume of capital he commands, this man is able to continue to exert influence over Paul well into early adulthood, using his strong social networks to offer employment opportunities to both him and his (first) wife in order to draw him back within his purview. Indeed, such is his influence it seems he arranged Paul's first marriage. Nevertheless, Paul is gradually able to challenge the coach's domination over him, both emotionally and physically, and what he has to offer becomes increasingly less appealing. Simultaneously, Paul establishes a sexually promiscuous lifestyle through his early adulthood and uses alcohol and other 'recreational' drugs on a regular basis. For a time he develops a reputation among his peer group; he is a successful basketball player, athletic and 'good looking' and is sought after for, and seeks out, sexual companionship with females. It appears he builds a lifestyle and identity which is overtly heterosexual and outwardly conforms to traditional notions of masculinity.

Paul states he was 'in denial' about the true nature of the relationship for many years. He would openly refer to it with acquaintances in a seemingly untroubled manner, until a friend categorized his experience as 'rape'. His wife supported this, and it clearly had a significant impact on

Paul: 'suddenly you have to understand yourself as a victim'. At this point, then, Paul is forced to confront a new construction of himself: 'I started to confront it and to talk to counsellors, who were unequivocally pointing out to me that I had been victimised – *you* were the victim'. Thus, he is presented with a very negative construction of himself, at least in so far as the notion of 'victim' was anathema to his habitus. Paul had developed professionally into a highly qualified and respected figure, providing support and guidance to others. He is strong, physically, emotionally and intellectually. He had re-married, had children, left 'drugs' behind (except alcohol) and worked hard to develop a successful career. Within the fields he was engaged in he gradually acquired significant cultural and social capital and was able to convert this into economic capital.

However, as he enters the field of 'therapy' he is confronted with an alternative vision of himself: the 'victim'. The ground shifts under his feet: 'It was an adjustment … it was delicate, and my marriage was threatened by it. There were some difficult times.' Instantaneously, he becomes a 'victim of abuse', the 'victim' of a 'predatory paedophile'. This is not to imply he was unaware of the exploitative nature of the relationship, but he is now forced to accommodate an externally imposed construction of himself. Furthermore, it must be appreciated that this is an identity accompanied by a whole scheme of objectifying discourse underpinned by notions such as 'damage', 'trauma', 'recovery' and 'survival'. He is, perhaps, a 'fish out of water', a habitus 'out of sync' with the grounds upon which it was formed, struggling to recognize itself in relation to its external surroundings. I am referring then to a 'durably installed' disposition that is challenged by a countervailing force – a force *field* – that imposes a whole new, external nomenclature, essentially a new identity, upon him.

This is not to challenge the very real emotional and physical effects of the experience of being subjected to sexual violence. During the abuse, Paul reports imagining himself as a female and this had long-term consequences for him and his sexual life as an adult. Within masculinist discourse 'sex' is unequivocally heterosexual (even while this is contradicted in practice); a thing, an act – a 'fuck', 'screw', 'shag', etc. – done *by* men *to* women. The dominated position is fundamentally constructed as female and the dominant position is fundamentally and necessarily male. Therefore, for a young boy raised in a heterosexist family and a conservative community environment, the only substantive frame of reference for sex with a man is a homophobic one, a 'queer' one. Thus, for a young, male athlete, adopting a female persona is perhaps a narrative that allows him to make sense of the experience in a way that is in keeping with the structures of his masculinist habitus as it offers an alignment with cultural norms that perhaps frames the experience as less transgressive, or 'normal'. Unsurprisingly, the psychological effort involved in this figures significantly in his young, evolving habitus: 'if you do that in your formative sexual years, how do you get that out of you? Well you don't.'

However, Paul's later encounter and subsequent immersion in the field of psychotherapy thrusts him into a new world of psycho-medical categorizations that carry with them their own historical, 'scientific' truth-claims. These may be, to greater or lesser extent, at odds with one's habitus. Given Paul's account of the powerful masculinist influences in his life, both individual (such as his father and his abuser) and cultural (such as the game of basketball), it does not seem unreasonable to suggest that his habitus – the generative principle of action – was durably structured in firm opposition to notions of victimhood. The designation of 'victim', then, offered a stark new lens through which Paul could view his childhood. He identifies the 'victim' label as one that can have a deleterious effect without a conscious and determined effort to reject it or distance oneself from it: 'once you accept the fact that you were a victim you have to let it go'. Paul also rejects the 'survivor' label, finding it problematic and inappropriately self-aggrandizing in the face of those that, literally, *don't* survive.

Again, this illustrates how in each field there is a struggle over what is considered valid and legitimate. The 'survivor community' is beginning to play an increasingly prominent role in this struggle. Indeed, the notion of 'survivor' has been utilized by the therapeutic professions but it is also a political category and carries out 'political' work. This is not universal, but the term seems to have gained particular traction in English-speaking countries. It is possible to speak, then, of a 'survivor community'. However, again, Paul rejects this label in relation to himself. He further illustrates the deep complexity of this problem which resists easy and comfortable capture in discourse: 'to this day ... if I say "I loved him", people cannot *stand* to hear that, but that's what happened.' Reductions of such accounts to glib pseudo-scientific labels is wholly inadequate.

The benefit of situating these more challenging and complex aspects of survivor stories within the whole story (or at least a condensed version of it) is that it is placed alongside other expressions which articulate both the exploitative nature of this relationship as it was encountered by the boy, as well as the deep and lasting damage it has caused. Indeed, as Paul's account testifies, other boys abused by this man were significantly less able to cope with the memories of what they had been subjected to. Equally, the politically powerful and necessary terms of 'sexual violence', 'sexual abuse', 'sexual exploitation' and their individualized effects of 'victim' and 'survivor' must not be allowed to overwhelm or erase the nuances and complexities expressed by those that understand most about this experience.

Mary Jo

My father was successful. He was very cultural. We talked about politics and art and we had diplomats and artists coming to eat. He swam and played football. My mother didn't do sports. While we were young she didn't work.

I was quite active as a young girl and fell in love with gymnastics after we went to see the Olympic Games. My parents saw that it was what I wanted to do, so they started me at a club. My father always said that when we first approached them they said I was too young and should come back at 14. My father said, 'at fourteen she should be at the Olympics!' So I started working out at age 7 and most of my childhood memories are related to gymnastics.

I was very focused and learnt very fast. After a year my first coach said that I had a lot of potential and recommended I go to the national training centre. They agreed to give me a trial and I was accepted. I started training there when I was 8 or 9. I left for school at 7:30 a.m. and I didn't get back home until 11 or 11:30 p.m. At 5 o'clock I would rush to the gym and train for 5 hours every day. You can only do that if you really, really, *really* like it.

We shared our warm-up with the boys. They were a bit older so we were like little sisters. We had a foreign coach. We trained very hard but I enjoyed it. They were very happy times. I was an open and happy kid in the early part of my life. It's important to know that because of how my personality changed later on. But I was always very disciplined and very obedient. I used to miss a lot of school but they helped me with rescheduling exams – and I was a good student. At 10 years old I competed in a national tournament and won three medals. That was my first competition and the only one where I competed in anything other than the senior category. I jumped directly to Senior at 13 and I became national champion at 15.

When I was 11 my coach went back home. The guy who was coaching the male gymnasts took over and he started a programme for those girls with potential to progress onto the national team. You know, *the future*. So I started with him and all of a sudden he started forbidding us from talking to the boys or even looking at them. Even if we looked up and there was a boy in front of us, we would be in really big trouble. He would call us all kinds of things, like 'whore! – you only come here for the boys'. But my family were very happy and I was quite famous. I was on TV and so girls would stop me on the street. But actually I did not like all the attention because every time we were in the news he would start telling us that we were 'bloody cows', that we thought we were better than everybody else. So we began to avoid any attention because we would get in trouble with him. We didn't understand, we just started to go more quiet. I stopped doing things with friends and we worked out like 5 or 6 hours after school every day and 8 hours on the weekends. He isolated us – we didn't have mobile phones. It was really easy to isolate a group of girls in the gym all day. Before we knew it we were all living in a bubble.

At the beginning we liked it when he would flirt with us, but he insulted us very often. Our parents asked us why we were looking down all the time in the gym, and we'd say 'well you have to concentrate, because you can fall'. We knew all the excuses because he had taught us what to tell our parents. His methodology was to make us almost like a religious sect. We were supposed to love him above everything and trust him above everything and he wouldn't let us speak unless we were spoken to. It was very hierarchical. There were the two 'chosen ones' and then there were the rest. The 'chosen ones' got to go to the toilet first, but no one else could go to the toilet until the chosen ones had been. Or when we were eating, he would be at the head of the table with the two favourites next to him and the rest in hierarchical order away from him.

It was very gradual. He insulted us and then the next day he just waited to see if you had told your parents, he went step by step. I went to a normal school with boys in my class and one day I get to the gym and he was screaming at me 'you've been talking to the boys ... you're a whore!' And I thought 'he's got spies in my school!' How does he know? Because I had just talked to a boy in my class about homework. Years later I realised that he hadn't actually known, it was just a trick. Sometimes he would go into the gym crying that his mother had died and all the girls had to crowd round him and comfort him and touch him. He did that very often. We actually joked about the number of times his mother had died.

He was married but we never saw his wife. We never saw her anywhere. He was well known for having sex with other women. A female coach that started working with us had a relationship with him; he was involved with a high-ranking official of the sport; with international judges. He was a dandy, a womaniser. He liked women around him.

Training was very tough. We had to work out a lot and we had to give up a lot of things that normal kids our age did. But we wanted to do it – we liked it. But he also used training as a punishment, say for looking at boys. You may have just finished training on the bars and your hands could be ripped, and he would make you climb ropes with bleeding hands as a punishment. Or he would make you do sit-ups just because a guy had walked by when you were doing vault. So the boys used to laugh at us because we would run past them looking the other way. They used to laugh a lot about that but we didn't want to get into trouble. You just wanted to be invisible. You just didn't want to get any attention from him. He could make you cry all afternoon with just a stare.

The workout was hard. But we liked it. I was very obedient and if he told me to do 100 sit-ups then I would do 101. I didn't miss one. If he told me to go on the beam and do a flip I would do it. I was very disciplined and very obedient. You can train that in a girl, but you have to have it too. Hitting was part of the educational method. Not in my home, I don't ever remember my father spanking me, not even a little bit. But there were other coaches that hit the girls really hard, and the boys sometimes got spanked. You know it was fairly common and extra training was a pretty normal way to punish the girls. But he would also tell you that you were a 'whore' and 'good for nothing'. When we were alone he would tell me that I was his favourite and that he loved me and he was going to make me a great champion – and how people wouldn't understand what we felt for each other.

But it was really difficult to understand at 12, because he told you that in private, but then he'd insult me in front of the other girls and ignore me and tell me to train by myself. Or he'd tell a secret to one girl while the other one is alone doing bars. So while you were risking your life learning a new routine on your own, he would start flirting with the other girls. So he would play on the envy and jealousy between us. It was a very tense, very sexualised environment.

There were lots of adults there. Some of those adults have come to us to say sorry for not saying anything at the time, because they knew what was going on. They knew that when he disappeared with one girl into a room alone – they knew when we all came up from doing the warm-up, except him and one girl. The boys would even make jokes about who was having the 'lucky massage' today. So later some of the boys said how sorry they were but they were also young.

I don't know exactly when the sexual abuse started because it started very gradually. So he used to play with us in the pit – like a pool but filled with sponge – it all started like playing, flirting. So he would touch you once and then he would wait and see if your father came with a shot-gun. And if not then he would go a little bit further and a little bit further.

In the gym the boys and the girls were together in the same room, but downstairs there were other rooms for music and ballet. On one side was a big mirror and a ballet bar and on the other side there was a training 'horse' with sections so you can make it smaller or bigger. He said we had to do our warm ups down there, where the boys were not allowed to go. So we would start the warm ups there and then he would put the horse on the other side of the room and he would give us a massage there, behind the horse, where nobody could see us.

That's when he started touching me everywhere. He would make me pull my leotard down and started touching my breasts and then penetrate me with his fingers. This was almost every day. I lived close by so I would often be there for about an hour before my teammates. So he would make me wait for him down there and when he got there he would close the door and lock it and he would abuse me there. He would penetrate me.

Sometimes I didn't even know what he was penetrating me with because when he started I would force myself to think about my floor routine and I would make myself hear the music louder than his breathing, in my head, so I would be going through my routine in my head with the music and everything so that I wouldn't hear him. This happened almost every day. I would hear people outside and I would pray that they would rescue me. But I also would pray that they wouldn't, because I was convinced that I was a slut, a little whore, and they would discover what a bad little girl I was. Sometimes on Saturdays or when my parents were out on holidays, I would go and stay with an aunt. He would pick me up in his car and take me for a drive. He would grab me at the back of my head and force me down. Again I would start thinking about my music and about other things.

On my first international competition I went with him and this other gymnast, a boy who was older – he wouldn't even let us have breakfast together. So I was alone in my room, and he could go in and out. And before the Olympics – I was fifteen – the team stayed in a hotel. We shared rooms with teammates. He would come in to give us a massage every night. He would always do my roommate first, then when she was asleep, he would rape me.

It was a very confusing period for me. I didn't understand what was going on. Sex was not spoken about in the open, so you couldn't ask somebody about it and we were pretty much enclosed in that environment and we just didn't have anybody to talk to about it. There was no sex education at school at all. It was taboo. At home we talked about politics, art, everything except sex. So we didn't talk about the sex, not even to our closest friends. We just didn't want to be discovered. I was convinced that I was a whore, a slut, but even my team didn't know what kind of a slut I was, so we never talked about it. Ever. If I thought that the subject was going to come up I went off or I changed the subject. Nothing would make me tell about it. When I wasn't training I remember lying in bed with the light off, just looking at the ceiling. My mother would come in and ask me 'what's the matter, why don't you go out?', 'I'm tired, I'm tired'. You got through like that. It's very easy to conceal.

One day after the Olympics I got injured. I just started physically breaking up – because I had other things in my head. He got really mad and would still make me train despite the injuries and tell me that I was a lazy, bad girl, and that God was going to punish me for being so bad. It was horrible. He got really mad at me. I was his first gymnast doing something important, so I was going to make him the great coach that he wanted to be.

My dad took me to a doctor and he put a cast on my leg because he knew it was the only way that I was going to be able to recover from that injury. But when I got back to the gym he just went into a rage and made me train on the bars. I have a newspaper cutting where I am doing a handstand on the bars with a cast on. The only thing I didn't do was tumbling or anything that had to do with standing up – he made me work all day on the bars.

Parents were not allowed in the gym – they were absolutely forbidden. So they had to wait for us outside. One day, after a lot of especially bad verbal abuse, I left the gym crying. I used to always collect myself before I went out to the car, but this day I came out crying. My father didn't need anything else, he just went after him and I could hear them screaming from outside. I was terrified. After that my dad wouldn't let me go back. It woke me up. I know I had another Olympics in me, I was 15 at the time and National Champion. I was at the top of my career. But my dad said 'it's not worth it, I don't want you with this bastard for another 4 years.' But he didn't ask any more questions and I didn't tell. I thought if I told him he would go and kill him.

After that I went abroad to train with another national team. The training was really tough – it was a communist country – but nobody raped me, or touched me. That's when I started to realise what happened to me. I came back and competed for a different club. Then – with him right next to me, just staring at me – I fell on my head in a major international competition. That's when I said 'enough, I don't want this anymore', and that's when I stopped. After I quit gymnastics I didn't know what to do. I was very troubled. It was too much for me, it was too hard for me to see these people. I developed bulimia. In the end I left the country. I did try to compete again then, and trained hard, but I got a bad injury. I haven't done gymnastics since. Not gymnastics or any sport. It was so traumatic, so I said that I would forget about sport and not have anything to do with it anymore and I completely blocked it. I haven't done anything.

I had lots of problems with relationships with people. I did not know how to relate with kids my age. I didn't know how to relate with adults. I felt like a weirdo in every environment that I got into. The worst was the relationship with boys my age. I didn't know how to relate to them; how to talk to them. I felt like I had nothing in common with them. I had grown in this closed environment and I had this hole in my personality and in my life experience. I had some very bad years, with the guilt, I was very insecure. I suffered from big fears but I didn't even know what I was afraid of. I had nightmares where I would wake up crying and sweating. I was bulimic for about 12 years (anorexic and bulimic). So they were very tough years. It's not easy, trying to act like you were normal, with that trouble in your head.

I had problems relating to my siblings and my parents. I always lived with the fear that my parents would find out. Actually I have never been able to have a normal relationship with my mother because I was always afraid that she would notice something and so I was always very distant. I guess if you don't do that as a kid, it is really hard to do it later on. Every time that – even years later – the topic of gymnastics came up, I would change the topic or just leave. That's one of the bad things ... I regret never being able to tell anything, as a normal child, to my mother. I was always trying really, really hard so that she wouldn't notice anything, so I wouldn't have to tell about it.

I pretty much isolated myself from everyone as much as I could. I had very low self-esteem and years of wanting to commit suicide. Until I got my kids. When I got pregnant with my first child, I stopped the bulimia and it got a lot better. From then I started recuperating a little bit and even thinking that somehow, at some point in my life I would have to tell the story. I think that's when I started to open up and realise what had happened to me. This was 12 years after I had left. It takes a long time.

I still have some problems. It's really hard for me to feel comfortable among people – I always feel like I don't belong. I still have nightmares sometimes. I still suffer from fear that I cannot explain. And I still have some sexual problems, in my relationships. I haven't had any counselling. I have not spoken about this, not even to a psychologist. I always felt that it was something that had happened to *me* and that I had to take care of it by myself. It's a little bit like gymnastics, a little bit – you are responsible for your own things and you have to take care of them. I had some short therapy for the eating disorders but it's been very specific and nothing to do with the sexual abuse, which is the cause. You need a psychologist that specialises in sport and who knows what drives an athlete. It's a little bit different than just a normal victim of sexual abuse because there are other aspects that influence the whole process.

Eventually I contacted a couple of team mates who I thought could have been victims – but they were not ready. Now they have come forward but back then they were not ready to talk. I also spoke to my friend, who was also a victim. She told me that she was with me and that we could do it if we wanted to, but we were not ready. None of us were ready then. At that time, he was very very powerful, not only in the world of gymnastics but also in society – we were very afraid.

Then one day I went down to the cellar and found some old albums and all of my gymnastics stuff in boxes. And I started moving inside. Besides that my daughter had seen gymnastics on TV and was asking if she could do gymnastics, and so I was freaking out. I was scared to contact some of my old teammates so I started trying to make contact with national team mates from a different club – who we had hated because he had it put in our heads that we should hate them, because they were 'bad' – and we started talking about those years. One day one of them asked me what I could tell her about the rumours back then, about him having a relationship with his gymnasts. I flipped out. I said what do you mean 'rumours'?

'He's still coaching kids!' She told me that everybody thought that the relationship between him and the girls was very weird and that people suspected. Then I found out that there had been a report made to the governing body. So they had known about it and not only had they *not* protected the kids, they had protected the *abuser*! They had made him more powerful; they gave him everything that he needed just to keep on abusing girls.

So we didn't know what to do. We didn't want to go to the press because our families didn't know about it – but a story did appear. Then I got a call from another gymnast that was much younger and she said that she had suffered it too and she contacted the newspaper. And after that we were contacted by some more girls. It was very confusing and very hard. In the end I felt like I had a moral responsibility to speak about it. There was a very hard campaign against me via social media – some coaches and gymnasts who were younger, who didn't know me and weren't even there at the time. There's been years of that. It still goes on today.

We didn't want to go public on the news but – after months of harassment on social media – we decided to go public after my abuser's supporters made our names public in the press. We didn't like how it went out in the news, they only pick the part about the abuse. We felt it wasn't explained correctly. We wanted to tell our story and not just the points about the abuse. He still coaches and goes around to clubs and doing private classes. He's been in an elite camp. He doesn't have a conviction and because of the Statute of Limitations, the police couldn't do anything. Unless there is a more recent case he will not be responsible for what he did. That's the sad truth.

My mum is having a hard time with it because she feels guilty that she could not detect it at the time and could not help me. She felt sorry but she also said that she was very proud of me. The first thing she said was that she now understood a lot of things, and now she understands a lot of my reactions and my personality as a little girl, and as a young woman. That is something that is still not resolved. It's something we are still working on. It takes a lot of healing.

Since I went public with this, I have had a lot of calls from athletes who need help and from families who need advice. Just listening sometimes helps a lot. Listening without judging helps people a lot, and trying to get them to the institutions that can really help them. And that is very good for me. It gives me a lot of satisfaction to be able to help people like that. The campaigning has made me stronger; it's made me realise how important it is and how necessary it is to work on this to help people come out and speak out.

In my country when people talk about 'violence in sport' they talk about fan-violence. I want them to look away from the stands for a moment and take a look at what happens down at the field, in the sporting facilities or at the gyms. I want to help institutions provide safe and healthy environments in which our kids and young athletes can do sport without any kind of violence. I want society to take responsibility for the protection of children and young athletes and to consider that responsibility to be above any possible sporting result.

Analysis

Mary Jo's father was well educated and successful and her family life appears nurturing and stimulating. Mary Jo's father achieved a great deal in his career and socialized with individuals who themselves had political and cultural influence. The family's trajectory (including international travel) seems to have revolved around her father and his work. She is exposed from an early age to her father's eclectic, intellectual and elite social network and encouraged to voice her views and engage in 'adult' discussion and debate from an early age. She was raised by parents who did not discipline her by physical means, such as smacking.

Mary Jo's evident physicality and her tendency towards vigorous, even risky exercises as a young child was not discouraged and her passion for gymnastics appears to have been cemented while attending performances at the Olympic Games. Her father's support for her early interest was strong and her parents encouraged her into serious practice and competition from a young age.

Thus, apparently against the initial advice of club administrators who felt she was too young, Mary Jo was enrolled in a local club at the age of seven. She was soon training on a daily basis and when she quickly outgrew her local club, she was accepted into a national training squad, also situated near her home. This involved a daily five hour training regime, which she was very happy to undertake and enjoyed. Her early achievements received positive media attention and her school was also supportive of her gymnastic career, arranging exams around her competitions. Her focus appears to have been quite singular, and this focus was explicitly endorsed and supported by all the significant adults and institutions in her life, especially her family.

Gymnastics, then and now, is a sport that has traditionally been wholly acceptable for females to participate in. With its aesthetic focus, gymnastics permits female strength and power as it simultaneously insists this is expressed through elegance and grace by bodies that must be *petite*, lithe and lean, and with minimum coverage. Within a wider patriarchal society, gymnastics coaching and administration, at least at the elite level, was male dominated almost without exception. The male coach placed in charge of Mary Jo's development had acquired high levels of *cultural capital* in all its forms (*institutionalized*, *objectified* and *embodied*). As a former elite gymnast and coach, he embodied the practice of gymnastics; he had acquired the objectified knowledge pertaining to the performance of gymnastic skills and the acquisition of these skills; and he had accumulated the institutionalized accreditation of gymnastic titles and awards. He is, then, a valuable means by which the field (and the particular governing institution) can valorize and reproduce itself. He is a powerful means of intergenerational exchange, validating and conveying the logic of the field to new members, guarding its 'borders' and promoting its symbols. As such he represents that which both the *field* and the children in his charge – including their parents – value and 'desire'.

Therefore, exerting control of the gymnasium – the *field* in its objectified, material form – is a relatively simple operation. His position in the field afforded him almost total control of the distribution of *capital* within the sub-field of the gymnasium. Within the social and cultural *milieu*, discipline and punishment underpinned pedagogy within sport (and beyond) and verbal and physical punishment was an accepted part of adult-child instruction ('coaching') within gymnastics.

For Mary Jo and her peers, a disciplinary regime structures their entire existence within the gym, extending across meal times and even access to the toilet. Thus, with himself at the centre of the field, the girls are rewarded or punished via spatial proximity to that which is invested with the highest volumes of symbolic capital: the coach. If he is pleased with them, they are located closer to him; the further away, the less favoured they are. Those *in* favour are explicitly identified through 'privileges' such as special attention in training and affectionate 'asides'. The children, therefore, compete to be close to the coach. If they want to be at the symbolic centre of this field 'elite competition' – and they want that very much – they understand the rules of the game: they need to be physically (spatially) and emotionally 'close' to those that already occupy this space. That is, they need to accrue cultural capital that is controlled and distributed by the coach, therefore, they must submit to the symbolic violence of the gymnastic field and the gymnasium. To stay in the 'game', they must 'play the game'.

The gymnasium (the dominant location of Mary Jo's childhood) is a material or objectified representation (or structure) of the wider gymnastics field where Mary Jo receives daily instruction in the field's *doxa* – that which 'goes without saying', that which lies beyond the need for explanation and, therefore, beyond question. Through systematic instruction (or 'symbolic violence'), which shapes her body as it shapes her mind, she comes to embody the *gymnastic habitus*. Through expert tuition, by those already endorsed (or ordained) by the field in its institutional form (a *national* centre of excellence with *national* coaches), she is inculcated, not simply in the gymnastic skills and routines, but in the *field* itself. She becomes a repository for all that the field is – an embodiment of the field – she truly becomes a *gymnast*. Thus, she values what the field values, including and especially those who are the 'ordained' tutors in and of the field.

For a child in such circumstances, their habitus is heavily structured by the principles, values and practices of the field in which they endeavour. In her mid- to late-childhood, Mary Jo's daily and weekly routines, as well as her aspirations for her future, were utterly dominated and thoroughly structured by the 'world' of gymnastics. In other words, *gymnastic capital* was central to her young life, thus central to the structuring of her *habitus*: what counted as valuable in the field of gymnastics, counted as valuable in Mary Jo's childhood.

Mary Jo's habitus, substantively structured according to the *doxa* of the field, propelled her effortlessly towards the man that would exploit her sexually and it held her, enchanted, frightened and 'silent', even as the coach held her, physically and violently. The symbolic capital accrued by this coach (as a national level coach) – his power within the field of gymnastics – is supplemented (and complemented) by the construction of childhood, gender and sexuality within the field (its logic). Through constructions of *childhood*: children are adults-in-training, becoming(s) rather than being(s), partial rather than full; commodities, valued for their exchange rate in the economy of elite gymnastics and international sport; *gender*: masculinist conceptions of females as passive, sexual objects of male entitlement and possession prevail; and *sexuality*: heterosexist and homophobic. These dominant constructions illustrate the contours of the symbolic economy of the field that the young female gymnasts were required to embody. Therefore, while the practices employed by the coach to manipulate these girls may be designated as 'grooming' strategies, this was not an environment that had to be created out of 'thin air'. In fact, arguably, the coach had to do very little to manufacture these conditions; rather they were already present in the *doxa* of the field.

The policing of their gender identities, especially their developing sexual identities, can be seen, not as contrary to the structure of the field, but entirely in keeping with it. While not included in Mary Jo's story, she also reported that her female coach would repeatedly encourage her and her peers, during practice, to 'be pretty'. Such language is not meaningless nor without effect; rather symbolically powerful, objectifying the female gymnast within a discourse of passivity and subordination to the male gaze. Doubtless young male gymnasts were not similarly instructed. Such discourse helps to reveal the structure of cultural capital within female gymnastic performance and illustrates the logic of the field.

Likewise, when Mary Jo and her pre-teen peers are labelled 'whores' and ordered not to associate with, or even look at, their male counterparts – to the point where they avert their eyes when running past the male gymnasts – this practice goes seemingly unchallenged. Similarly, when Mary Jo appears at the gymnasium in a leg cast, administered in order to allow sufficient time away from training for an injury to heal, she is forced to continue to train; and this is apparently documented by local press. Thus, not only does such practice go unchallenged, it is seemingly celebrated. In fact, this coach's training practices were highly valued by the governing authorities.

Rather than emphasizing the idiosyncrasy of this coach's practice and constructing this through the language of 'grooming', sexual deviance and psychological abnormality, following feminist writers on sexual violence, I contend that this coach's practice (or 'training regime') was in fact 'all too normal'. This coach was not alien to the *field*, but in fact the embodiment of it; similarly, the gymnastics field was a sub-field of the wider sports culture and indeed, the wider culture. Therefore, Mary Jo reports the feeling of having nowhere to turn: 'At home we talked about politics, art, everything except sex'. In the wider national culture, sex was not generally a topic that was discussed with children, and certainly this was the case in Mary Jo's family, despite their liberal and progressive views on other matters.

Conversely, the coach had gone to great pains to sexualize the gymnasium and to construct Mary Jo (and her peers) as 'whores' and as girls with deviant sexual appetites. Faced with the seemingly incontrovertible evidence of the sexual activity she was subjected to, Mary Jo comes to identify herself in those terms: 'a whore, a slut'; she comes to 'believe in the game' established by her abuser. Thus, she is objectified and positioned as the 'lowest of the low', powerless except through the exploitation of her own body, and of no value except for what her body can offer, as an athlete and a sexual object, with the former seemingly dependant on the latter.

She lies on her bed in the dark, unable to talk to her mother and unable to see any possibility for extracting herself from the daily childhood routine of rape, gymnastics and deception: 'It's very easy to conceal' seems a particularly chilling statement. It is perhaps possible to challenge, or at least extend, Mary Jo's account on this point. Certainly, the alternative – revealing herself as a 'whore' – was impossible to contemplate. As she imagined herself out of, or away from, the corporeal experience of sexual violation, she fantasizes about being rescued, simultaneously dreading the possibility of her 'dirty' secret – her 'dirty' *self* – being revealed. However, the concealment of her daily ordeal, as a child, could only have required a constant and substantial emotional effort. She may have been silenced within her suffering and the persistent violation of her body, but maintaining the appearance of a happy child and an elite gymnast while experiencing one's self in very different terms, clearly demands a constant vigilance and a considerable effort of will: 'I was always trying really, really hard so that she wouldn't notice anything, so I wouldn't have to tell about it.' Concealment and deception, therefore, become a daily necessity;

but far from 'easy'. They become, then, a feature of her habitus, an incorporated disposition.

She reports developing a hypersensitivity to situations and conversations that could lead to discussion of her gymnastics career. Thus, long after she had finished competing she was forced to distance herself from her own achievements – her own childhood – lest mention of them lead to the uncovering of her secret. Her childhood relationship with her parents and siblings, viewed from adulthood, was constructed around her concealment, around a falsehood she had actively maintained from a young age and throughout her life. The repercussions of this are deeply troubling for her. Arguably, the act of concealment becomes a practice of concealment, or rather a durable disposition. Her own childhood, then, becomes objectified – an object of shame and guilt, her *self* alienated from its-*self*, not to be spoken about, rather to be hidden away in boxes, in dark cellars.

It would be glib to state that it is simply the passage of time and her own maternal role that prompted her to reconsider her silence and concealment. However, it is perhaps through her new parental/familial priorities in raising and protecting her child that she musters the fortitude to re-establish contact with women who were once defined as enemies. In a sense, she re-enters the field from which she was forced to exclude herself. Her previously high volume of cultural capital in the field and her growing desire (or feelings of responsibility) to speak out generates interest within the press, although this is in fact something she is forced into by others revealing her name. She gradually re-enters the public arena as a 'victim' and 'survivor' of sexual abuse. However, this act also establishes her as a target for verbal (online) abuse from some *within* the field who refuse to accept that she was abused by this man. His capital in the field continues to produce a (masculinist) dividend and this is protected by the (masculinist) judicial field that prevents assessment of the allegations in court. Thus, Mary Jo's decision to speak out brings a further form of abuse, perhaps reinforcing the fears of other victims about the risks of voicing their experiences.

Stephen

My early childhood was ok, if a little strained. My father wasn't around and my mother was trying to look after me and my teenage sister, which by all account was a challenge. She was working part time. It was happy enough but by no means idyllic. We didn't have that much money and I suppose I felt different from the other boys because I didn't have a father.

My mum had taken me to the local swimming club and she met an old school friend there who happened to have two children around my age. I became good friends with the boy, Tim. In a fairly short time we all became close. This woman's father also happened to be the treasurer of the swimming club. He was a retired police officer. He was around 65, possibly older. He used to take me and his grandchildren swimming. I was really interested in swimming and wanted to become a swimmer. I was around 8 at this time. I received training from a few coaches at the club, all of which I liked. I remember going from sort of average to above average in a relatively short space of time. My confidence grew and I was very keen. In the end I didn't compete seriously, but I represented my school.

The relationship between the two families continued, we even went on holiday to Wales together, but without my mum who was working. And at times I slept at the grandfather's house, in the same bed as Tim. I suppose I looked up to the grandfather. He was influential at the swimming club and was 'high up' in swimming circles – or so I thought – he probably wasn't but this is what he made me believe. He once took us to the Olympic pool. I remember because he made a really big deal about how he knew a famous swimmer who was there competing. She was there but I remember she just looked at him like she didn't know him.

He liked to play the clown, I remember that and he was very overweight which made him seem 'clown-like'. I have the impression that he wanted to be thought of as a figure of fun, but at the same time with gravitas. I guess he used that 'figure of fun' mask to fool people into trusting him. He liked to punish me and Tim, not physically or sexually, but with coldness and cruelty. On one occasion I didn't finish my breakfast cereal so he wouldn't let me go swimming that day. I became fearful of him.

He and his wife booked a trip to Australia, but he was going to follow his wife out there after a week. His daughter (my mum's friend) drove me and Tim to the airport, while he drove with his wife. We saw his wife off at the airport. Because Tim and I had been misbehaving in the car on the way there, he said that he would take me back alone. This is when the first incident of abuse took place. He put his hand inside my track suit bottoms, all the way home. It felt unnatural and I wanted him to stop touching me, because it didn't feel right, but at the same time it felt 'nice' and my body responded to the touch. I had the vague sense that what he was doing was wrong – he wouldn't look at me, he just focused on the road, as though it wasn't really happening. It's difficult to think about. It was confusing, and embarrassing. But it's also so long ago – it's very hard to recall, like a surreal experience. I knew it wasn't normal behaviour. I remember that he came back from Australia with a boomerang for me.

The only other incident was at my house. He dropped me off. My mum didn't have a car and Tim lived quite far away, so it wasn't out of the ordinary. But he offered to put me to bed. I don't remember how many times he came to my house, but my mum felt comfortable enough to let him put me to bed. We were fairly close. It was the same as the first time, but not so long. I think this time the feelings of unnaturalness were heightened and I really felt uncomfortable. Again, he didn't say anything before, during or afterwards. It was bewildering, but I was aware that something was happening that wasn't supposed to be happening. But at the time, it didn't feel traumatic.

I think I picked up on his perverseness and that made me question what he had done. It's really hard to describe, it's emotionally charged and because it's so long ago I'm not sure if I'm making things up about the way I felt. But by this time I knew it wasn't right and I told my mum what he'd done to me. I remember the night I told my mum quite vividly. He was at my house and we were playing chess. I think I was beating him, anyway, he went into a strop and left without saying goodbye. That was the last time I saw him. When my mum came to my room to say goodnight she asked me what was wrong and I just came out with it 'he's a pervert!' Obviously she pressed me to explain what I meant and so I told her what he'd been doing. She was horrified. It was an easy decision to tell her because by this time I knew there was something wrong and I didn't want to be in his company any more.

She went straight to the social services who went to the police. I remember acting out the offences with toys in front of a two-way mirror. But no charge was ever brought. He was an ex-policeman – I don't know if that had anything to do with it, but I suspect that the case was too weak anyway. I remember being very confused about it all, like I was in trouble, because the authorities were involved. It felt 'heavy', which I suppose it was. I also felt sad and disappointed because I couldn't see Tim anymore and – like I'd 'upset the apple cart' – like I'd put into motion a serious chain of events that I didn't really understand. I remember Tim's mum dropping him at the end of the road and him saying that we couldn't be friends anymore. We broke all contact with the family and I stopped going swimming.

But I remember – after I'd told my mum about the abuse – I came home one evening and my mum and Tim's mum were sat on the floor talking. I could tell it was serious and my mum asked me to tell them what had happened. It wasn't until years later that I found out that Tim's mum believed me, which makes me wonder if he abused her too. I don't know.

The realisation of what had happened to me took place quite suddenly, when I was 15. I remember being sat on my bed and feeling distressed and having flashbacks. I don't remember if it was caused by anything in particular. It was only then that I realised – the grooming, manipulation, the horror, trying to make sense of the whole situation and what it meant for me – and that, I think, was when the damage occurred. It was referred to a few times in my 20s but never really dealt with. It was always too painful a subject to bring up if I'm honest and I didn't want to subject my mum to any more torment than was necessary. But I also felt resentful towards her and blamed her for letting it happen.

I was addicted to heroin for about 5 years during university. It took me two years to get clean and I had to go to a treatment centre. One of the things that came up in the 'family meeting' with the counsellor was the abuse. Since then it's been a topic which my mum and I have discussed productively. I feel much more comfortable talking about it with her (and others) now. It isn't so much of a dirty little secret anymore, although it can still be difficult to talk about sometimes.

For a long time I didn't tell anyone. Because for a long time I wasn't sure if I'd dreamt it or fantasised it or something, so it seemed like I was going mad. But very slowly the facts came to the surface and it's only quite recently that I've been able to start to draw some kind of line under it. I don't think it will ever be fully eradicated from my psyche, but I have more acceptance around it. And gradually I've felt able to tell more people about it. Friends from the treatment centre I went to and friends from a support group on drug addiction which I attend. But most of my family still doesn't know.

The damage it's done has been immense. To my mental health, my relationships, self-image. The damage was most destructive in my late teens and 20s when I would drink and take drugs to escape the feelings. I'm 36 in 2 weeks and can honestly say I'm dealing with it, for the first time. I've recently revisited it and got a witness statement from the social worker that worked on the case. My girlfriend knows and I've started to see it as not such a big deal. After all it could've been far worse. But I still have bad days. There's some days where I've said he's ruined my life, and others where I forgive him because he's irrelevant. He's been dead for many years. I get triggers all the time but I've learnt to cope with these. For example anything to do with swimming will trigger me and I'll start to feel unwell.

Analysis

Stephen's story is distinct in relation to the others presented here. After two episodes of contact sexual abuse (masturbation) perpetrated by a family friend, who used swimming as a means of gaining access to the boy, Stephen was able to confide in his mother about what had happened. His feelings about the abuse are not distinct from the accounts of other men and women presented here (with the exception of Jack), but unlike the others, he felt able to tell a parent and in doing so, he was able to stop the abuse from going any further. Clearly this is significant and must also be examined using the same conceptual tools employed to analyse other accounts.

The grandfather/club official was endorsed by his mother, no doubt because of her friendship with his daughter, and he seems to have begun to insinuate himself into the fabric of Stephen's family life. He used swimming as a means of establishing himself as a useful individual for Stephen's mother to rely on, especially given his access to transport, and someone who could help Stephen progress with his sporting ambitions through his social capital at the swimming club. As the club treasurer, no doubt combined with his ex-police status, he was clearly viewed as a trustworthy male influence who could be relied upon to look after her child, even to the point of putting him to bed.

Given his father's absence (and his difficulties with this) and a mother who was having to work hard to keep the family financially stable, Stephen may be viewed as a particularly vulnerable child. Perhaps this is, in fact, what this man saw when he came into contact with the family. His strategies of insinuation are not uncommon or surprising. His comparative economic capital allowed him to assert himself as a significant presence in Stephen's family life, offering material support to a young, single mother of two. He clearly used his position at the swimming club to try to impress Stephen, and impress upon him his cultural capital within swimming. However, as club treasurer, rather than a coach or a competitive swimmer, this man did not command high levels of cultural capital and the boy appears to have seen through his attempt to establish an image of himself as a member of swimming's elite.

Stephen began swimming aged 8 and developed an enthusiasm for it. He progressed and swam competitively, but not beyond local competition and school galas. It seems reasonable to characterize his interest in swimming as a relatively fleeting childhood leisure pursuit and not as an activity that structured his daily life. His family (mother) was obviously encouraging of his interest in swimming, and it would appear that swimming presented an opportunity for socializing and developing family networks, but far from an overwhelming feature of the family's life. He reports that he gave swimming up after reporting his abuser, therefore, by the age of 9 or 10 his interest in competitive swimming was over.

Stephen's childhood habitus, then, seems only partially and temporarily influenced by the field (swimming) that his abuser occupied and used as his primary sphere of influence over the boy. Thus, there seems considerable distance between Stephen's disposition towards sport, and, say that of Paul or Mary Jo.

Furthermore, it seems clear that a central, albeit understated feature of Stephen's childhood, is the absence of his father. Indeed, this also distinguishes him from the other 'survivors'. It is perhaps not unreasonable to suggest that, in the absence of his father, the family unit, including an older sister, provided Stephen with an atmosphere which viewed discussion of personal and emotional matters as positive and normal. It does not seem overly speculative to suggest that the masculinist ideology that seemed to dominate the early childhoods (to greater or lesser degrees) of the other 'survivors' was largely absent from Stephen's family. Arguably, his early boyhood habitus was not structured *principally* through narratives of athleticism, and this in fact facilitated a much wider range of possibilities for the expression of 'weakness' and associated emotions in this young boy while not disposing him to the wholesale investment in athleticism that seems so apparent for the other participants. There certainly isn't the sense of being *bound* to an institution (field) and a destiny as there is in the other accounts.

From this point of view, Stephen's disclosure – his capacity to tell – may be seen as the product of the familial field, and his embodiment of it, just as the silence of the other children is associated with the fields that dominated their young lives, especially the athleticist field. For Stephen, masculinism and athleticism while no doubt far from absent in his life, was perhaps challenged by principles emphasized in other fields that were more fundamental to his young habitus. Stephen's abuse was connected to his sports participation, but this was not a field in which he or his mother were heavily invested. Stephen may have appeared as particularly vulnerable, however, he was in fact able to tell about his abuse, despite it already having begun and at a relatively young age, very likely avoiding further sexual encounters. It is also very clear that the effects of the abuse have been significant and have seriously and negatively impacted on his life, and he continues to work through them.

Elaine

My dad came from a very large family. His dad was extremely abusive emotionally; his mum was an alcoholic. We were wealthy. We went overseas as a family at least once a year and my mum and dad went overseas on their own at least once a year. We lived in a really big house, which had been paid for by cash. Dad had five cars. He was away a lot and worried about his business, but he was a fantastic provider. I was never short of anything.

As a little girl I was into ballet, but when I was 5 I started tennis. My mum and dad played. My dad was quite good and won a lot of club championships. They were either playing tennis or watching it on TV. All their friends were tennis players or in the club that they belonged to. I don't remember my parents having a lot of friends outside of the tennis circle. Any parties or 'get-togethers' were at the Tennis Club. I practised a lot with my dad and my mum was actually my doubles partner until I was 13 or 14.

School came pretty much second to tennis, although I had very good marks. From the age of 10, I was on the tennis court about 7 hours a day. I would get up around six in the morning and play from 6:15 a.m. to 7:30 a.m. before school. When school finished I would be straight back on the tennis court for 4 to 5 hours every single afternoon. I spent a lot of time playing with my dad, and we would have squads and group tennis, but I really don't recall him watching me compete.

I had some privileges at school. If I needed to play tournaments I was given the time off and instead of normal PE I would go and play tennis. If I couldn't finish a project or homework, which was often the case, I'd be given an extension. When we had school outings, I wasn't allowed to go because I needed to play tennis so I stayed at school and helped the teacher prepare schoolwork or whatever. One or two teachers didn't really appreciate me getting special treatment but generally I had a very good relationship with all my teachers. But I was very diligent and didn't get into trouble. I didn't go to school parties, or to sleep-overs. I didn't know all of that kind of stuff, which was really difficult. My friends were all elite tennis players. I never really had much time out of tennis so I never experienced the full privileges of childhood. I didn't know what it was like to have a *social* life. But I always got a good feeling from winning. I have an intense desire to win – I don't know if it's a desire to win, or more a need to be recognised. That desire, or need, comes from – well love was withheld from me if I didn't win. The only acknowledgement I got was if I really excelled at what I did. Sometimes even that wasn't sufficient. So I tried to just be better and I was scared of not being good enough.

There was a lot of stress involved in every single match that I played. I think it didn't make me a very nice person – I knew that I wasn't a very nice person. I had a foul temper and my mum was quite well known for her misbehaviour on the court as well. I broke a few rackets, I'm not proud of it but I did. I had a bad reputation. But there were very few tournaments that I didn't win. There were a lot of people that were interested in me. I had coaches coming to me because they wanted to coach me. I was sponsored, I was in a magazine – I had a lot of attention. But I wanted to go to Junior Wimbledon – that was what I strove for.

At some point my mum's work became much more flexible and she started spending a lot more time at the tennis court. She was at the tournaments pretty much whenever she could be. Then it started becoming really unpleasant. She pushed me really hard. She had a dream that I was going to be this really awesome tennis player, and even support her. So she had her little protégé and it kind of became her life. So my tennis became – not about me winning, but about *her* winning. Her social standing was based on my results. So losing wasn't an option and our relationship was about me striving to please her. I think our relationship was very strained. After a loss I was always nervous to come off the court. The beginning of the conversation would be that we would have to lie to my dad. Generally I would be sitting in the front seat looking out of the passenger window, crying because of the lambasting I was getting. Even if I won, there was invariably a lecture about how I could have done a little bit better. It got to a point where I would just switch off completely. So if I had lost, most of the time we would go home and tell dad that I had won, just to keep the peace and stop him from ranting and raving about how he was spending so much money on my lessons and my coaching. We lied to him a lot.

Steve coached me from the age of 5. Steve was always there. I did every-thing with him. By the age of 7 I was already winning tournaments. It was a lot of fun. By the time I was 8 I was already up on my wall at school and by 10 I was playing in the senior leagues. At under 12s I was number 2 nationally, but I was only 10 years old. I was competing overseas by the time I was 11. The relationship with Steve was good, I trusted him com-pletely. But Tony was a real hero. I just remember whenever he was there, you could *feel* his presence. Then one day he came to me and said he had been watching me for a while, had seen a lot of potential in me and would really like to coach me. When I left Steve it all went very sour. I remember him and Tony having a massive fight at a tournament. Tony poached a lot of his pupils.

I was embarrassed about leaving Steve but Tony had promised the world. It was up to my mum and dad – they paid – so I just went to Tony's squad when I was 11. The people were all very familiar, it was comfort-able, and before long I was with him about 4 or 5 days a week. I was having lessons with his squad, lessons with him at regional level and I was having lessons at his home as well. It was great to have him as a coach and I thought I had a really good relationship with him, I thought I was really special.

There were 22 of us in his elite squad; about 6 girls and the rest were boys. The ages ranged from 11 to about 16/17. We had some much older boys who were on the squad who were 16/17 years old. Maybe the oldest girl was about 14. The boys always used to play on the top court and the girls on the bottom court. He spent a lot of time with us. The regional squad was an even mix of girls and boys. But it was also the same girls and boys that were at his elite squad. So we were together all the time. And then my mum used to take me to private lessons at his home. By the time I had left him I was playing beyond my age group. He got me into the senior squad before I was even finished with the junior squad. I think I was quite a bit ahead of everybody else.

Tony was always very concerned about the way we looked. He was very clear on what we were allowed to wear to tennis – skirts only – and what we went out in after tennis. He would put me down by telling me I was putting on weight or make other comments about what I was wearing. Very subtle comments that made you think, 'hold on, maybe I need to just change this'. He also had a habit – while we were on the ground stretching – of standing over our heads so we could see up his shorts. It was very, very awkward. Then he asked me about one of the other players – about whether or not she was a virgin. I didn't even know what that meant! Then one day during practice, I was about 12, he called me across the court and told me that my mother had asked him to discuss 'the-birds-and-the-bees' with me. I almost died! I just wanted to crawl into a hole. I couldn't work out why she would have done that. Anyhow, he sat with me on the steps of the tennis courts for about an hour explaining all the ins-and-outs of sex and sexual relationships. I listened and endured the awkwardness. I was very embarrassed. But I didn't have a relationship with my mum where I could discuss that with her. It was all very awkward and I shoved it into the back of my head and I didn't tell her anything. Over the next few months it progressed to him wanting to look down my top and down my pants. Then when I went abroad with him, he called me to his room to collect pocket money – and he was naked! So all the alarm bells went off, but I didn't know what to do or how to handle it.

That kind of stuff continued until one afternoon he picked me up from school. I never questioned why, but he didn't normally do that. Half way to the tennis complex, he just started speaking about sex and all that kind of stuff and then he took my hand and he put it on his crotch. I just sat there absolutely frozen. I didn't know what to do. And then he started telling me that he loved me and that it was time for me to grow and become a woman and that we needed to do this. There was all this talk about how he was the one who was going to *transition* me into becoming a woman – by having sex with me – this was his agenda with everybody he abused. He took on the role of *transitioning* me to being an adult. Which he did.

When it was over he drove me to the courts, told me to get cleaned up, which I did, and then I went on court. It was a very strange afternoon – kind of surreal. I remember very clearly the leaves on the trees; I remember the sky was exceptionally blue; and my sense of smell seemed heightened. But what was bugging me most was the smell – of sex. I was worried that the other people on the court could smell it as well! That was my biggest concern that afternoon: were they smelling what I was smelling? To this day I gag and I can't handle that smell. I went home. I couldn't process it. And I became very withdrawn.

He only had intercourse with me once, but the abuse went on for about two or three years after that. He always wanted oral sex and so any opportunity he got, that was the thing. Somehow he had convinced me of this whole love affair – and I bought it! I knew that what he was doing wasn't right but I was brought up in such a way that I respected him. He told me that this is what needed to be done – I didn't question it. But I knew that if we were going to his car, there was a reason for it. It was always in his car. There were incidents in the club, but they were only minor things in comparison.

But after the abuse began I think I was trying to hang onto something that I suppose wasn't really there. I think that I might have even become a little bit jealous of him as I was always wondering where he was. I do remember seeing him with other girls and seeing them in the car and wondering what the hell was going on. A lot of anger came out on the tennis courts after the actual incident. I also think I might have started to try and own him. But it was not something that we ever discussed openly. Life just carried on.

Shortly after my thirteenth birthday my mum asked me if I was pregnant. I was so shocked! She said she asked me that because she knew we were 'sleeping' together. I'm very angry because she should have stopped it. She hasn't explained it. Some years ago I started to confront her about stuff that happened, but I was pretty much shut down and I've barely spoken to her about it. I'm very bitter and angry at her – although some days I forgive her.

All the stuff that happened with him was before my thirteenth birthday. So it was all in the space of a year. That was all the grooming process, which we know about now, but I didn't know then. Making me feel special – in hindsight I know that it was all just a ploy – it was all a game so to speak. I left him when I was about 15. I changed coaches.

My new coach was great. I don't know if it was my decision to go to her or my mum's. I actually don't know how I ended up with her, but she got me back on track and at 17 I was back at the top. I never really spoke about him all that much but then when I was about 20, I kind of very quickly told my friend what had happened and then just as quickly shut it down and carried on with the evening. So it was kind of like 'I've said it, now put it back in its box – just leave it.' So that was the first time I really talked about what had happened.

The OCD started when I was away at university. It started with cleaning. I had my own dorm and stuff and I started cleaning. And from cleaning my dorm I started cleaning myself. I started bathing in bleach. I just never used to feel clean and I lot of it came from what happened with Tony. I used to bathe in like half a bottle of bleach. I was still winning tournaments but the pressure was intense and I actually became extremely homesick. I was very confused. I wasn't happy. I just didn't want to play tennis anymore. I kind of got to a point where I didn't enjoy tennis. Everything was just wrong. I'd been away for about 18 months. One day my dad phoned and said that if I wanted to come home he wouldn't judge me or be upset with me. I was home within 4 days.

When I came home expectations were high. I carried on playing tournaments but I just wasn't enjoying it. I joined a new club where I knew a lot of people – but then Tony took over the coaching there. He kind of moved into the club and I felt I had nowhere to go. It was just like the ultimate thing and that was just the end of it. During a tournament I said to my mixed doubles partner that it was the last time I was playing. It was like night and day. I packed my rackets away and that was it. I left and never picked up a tennis racket again. It was just after my 21st birthday.

At that point my life just started to fall apart. I pretty much cut myself off from everybody. I developed an eating disorder. I think a lot of it was about self-worth. Somebody told me that I was fat. It was only a joke but that kind of triggered it. It had a real impact on me and it just got completely out of control. I used to weigh myself if I ate, I used to weigh myself if I drank a cup of coffee; if I went into the bathroom I would weigh myself. I'd weigh myself I don't know how many times a day. I suppose it was something I could focus on, so that I didn't have to think about the other stuff. But I almost died because of it. I guess I got to a place where – I just *couldn't* anymore. In the end they were either going to put me into care and I was going to lose my daughter or I could sort myself out. So I started going to therapy and they kind of got me to start putting on weight and feeling a bit healthier and I started to look after myself a bit better. I was a single mum with a full-time job. I had a good job but my life pretty much revolved around her. She started playing sport at an early age so after work it was off to whichever sports she was doing that evening.

I suffered from severe depression. I've had severe outbursts, almost always related to intimacy. They can be really nasty. In a moment of rage I would trash a room. I haven't done it often but I've done it a few times. I'm not proud of it. I tried to commit suicide and as a result I ended up seeing a therapist. We started digging into what could have caused me to feel that way and what triggered me. All this stuff was just coming out; it was unbelievable! It was as if it was the right time. When I did the in-depth stuff with my therapist it was quite mortifying to know that this was ultimately what had been affecting me all my life. And I became really very angry about it.

I lived with the shame for so long but I had started dealing with it when a reporter contacted me. After a discussion with my psychologist we agreed that this was something that I needed to get out there; we needed to expose him for what he was. It was also a joint decision with other victims. It was a long process – about 6 months – of back and forth messages. It was a huge decision to be identified. In the first article other girls were identified also. I don't know if it was a good idea to put my name out there but I did and then had to deal with the consequences of that choice. My parents were mortified, just absolutely horrified. My dad's response to it was that I should get over it and not let it destroy my life. His take on it was I was never going to get anything out of Tony so I should just move on and get over it. Which was quite a difficult thing to deal with.

In terms of the tennis fraternity, a lot of the people said that they had thought that something wasn't quite right. I know that three sets of parents complained to the tennis union at the time, so it was very much known about. I've recently hooked up with a lady, who hasn't come forward, but was a victim of his – I remember seeing her in the car with him – and her parents complained. So the authorities knew about it. It doesn't matter who you speak to, everybody seems to say that there were '*rumblings*' but no one did anything about it.

The governing body have never taken any responsibility. I wanted to speak to the people who were there at that time but you just can't get hold of them. They haven't come forward to say they believed us, or were sorry that they didn't protect us. It would have been nice if they had taken some responsibility for it. Maybe they feel that they just can't face it but it would be nice if they said 'how can we support you now?' and 'how can we get you back on track?'

I have had a lot of support, I suppose as a consequence of disclosing publically, but we've also had people accusing us of conspiring to make money. Mostly on social media and it's mostly men that say we're after money – it's very seldom women. And we've been accused of being prostitutes. I get messages from men wanting to know if I'm 'available' and stuff like that. People don't really see that I was 12 years old, they see me as I am now! They don't see the little girl. I have had one or two stalkers, some quite bad – death threats to me and my family. I had a couple of instances when I had to involve lawyers. I've also had a couple of women, including women in my circle, who have become quite antagonistic towards me.

I still bathe in bleach, but only a cap-full at a time now. But when it comes to house-cleaning I am completely out of control – everything must be in its place and facing the same direction. It's really out of control and it affects a lot of my relationships. While there's been a few disappointments, things have gotten a bit better in terms of my emotional wellbeing. I am a lot more at peace now. I'm sleeping unaided for the first time in about 10 years. I used to take medicine so that I could sleep every night and I haven't for 8 weeks now. So all the anti-depressants – all the crap I was taking to try and help me cope – I don't need it anymore, which is a really nice feeling. I think I've forgiven him. I don't even care if he goes to jail or not. I'm really not too fussed about it. I just want to get on with my life now and start afresh.

Analysis

Elaine's father and mother were both very keen tennis players and were heavily involved in the local club. Indeed, the tennis club, and their association with its other members, seems at the heart of the family's life (its social capital), alongside her father's (financial) business interests. Their membership of and status within the club – and the rather exclusive nature of tennis as a leisure pursuit (in comparison with many other sports) – helps to locate the family in terms of a *habitus* that is seeking distinction and has significant material means to do so.

Elaine took up tennis at the age of 5 and reports being on the court for approximately seven hours a day from the age of 10. She received coaching from a young age and was regularly given special dispensation at school because of her tennis competitions. She recalls a strong desire to win and parents whose love she perceived as conditional upon her win-loss ratio. Her relationship with her father seems to circulate around her sport: he was both her practice partner during her mid-childhood and her source of finance to support her development. She was emotionally (and occasionally physically) abused by her mother who appears to have been wholly invested in her daughter's tennis 'career': 'She pushed me really hard. She had a dream...'

Elaine's childhood is best characterized, then, as a 'tennis childhood': 'My friends were all elite tennis players. I never really had much time out of tennis'. She was raised (socialized) within and through the traditions, values and mores of tennis with seemingly few outside influences. From a very young age, her childhood is structured around the objective of turning her into a 'tennis champion' – with apparently token resistance from a few teachers – within a thoroughly supportive school environment. Thus, her early pursuit (and achievement) of elite performance was seemingly fully endorsed by all those around her.

In a short space of time, she managed to capitalize on her early potential through competition, in which she dominated her peers. Elaine's *habitus*, then, was structured according to the principles of elite sports performance and the logic of the 'tennis field'. Her status (and self-esteem) quickly became heavily dependent on her tennis performance, not just outside the family, but also inside the family. Indeed, she reports feeling as though her mother's reputation in the community was dependent on her tennis results. That is, her mother's social and cultural capital was closely associated with the volume of 'wins' she accumulated: 'our relationship was about me striving to please her'. On the other hand, losses had to be concealed from her father, at her mother's instigation, so as to avoid recriminations regarding the financial cost of coaching lessons and competing at the elite level. In other words, the investment her mother and father made in her – her mother's time and emotional support and her father's financial support – was expected to generate a 'profit' (*capital*, in all its forms), and the continuation of this family investment was dependant on this. Doubtless, Elaine experienced this as 'pressure' and 'anxiety', and so it is far from surprising to learn that this manifest in 'poor' behaviour during competition.

It may well have been her parent's desire to generate an increasing 'return' on their 'investment' – to capitalize on their daughter's raw potential – that led them to facilitate a change of coach, from one with a strong local reputation and a good relationship with their daughter to one with much higher status in the field. Elaine's new coach was a thoroughly dominant figure within the field who possessed high levels of cultural and social capital and had been able to efficiently transform this into economic capital. Therefore, the decision to invest in this coach – to purchase his coaching skills and access to his social network – represents a significant symbolic decision that surely left Elaine in no doubt about how fortunate she was to be there. Indeed, it perhaps reinforces and emphasizes the narrative that Elaine had received since early childhood: 'losing wasn't an option', indeed, while she now has 'everything' to gain, she also has 'everything' to lose. Thus, tennis is far from simply a pleasurable 'ludic' pursuit, but something that the family is wholly invested in. It seemingly becomes symbolic of their success as a family, and Elaine's performance on the tennis court becomes the centre of the family's life.

Elaine recounts the interpersonal strategies of coercion employed by the coach. He sought to undermine Elaine's confidence through critical comments about what she wore and how she looked, including her weight. The wider sociocultural milieu was deeply patriarchal and masculinist with clear disciplinary narratives about acceptable/preferred femininity and what constituted a 'successful' female. Therefore, such intrusive and personal observations were seen as unremarkable in a culture where women and their bodies were viewed as the property of men and subject to the 'male gaze'. This 'symbolic domination' is the precursor for physical (sexual) domination.

When the sexual abuse begins, she sees no alternative but to go along with the demands this man makes of her. She has no access to an alternative vision that might enable resistance. Her life was wholly constituted by succeeding in tennis, *becoming* a tennis player, therefore, obedience and subordination to those who could help realise that goal was all she knew. The man subjecting her to sex (rape) was also the tennis field 'made flesh'. He represented the most potent form of symbolic capital – he embodied the field and was fully endorsed by the tennis authorities and the wider tennis world. Therefore, to speak out against him was to speak out against the *field* that she so fervently wanted to become a part of. She had been trained, from early childhood, to 'desire' this 'game', therefore, to desire those that embodied it. He was everything she hoped to be and represented everything she (and her family) hoped for in her future.

The coach begins to sexualize the relationship by displaying himself (his genitals) in a way that could, no doubt, be construed as accidental – a 'misunderstanding' – if he was ever challenged about it. This appears to be part of a test to establish if Elaine or her peers would challenge him or 'tell on him'. However, their embarrassment was the natural, and anticipated, response, as was their silence. Elaine and her peers knew what they had to lose by jeopardizing their relationship with their coach.

The effect of his actions is to alter Elaine's relationship with him by immediately positioning her as a *keeper* of his (illicit/'dirty') secret. This was clearly the thin-end-of-the-wedge, thus, he then tests her further through a one-to-one sex-talk and by inviting her to his room while he was naked. Thus, her coach gradually positioned Elaine at the centre of his life (albeit that this was something of an illusion), conveying upon her the unspoken but explicit responsibility for his gratification. The relationship can be represented as one of 'gift exchange': he provided the gift of himself as mentor/master – a highly prized, sought after commodity in the tennis world. This is, then, a gift that Elaine could not match, leaving her in extreme 'debt' with little capacity (*capital*) to repay. What she did have – her embodied capital, her physical labour – was, therefore, his to demand and to possess. Indeed, whatever he demanded, she was bound, by the principles of the *game*, to provide – to give her 'all', 'one hundred and ten per cent' – to provide recompense for the 'gift' he offered, on a regular and persistent basis.

Her young/emerging *habitus* had been structured by the *fields* (principally the family and tennis) that she had come to embody and she was violated by a man who was dominant in that *field*, who was the 'field made flesh'. As she says: 'I was brought up in such a way that I respected him. He told me that this is what needed to be done – I didn't question it.' And this dominated position, subordinate and subservient, is exactly representative of the *doxa* of the sports field – 'if I say "jump", you say "how high?"' The mentor/master-apprentice/servant relation is a requirement of the field for those who want to succeed in it. The young athlete does as s/he is told and in their servitude they labour intensely to become that which dominates them, working daily to repay a debt that cannot be repaid. If an element of this work is also 'sex-work', their habitus is well versed in the stakes of the game and what it takes to succeed.

Elaine was of course deeply affected by the sexual violence she was subjected to. Her description of the day she was coerced/forced into sexual intercourse is vivid and significant. Following the rape, she was taken straight to the training facility where she practiced as usual. Her habitus was fundamentally structured around tennis and performance, she was a *tennis player*, wholly invested, *interested*, in the 'game', therefore, what else was there to do? Nevertheless, it is clear that this event had a significant impact on her: 'I couldn't process it. And I became very withdrawn.' Arguably her habitus becomes suddenly misaligned with the field that she had been trained to resemble. There is perhaps a *hysteresis* of habitus so that the game is no longer simply an extension of herself but a game that simultaneously represented her dreams and her nightmares.

She doesn't, of course, simply lose her skills on the court. Like habitus, these are 'durably installed', practised to perfection. But her position in the field is no longer dependant simply on her ability to perform on the tennis court. The game has fundamentally changed. It is no longer wholly encapsulated within the patterns and routines of athletic performance. The form of cultural capital – what counts – has been repackaged and restructured in a form – a new 'deal' – that her habitus must accommodate, but is unprepared for. Her position is no longer simply dependant on pleasing her coach in athletic terms, but also in sexual terms. Unsurprisingly, she is deeply confused and disorientated, and this is manifested in her performance and her behaviour. She relays that, following her public disclosure, women she had competed against as a child told her that they hadn't understood why they could suddenly beat her.

It is approximately two years after her mother questions her about pregnancy, and after an apparent decline in form, that Elaine leaves – or is moved – from her abusive coach to another (female) coach. She states that she gave him little thought in subsequent years until she eventually discloses to a friend when she is about 20 years old. This appears to be the first landmark on her long road to official disclosure many years later. However, significant emotional difficulties manifest in her late teens, at a time when she is living away from home so she can continue to compete at the elite level.

As she matures, the possibility of performing at the very highest level fades, and so her position in the field is adjusted, 'downgraded', and her symbolic capital is restructured accordingly. She reaches a point – seemingly prompted by her abuser's renewed intrusion in her tennis life – where competing, even just playing, simply is not 'worth the candle' anymore. She 'quits' tennis abruptly and completely – like 'night and day' – and 'at that point my life just started to fall apart.' Her position in the field in which she had invested so much shifts dramatically – she is no longer 'number 1', no longer a 'Wimbledon hopeful'. She loses her *place* in tennis (literally and figuratively) and the field moves on, but now leaving Elaine behind. She is no longer as a fish in water, rather a fish out of water.

She perhaps experiences a more potent *hysteresis* effect – a 'disruption in the relationship between *habitus* and the field structures' (Deer, 2012: 129) – but this time with more severe consequences. Not only has her investment in tennis – 'body and soul' – not been rewarded (nor fulfilled her parents dreams) as she had hoped, but she has paid for the privilege through having to give the most intimate and private aspects of herself to a man who also appeared to care little for her once he had 'acquired' her sexually. She loses her place in the field she had inhabited – and which had inhabited her – since early childhood, and she experiences a further violation as she is hounded out of the sport by a child sex abuser who continued to receive the admiration of the field.

Her relation to the game that she had invested so much of herself in is broken, or destroyed and she is, perhaps, 'out of place'. She can no longer believe in 'the game'; her belief is, in fact, shattered. She not only loses her place in the field, for a time she appears to also lose her place in life and the emotional/psychological consequences are severe. She attempts suicide and experiences a range of conditions, most particularly an eating disorder, obsessive-compulsive behaviour, anxiety, sleeplessness and aggressive emotional outbursts. She receives therapeutic support, but seemingly, at her lowest, most desperate point, it is the strength of her conviction to fulfil the role of mother to her child that eventually provides the grounds for her to move beyond the most debilitating effects of her experiences. Through motherhood and employment, she is able to invest in herself and generate cultural, social and financial capital.

As her capital resources increase, she is able to establish a wider support network and make contact with other victims. With the encouragement of a therapist and through an opportunity presented by a journalist, Elaine chose to report her abuse officially and disclose publically. Gradually, it has emerged that others within the tennis field knew about the coach's behaviour and failed to act. She continues to be disappointed by the lack of response from the governing body to the victims.

Jack

Both my parents worked full time. I was looked after by a nanny. My father was very intelligent but didn't finish high school. He was expelled in his final year for hitting a male teacher for being too friendly with my mother. He was a man's man, admired for his abilities as an athlete and his general physical strength. He played hard, was easily provoked and won every fight he was in. He settled his battles with his fists. He wasn't a bully, but very much a product of a merciless father who used to beat him senseless. He was raised to wear the pants in the house – but he met his match in my mother.

I didn't think he loved me. I loved him, but didn't like him. My father was a very weak man in my eyes. He was afraid of taking risks and allowing himself to grow as a person. Once, I did something that royally angered him and he beat me with a belt. My mum protected me but he beat her as well. He was arrested and she threw the book at him. It was a one-off incident, but they were at divorce and separation's door on numerous occasions; she stayed with him though, and made it work. Yet he was perceived as this giving and caring individual and he had the world believe he was the nice guy and my mum was the difficult one. But I felt as though I was the problem.

My mum was also an abused child but she vowed that her children would never endure what she had to endure. As a parent she was ahead of her time. She understood the value of allowing a child to be whom and what s/he was intended to be and believed in allowing a child to learn through exploration. She let me choose my own clothes – lime green and purple was a favourite! I am sure she deliberately antagonized my father. She actually became the main breadwinner.

My favourite past times were reading – fantasy, science, horror. I also engaged in the arts such as painting and drawing. And I had a great doll collection my mum got for me. I am certain it contributed to me being a more nurturing male. But my father was deeply ashamed of it and we had to keep it under wraps. Although he did make wardrobes and such for me, for my dolls – but he did eventually take it away from me. Boys did not play with dolls.

I was the pale, fat boy who was overprotected by a loving mother and pushed to conform by an overly masculine father – to play sports he excelled in, such as rugby. I tried to emulate him, but he was embarrassed by a son who could not do what the rest of the boys in the family excelled at. In his later years before he died he told my mum how much he loved me and how he had wanted a different relationship with me but he didn't know how. I do think he tried to break the cycle.

When I had my teeth broken during a rugby-type game at school – which in reality was more a case of being bullied – my father decided to enrol me in a karate class. I was good at it but not a fighter. After obtaining a blue belt it came to a screeching halt when I was shipped off to boarding school. My father couldn't keep his hands to himself, but my mum refused to break up the family for his indiscretions. So in order to find time to reconcile their fast deteriorating marriage, my parents sent me to a boarding school when I was eight. The transition was hard but the events that occurred there were not all that unusual. I saw a lot of smaller boys being hit by older boys and there was a lot of fellatio performed by the younger boys for the older boys. The older boys were assigned to be monitors during bath time and much of this occurred during bath time. One boy in particular was sought out more frequently because he did whatever was asked of him without the tears or beating. But I was not subjected to anything physical and my stay only lasted six months.

But this was not new to me. From the age of five, an older male relative, who I had previously adored, had engaged me in sexual activities – he raped me basically – during school holidays. After boarding school we moved into a brand new house with the intent of a new beginning for the family. But my sexual abuse wasn't left behind, it came along. It only ended with this relative when I was about 12 years old.

After boarding school my parents worked very hard at rebuilding the family unit. But I did not fit in. My friends at school were the 'sissy-boys' and 'poofs'. During that time I discovered roller skating which I loved. In his efforts to accommodate me and have us do more structured family activities, my dad took us to a roller-rink every weekend. But it was a long way and this soon stopped. In an effort to keep our relationship going he took me to an ice rink instead, closer to home. I hated it but I could go more often. My father would take me to the rink and wait in the car. One day a lady approached my mum and said I showed great potential and told her to enrol me in a class. Done! I was snagged in the world of figure skating. I was a bit too old really but I knew I could do it and I knew it would get me away from the relative who came to visit each school holidays.

My first coach told us that I was one of the most gifted skaters she had ever seen, but I did have a difficult road ahead of me as I'd started very late. But I knew this was my destiny. All I did was eat, sleep, school and skate. I didn't apply myself at school – I had to skate – I had to conquer myself and be a success with this. I put everything into it. I also wanted to make my mum proud. Eventually, I caught up and surpassed my competitors. At 14 I was selected to represent my country in a senior event. The school bullying stopped because I was protected by the principal because of my sportsman status. I experienced a huge growth spurt. I was tall and thin and girls began to find me attractive.

I discovered I had a talent that set me apart, but I was still tormented by the hockey players where I trained. I was labelled as a poof, etc. which would infuriate me. The gay label was always something to be ashamed of because it was such a huge sin in the eyes of God. This whole culture was raised on the Bible and we also had Bible Study every year as part of our school curriculum. That was 12 years of God and all the punishments He had installed for the sinners. Add in going to Church regularly, with home visits from the deacon and the minister and you basically live in fear of your eternal soul's survival. One of the big sins was being a queer.

One day a new guy showed up at the public session and he was really pushing the gay issue. My coach's husband intervened and had him removed from the session without me knowing. After the session I went to the locker room to take off my skates and relax while the hockey session was under way. This guy was in there waiting for me. He was angry and was throwing every homophobic term in the book at me. I asked him to leave me alone and he walked right up to me and asked me what I intended to do about it. I told him I didn't know but I could have him barred from the rink. He laughed and hit me. I fell down. He stepped forward like he was going to kick me when a voice calling him stopped him. He turned and walked out. I got up and sat on the bench to lick my wounds and I started to cry because I was angry. I felt my sanctuary was invaded by a bully. An assistant hockey coach found me, crying. He sat with me and comforted me.

About a week later I was at the rink and so was my attacker-friend. Near the end of the session, during a spin, I was side-swiped and knocked right off my feet. I managed to get to the locker room. I don't know how long I sat there but it became very quiet. I was hurt, wet, freezing cold, and very upset. I was trying to get my sock off when the assistant coach appeared again. He apologized for not being around to help. He took my socks off, but then held onto my foot, stroking it. He asked if I was hurt and offered to help me change out of my wet stuff. I didn't know what to say or do. He seemed to be such a kind and gentle man.

As I stood there in my underwear he turned me to the side to check the damage. I was shivering and sobbing. It hurt. He gently massaged the spot and then asked me to sit down. I did and then he inspected my elbow and arm and he rubbed and massaged it. Next was my knee and thigh. It felt good and I felt safe. I started to cry for no reason other than the relief of feeling safe.

Then he pulled me to him and held me. He rubbed my back and kissed my head. I was so grateful. He continued to rub my back, his hands moved down to my buttocks. He then chuckled and asked me what we had here. He was referring to my erection and he touched it. I was so embarrassed. He sat me down again and told me not to be embarrassed and that it was normal. I tried to cover myself but he assured me it was okay then promptly pulled his sweats down to show me his aroused penis. I did not know what to do. He put our penises together and said: 'See, yours is almost as big as mine!' and then I ejaculated. He then masturbated until he ejaculated. After that he cleaned us both up and helped me to get into my street clothes. I didn't say a word. I didn't know what to say. He packed up my bag and we walked to the exit of the locker room. At the door he stopped and told me that I need not worry about those guys again. He would protect me for as long as I can keep our secret safe. I understood and I agreed. It seemed like a small trade to get what I wanted.

After that, we generally engaged in sexual activity of some sort at least once a week and this typically was at the rink in the locker rooms. It occurred more frequently during the school breaks when we were at the rink a lot. I didn't mind the sex with him – it was not painful and it was pleasurable for me. He was always very gentle and never hurt me, even when we had quick interludes at the rink or someplace. He did develop it into more than just masturbation. I learnt about fellatio and sodomy – from both perspectives of giving and receiving.

He was always very gentle and never hurt me. Even when we had quick interludes at the rink or someplace other than his place. I was totally captured by him and his attentiveness to me – if I didn't know any better, I can almost say I could have been diagnosed with a form of Stockholm Syndrome, only I knew that in this case he provided protection. I am not even sure if I truly did need it after a while. I believe that after the initial bully was gone – and I don't know where he went (and the other two guys) or how it was orchestrated and by whom – I didn't need the 'protection'. I never had to face or deal with anything like that day.

He was very well liked, outgoing, and very professional, and also the epitome of heterosexuality. He took care of himself and had a large following among the girls at the rink. He dated two or three who were about his age. When I was about 16, I was very much aware of what homosexuality was and the stigma it held. I was not sure if I was gay or not – I just didn't want a label of any kind. I was aware of my own feelings towards a few girls *and* a few males so I didn't want to be labelled as either gay *or* straight. I felt it would interfere with my own choices and limit my own access to a person I truly could fall in love with. Once labelled 'gay', I would not have a shot at a heterosexual relationship. I was also afraid my mum would find out and I just knew she would hate me for it.

Sometimes he would pick me up for the afternoon and I would go to his flat. On a few occasions he brought over a friend or two who would participate. They were roughly his age and there were about six or seven different men. They were in really good shape and they were clearly wealthy. It all seemed very familiar and routine, like this was not something new. My role in these encounters was an object for display, I think. It felt as if he was showing me off. Initially I was very fearful but he pretty much kept the routine familiar and he set limits for them and he always showed he was in control. A few of the friends did have anal sex with me, but it was not all that often. On one occasion one guy was a bit more aggressive and it all came to an abrupt halt. The two of them left the bedroom and Coach returned alone and he continued as if nothing happened. The same guy did return two or three times, but he was not aggressive at all. That showed me just how much control he had and that he was still protecting me. There was always classical music in the background and I never saw any evidence of any alcohol. This went on till I was almost 17. I think for the duration of that relationship, I only viewed it as some arrangement to meet our individual needs. I never hated having sex with him and whenever he had a new girlfriend, I would see less of him. I didn't mind not seeing him as much and I was not jealous of these girls. I think this was because I knew that if, and when, the girlfriend did leave, he would seek me out.

As I got older he seemed to find more reasons to watch me skate and he did actually show up at a few championships at other rinks. He told me he loved watching me move while I skated. There were still the occasional quick sessions at the rink but by that time I knew fully what he was doing – but I was not too sure how to get out of it. When my figure skating coach emigrated it seemed the perfect excuse. I knew he wanted a typical family life and to have children of his own. So when we went our separate ways it was done in a matter-of-fact manner. I moved to another rink and he stayed behind. He seemed fine with it.

Looking back onto this relationship, he was clearly possessive of me and I allowed him. But it was not very difficult to comply with his requests because he was not violent or forceful. He was cleverly manipulative and I always believed he was protecting me. I do believe he was a pervert who liked to control the situation fully, so, I guess I am certain he was at the rink for another reason and I just – happened. But I can say this for him, other than being very inappropriate with a minor, he kept his word. I was never bothered by another hockey player. I also was cognizant of the fact that it was perfectly acceptable to have a same-sex lover because I knew I wasn't the only one who would enjoy sex with men because of the exposure to the experiences he gave me.

In truth I think I only viewed it as some arrangement to meet our individual needs. He never hurt me physically, he was very gentle with me and he gave me the warmth and admiration I wanted. I never felt used. But I also know he was just another predator who saw an opportunity of vulnerability and reacted to that. The down side to that is I was never afforded the time to build relationships with my peers.

It was very interesting when I saw him a few years later when I was coaching. I made very sure that all my male students were accounted for at all times and they were never left at the rink alone. Our relationship/agreement was never spoken of again. He did get married and by the time I left, he was a father himself of two little girls.

I never told anybody about him. I didn't think of it as being particularly traumatizing or physically harmful/painful. I also think that I saw skating as a sanctuary. I still feel somewhat guarded about that period, and letting anybody in to my world that gave me so much. If I told anybody, I would lose that altogether and I would have betrayed myself and what skating had given me. I have not shared this with anybody else. But I do believe I had to tell it for the sake of others who may be in the same boat or potentially walking into something like this.

After I changed rinks and coaches, I landed with a male coach. On a few occasions he tried to get into my pants – I left after about two months. I knew what he was about and what he wanted and I didn't want to go that route again. I also knew his wife and his children. This led me to re-evaluate myself and that's when it fully sank in what had happened to me, how inappropriate it all was and how I sold myself to get what I needed. But I have long since worked through that; I was a victim – too young and uninformed to know any better. The blame belongs to my perpetrators.

I would be lying if I said that the sexual experiences were horrible. He did take every step to ensure I was comfortable and he did everything to pleasure me. But for the pleasure, I carried huge amounts of guilt and I did not know how to deal with that. In my mind, homosexual sex was supposed to be painful and violent, as it was when I first was introduced to it. Had it been, I think God would have forgiven me more readily, but with the pleasure I derived from it, how would I justify it to God when asking for His forgiveness for engaging in acts of homosexuality?

This all contributed to my self-esteem and self-worth being in the toilet and I never felt deserving of anything because I knew God did not approve of me and this was the main reason I was not as good a competitor as I could have been. Competing was about being judged and I did not want to be exposed because I thought people would see how bad I was. I was afraid to be judged and my dirtiness be put out into the open. It was all about my own shame. After having won the National Men's title, I turned to coaching and my students were very successful. I ended up on the show circuit for a few years and made a very good living until I changed careers.

As of right now, I haven't skated for years and barely watch it when it is on television.

Analysis

Jack's parents were sufficiently affluent to send Jack to boarding school for a short period while they tried to overcome marriage problems, seemingly at the root of which was his father's infidelity. Jack describes his father as a weak man, but physically strong and aggressive. There was considerable conflict between his parents, including domestic violence, and Jack also suffered physical abuse at the hands of his father. While this appears to have been rare, Jack partly attributes this to his mother's willingness to report her husband's behaviour to law enforcement authorities. His mother eventually became the main breadwinner in the family despite her husband's apparently traditional and entrenched views regarding gender roles. Jack credits his mother for keeping the marriage together and ascribes a particular strength of character and fortitude to her.

It seems that Jack was caught between his arguing parents who had conflicting views on parenting. He tried but failed to emulate his athletic, masculinist father, but found support from his mother who was seemingly content to encourage his desire to play with dolls and permitting him to dress in non-traditional 'boys' colours. Jack also perceives that this may have also been a conscious attempt to antagonize her husband. Similarly, it also seems as though his father, while exhibiting a deeply masculinist habitus, also attempted to accommodate Jack's inclination towards non-masculinist activities by making furniture for his dolls house, although this was eventually withdrawn.

As a young child, Jack was subjected to anal sexual intercourse by an older cousin. This continued infrequently (during school holidays) for much of Jack's early childhood. During the six months he attended boarding school, he also witnessed a great deal of sexual abuse of younger children by older children as well as abuse of older children by the school warden (matron). It is reasonable to assume that these early experiences had a significant impact on Jack. He felt that this had made him more susceptible to the abuse that followed within the context of the ice rink.

Jack spent most of his childhood in regular, state schooling. There was a strong sports culture – particularly traditional team sports – and Jack found himself isolated within this, along with other 'misfits'. He tried to engage with the dominant rugby culture, in part to please his father, but experienced homophobic bullying and a violent assault. He describes himself as something of an outcast in school whose friends 'were the "sissy-boys" and "poofs".' His cultural capital within the school – and within boyhood culture – was very low. He also found himself within a heavily religious and homophobic community with a developing bisexual identity.

His discovery of roller skating, and his subsequent aptitude for ice skating, therefore, provides Jack with the means by which he can resist his tormentors and change his boyhood fortunes. He certainly sees ice skating as a form of escape, a 'sanctuary'. Although he's a 'late starter' (11 years old) he quickly organizes his life around the goal of becoming a figure-skater: 'I knew this was my destiny. All I did was eat, sleep, school and skate. I didn't apply myself at school – I had to skate – I had to conquer myself and be a success with this.' He achieves this, ultimately competing for his country in international competitions and being selected for the Olympic team. His success at ice skating enables him to greatly increase his cultural and social capital in adolescence. In a pro-sports culture, his achievements are well received by the school and local community. The bullying at school stops and as his body develops from an overweight child to an athletic youth, he is able to establish a much higher status among his peers.

However, within the hierarchy of male/masculinist sport, figure skating is a relatively exclusive and 'unpopular' sport, receiving almost no media coverage in most countries (and certainly in Jack's country) with the exception of occasional major events, principally the Olympic Games. In addition, it has been often viewed as a non-masculine/feminine sport due to its emphasis on the aesthetic. This position in the field of competitive/organized sport is relative to other ice-based sports, particularly hockey and to a lesser extent skiing, that clearly have a very different principle or logic at their heart (or history) that has established them as firmly (hyper) masculinist. It is this logic that often sees them aligned with the logic of the nation-state, a symbolic expression of it, hence, *national* sports are often of-a-kind (at least in 'the West'). In contrast, aesthetic sports have been seen as closely aligned with the feminine, thus, sports such as figure skating are usually marginal within national hierarchies of sport.

Within a heteronormative and frequently homophobic culture, male figure-skaters, emphasizing the aesthetic and, thus, the feminine, through their sports performance, can be conceptualized as threatening to the established, normal ('natural') order; certainly as 'intruders' or 'outsiders,' even as they are part of the sports-athletic 'family'. Thus, it is not particularly surprising that Jack experiences homophobic bullying at the ice rink by the young hockey players, albeit that the more extreme manifestations of this appear to be challenged by some adults at the rink where he trains.

In Jack's account, the bargain struck between the boy and the coach for services rendered is recollected explicitly: 'He would protect me for as long as I can keep our secret safe. I understood and I agreed. It seemed like a small trade to get what I wanted.' This bargain, or exchange, is made immediately after the first commission of sexual abuse. Given the homophobic environment that clearly surrounded Jack, as he developed his (bi-) sexual identity, it is not hard to imagine that his silence about the encounter had already been achieved, instantaneously, at the moment the coach touched/caressed Jack without objection. The coach need not be aware of Jack's personal struggles over his emerging sexual identity – the homophobic bullying was clearly quite public and evident at the ice rink. The achievements (cultural capital) Jack was beginning to accumulate, through his commitment to skating, would be immediately undermined by an 'objective', explicit homosexual label/identity. Therefore, the point of ejaculation would certainly seem to symbolize the 'point of no return'. Jack's father represented an unambiguous heterosexist force in Jack's childhood, but in addition, 'I was also afraid my Mom would find out and I just knew she would hate me for it.' Thus, held within the heteronormative-homophobic forces of family, education, sport and religion, Jack felt he had to protect himself by concealing his (homo)sexual activity.

Clearly the same threat existed for the assistant coach, but with potentially more severe repercussions should the sexual activity become known within the community. This perhaps goes some way to explaining his 'considerate' and 'caring' approach to Jack, for which the cover story of protecting him from homophobic bullies neatly fits. Therefore, Jack sees this as a relationship that benefits him. His childhood habitus had been substantively influenced by experiencing the disempowerment of sexual violence by another older male from a young age while situated within a deeply homophobic environment. 'Coach' clearly offers him an alternative vision of sexual relations – one in which he is *subject* to sexual activity, but not (at least ostensibly) simply an *object* in it. This is, of course, an illusion as he is also being 'prepared' for organized sexual activity, where he is most obviously objectified as an instrument ('tool', 'piece of meat') for the sexual gratification of (apparently wealthy) adult males who had no doubt 'purchased' him from the assistant coach, himself an educated, well-travelled and independently wealthy man.

The persona of *protector* is further cultivated even while Jack is subjected to sex with multiple offenders. As with other male survivor accounts, he finds pleasure in the sexual activity and it becomes a regular, 'normal' feature of his later childhood and youth. Silence is essential as disclosure would threaten his newly acquired and much treasured athlete status and his aspirations of 'making it'. Therefore, Jack's *habitus*, structured around the *field* (the 'dream') of elite skating, with all the promise (*capital*) that it proffered, is happy to construct the relationship as a service-rendered in exchange for the protection of his 'sanctuary': 'If I told anybody, I would lose that altogether and I would have betrayed myself and what skating had given me.'

Given the homophobia that surrounds him, both in his family, his wider community and within the culture of the ice rink – a symbolic violence that structures an arbitrary social hierarchy in which he is positioned at the base – it is perhaps not difficult to see the attraction of engaging with adults that elevate him to the centre of their 'vision'.

Throughout these encounters, he is made to feel valued and protected. In this circle, his capital rises exponentially, and he has status without having to conceal his sexuality. Within his peer group, his sexual experiences afford him a new confidence, alongside his developing athletic body, so that he is able to acquire a social position that he has been unable to come close to previously.

Thus, Jack's young life and his experience of sexual subjection has to be viewed in terms of his personal history (*habitus*) and the cultural environment (*fields*) he was situated within. It is only through this double-view that his experiences, and his actions, can be understood. This analysis also allows a view of child sexual exploitation that elucidates the agency of the child. Despite being subject to organized sexual abuse ('a paedophile ring'), Jack nevertheless forges his own path through the difficulties and challenges he is faced with. His 'struggles' become visible through his story, so that we are able to see much more than simply the victim of sexual abuse. Instead we are able to see more clearly the life that was lived and a child that suffered, certainly, but also who negotiated, fought and strove against the social forces (or force fields) that cast him as 'other'.

Will

My parent's married fairly late. My father had been married twice previously. Both his wives had died of cancer. He was a successful trucker, a working-class lad 'done-good.' He was a colourful character and had plenty of money. For whatever reason he was a *huge* supporter of the Mason's and an avid attender of the Masonic movement. My mother's background was one of abject poverty – I mean, it was *tough*. She'd been orphaned at a young age and her brothers were sent abroad. She was prickly, determined and sort of the ultimate in aspirational middle-classdom. She needed that label, she needed that badge and she very much wanted all those things that were good in life.

Home-life was pretty good. We were in a large semi-detached house which my father liked because it was convenient for his yard. He barely had to get out of bed in the morning – even though he always did. He just watched the trucks go past and made a fortune out of it – and loved it! We moved to a more affluent area to a lovely period property with gardens all the way round – it was great. But my relationship with my dad was non-existent. He was always working. When he wasn't working he was boozing and going out. He enjoyed his drink, loved his food. But then started having heart attack after heart attack. That meant no sport, no play. Frankly, at that stage, I was in the way.

It wasn't until a year before his death – when I was 17 – that I really started to get to know him. We did a lot of fishing. He wasn't supposed to Salmon-fish, but I bought him a referee's whistle in case he got into trouble. I got to know him during those trips, it was fabulous. We became really very, very close – quite inseparable. But prior to that – very distant.

I'd been bounced around to quite a few schools but when we moved, the local school was clearly where the right sort of people sent their children, and my mother wanted to be a *right person*. I think I failed the entrance exam but there must have been places spare so I got in. I was about eight. My mother was delighted, she desperately wanted to be part of a community that was respected.

I remember my first rugby session. These two guys were on the pitch, and I can remember Jackson booting the ball. I came across and gathered it smoothly and I remember Jackson gesturing to Simmons as if to say 'this boy's got something about him,' and from that point onwards – from that one pick-up – it all started. I had a talent for the game and I practised insanely. But this was the *thing* – this was the *culture* at this school. That's what you have to realise, the culture *was* Rugby ... the culture of this school – was *sport*, was Rugby.

And the head of sport and the rugby coach was this guy Jackson, in his 30s, single, independently wealthy and living in at the school. This man almost controlled the school – the extent of his influence was *phenomenal.* He would encourage people to come and work at the school. I don't actually believe he could really play the game but I think he was a very good rugby coach in terms of his knowledge of the game. He knew the theory of it and he could impart that theory to us. But we were like thirty pieces of blotting paper on a pitch. Jackson would go and watch the start of the *Colts'* matches before the first team kicked off because he wanted to see the boys who were really showing potential. And believe-you-me, for any child going to this school, you want to be in the first team. But we didn't know what that really meant.

I suffered from dyslexia, although it was not diagnosed. So I wasn't enjoying the academic work, but I was enjoying sport. I could prosper at sport. It was like following a drug trail. I was in this high-profile position, I was wearing special tassels on my socks, I had this rugby cap – I was *leading* the team! So I *wanted* to go down that route. I found my rugby cap the other day ... I thought I'd thrown it away, but bizarrely I've still got it. My father would come and watch me play rugby for the school, and cricket. He enjoyed watching the sport but it was still quite a distant relationship. There was a distance without any doubt. That didn't change until much later.

There wasn't much chuckling during rugby training, it was a *very* serious business. If you played crap, punishments were dished out. It was nasty, he was a nasty man. I mean it's *that* simple. But you wanted to be the best, because what you wanted was praise from this man. He wrote match reports for every player! This is what you waited for – *praise*. We were all slaves to this praise and we were willing to do all sorts of things, because it meant so much. He was treated with a mixture of hero-worship and fear. He was a bully, no doubt – but he could also be great; and you wanted to be on the right side of him, you wanted the warmth of that sunshine. He was *alluring*, a bit of a man-about-town, with an expensive flat in town which he called his 'fuck-box'.

But part of what he could give you was power. And power is very sexy. I had his hand on my shoulder, and everybody knew it. It was like a divine right – I was captain of rugby! – and being bedded when there wasn't a rugby match on. It wasn't only the captain of course, far from it. See – looking at my old school team photographs – here we are, *god* – looking along the front row here, from what I *know*: *he* was sexually abused, so was *he*; *him*; *him*; *him*; *him*. *This boy!* He was abused and so were his brothers – and his *mother* was having sex with their abuser! *This* boy's mother put a rumour around that Jackson had an interest in boys because she saw him with his arm around a boy. So the balloon went up, but *my* mother quashed the parental revolt! My mother actually became a cheerleader for my abuser! And so it goes on. And this was just one man. The police conservatively estimated that he abused in excess of 180 children.

Nothing happened *on* the pitch. But if you became part of the elite, you were allowed into his room. He'd sit there, and he'd get whisky tots out – *Teachers* or *Hague* – and he'd like a boy on either side so he could stroke their leg. That did away with the personal barriers, so you started to be compromised. At one point he issued me with a jock strap – I wasn't being abused at this stage – and he said 'oh when you're as big as us you've got to wear one of these'. So I was handed one of these jock-straps, which I was very pleased about. And he'd share stories with you about how he'd been 'poking' mothers. And so it almost became acceptable behaviour, but actually with all these barriers being dropped, your defences were down, and then of course the abuse started. That started in all sorts of different ways.

You are in such extraordinary denial about what has happened. I mean, *everybody* is. It's a *confusing* mixture, an extraordinary mixture of denial and guilt – it's a terribly powerful mixture. You see most of us – most of us have this problem with the fact that, not *all* of these processes are bad. You know, you have this ... I mean for me, for me, you know, ejaculation, the first time I ejaculated – I'm sorry to use these terms – but the first time I ejaculated was at the hands of this man. Whatever one says, the process of orgasm is quite pleasurable. And of course when that happens – you know, you have this immense guilt that comes with it. Are you *encouraging* the man? *Are you?* I mean, I felt complicit – and that silenced me.

I was never told to keep quiet. Never. *Never!* That was never *ever* suggested. He knew perfectly well I wasn't going to say anything. I had a secret relationship with an adult, and that's the biggest secret you can have. You *see* – guilt! I was complicit. I felt as though I was motivating some of it. Why on earth are you going to own up to *that*? When you *know* what's going on is terribly bad. And you just see that this is going to be *all* your fault, it's all going to implode. When my mother said to me 'has he ever interfered with you?' I said 'no!' I could never, ever, *ever* say 'yes.' *Never, ever* could I say 'yes'! It would have been abysmal. I just don't know where it would have ended up. It would have been a nightmare. It was that *complicity* – complicity silences. I mean I was eleven, twelve, I mean *fuck me*, give me a break! But I remember thinking – it was my fault, I was part of it. It was to do with me.

But when you keep quiet about this for so long, you have this *emotional tsunami* right behind you. You know it's getting closer and closer and suddenly there was that combination of events and there it was – then the world imploded. Then I had to face it all. I ended up in a secure institution because I was very keen to find a bridge. I was in a very big black hole. It made me pretty unstable – it's been quite a voyage. I'm much steadier about it now, although I still find some of the bits very difficult. It's impossible to erase them. The whole process has been one of coming to terms with all those things that made me so *unbelievably* uncomfortable that I couldn't speak. That's what it's been all about. *Now I can speak* – and without the benefit of drugs – I can speak about it. Also, when parents die you can speak. I didn't know that.

I found out that this guy ended up coaching at a very good rugby club, only a mile down the road. I said to the president of the club 'You may not know this but he's a career paedophile and has been cited in complaints to the police. Were you aware of that?' 'No we've never had anyone by that name.' I said 'it's in the papers, for fucks sake, all one has to do is speak to the local paper!' 'No, we've never had anyone by that name'. When you hear the president of a club speaking like that – don't they realise that all they're doing is completely discrediting the organisation? But they *don't*. It's beyond me – *why*? It's about surely the children who are there. *It's about them*! It's not about *reputation*. It's very strange. I've noticed whenever you start discussing child protection with any of these organisations, they start speaking in a very weird way and logic suddenly vanishes. Everything's got to be confidential, even the child protection policy is confidential – *what*? Which is why I have no respect for people in authority at all. Very few of them have the moral fibre to say well we've got a problem here, let's get to the bottom of it. Until you let the light in onto the problem it will never heal. In child abuse the Holy Trinity is power, secrecy and opportunity.

If at all possible I'd like to open the door for more people to come forward and finally speak. I was silent for 38 years! So I've left it a bit late, but silence assists abusers. It's one of the things they require – they need silence.

Analysis

Will and Simon were both abused by rugby teachers (who were also players) within boarding schools. While the focus here is on the sports context, it is evident that for Will and Simon, the school/education context was also a factor in their abuse. However, the depiction of the logic of athleticism outlined in Chapter 4 would also apply to the all-male boarding school. Indeed, given the origins of organized sport within the very institutions such as those attended by Will and Simon, it seems evident that the ethos of athleticism is particularly deeply embedded within the logic and practices of such institutions. Indeed, this is very apparent from their stories.

Will's father was from a traditional working-class background and a successful businessman. Will explains his relationship with his father as 'very distant', at least until his late teens when his father was near the end of his life following a number of strokes. His father provided materially but appears to have spent relatively little time with his son, partly through ill-health. Will's account of his mother represents her as both independent and fiercely aspirational, especially for her son. He also recalls a temporary split in the family unit when his mother took him out of the country, seemingly without his father's approval. However, he recalls a happy early childhood during which his father's industrial business thrived and the family became affluent.

A place at a local fee-paying school with a strong reputation became both financially possible, while perceived as highly desirable. While Will explains that he felt he did not meet the academic entry requirements (he discovered later in life that he is dyslexic), he was nevertheless offered a place at the school. It seems evident that he was fully aware that a position at this school carried a great deal of prestige and his mother's determination to secure him a place, and thereby secure his future, frames the context within which he entered this environment. In short, he was 'lucky' to be there.

Will describes himself as a 'sporty' boy, and his ability on the rugby pitch was recognized shortly after he started boarding school. In Will's terms, 'the culture of this school – was *sport*, was Rugby' and, therefore, those that excelled were explicitly awarded high status in the school. A range of symbolic capital explicitly associated with rugby is evident at the school, such as sock-tassels and rugby caps, as well as the conspicuous display of trophies and photographs of past teams. The power of these symbols is perhaps illustrated by Will's reflective acknowledgement that he still had his rugby cap, many years after leaving the school, and, seemingly despite the experiences he was subjected to within the rugby environment.

Will's abuser was the rugby teacher-coach (or 'master'), and as Will puts it, 'the extent of his influence was *phenomenal.*' He clearly displayed, in conspicuous fashion, his social connections beyond the school, attracting past players with high public profiles ('stars') to attend school events.

In other terms, he had acquired high volumes of social capital and used these connections or networks to enhance the status of the school and, thereby, his position within it. Therefore, as Will observes, 'what he could give you was power. And power is very sexy. I had his hand on my shoulder, and everybody knew it. It was like a divine right – I was captain of rugby!' As with the other accounts presented here, Will had acquired, through his *athletic capital*, a high status among his peers. He was quite visibly 'succeeding' at boyhood. In a world (*field*) where selection to a sports team was the pinnacle of achievement, he had excelled.

It seems inappropriate to describe him as an *especially* vulnerable child, but his 'vulnerability' was closely associated with his high athletic (bodily) capital – his sporting ability. From a young age, his habitus is shaped according to the athleticist vision: strength, independence, vigour, domination – all of which was embodied by the rugby master. Thus, Will (and perhaps his teammates) had been well-prepared to acknowledge and value the habitus of the rugby coach. His father's business acumen and his mother's fervent desire to climb the social 'ladder' seemingly provided a robust familial platform for the development of a habitus shaped according to the principles of economic and social success. His education in these matters sharpened upon entry to a prestigious all-male boarding school – an environment designed to quite literally transform *boys* into *men* in an environment where *ends* were far more important than *means*.

The relationship was sexualized, no doubt in a very practised and matter-of-fact manner through reference to jock-straps, genitalia and tales of sex with the mothers of other children at the school. Alcohol was also used. All 'part-and-parcel' of the field of athleticism. Again, Will (and his peers) were being recruited into an illicit and exclusive world and their participation in it – coupled with their desire to *be* in it – secures their complicity and, therefore, their silence. Their young *boyhood* habitus, shaped by masculinism thus searching out the true form – *manhood* – desires the 'forbidden fruits' that symbolize the transition from boy to man: sex, alcohol – that this fully paid-up member of the masculinist fraternity offers access to. Rugby, as a kind of symbolic centre of the masculinist tradition, was and is a highly valued route to success in the masculinist field. As Will says, he 'was the ultimate sporting chap', therefore, the disposition to be 'in the team', was central to his young habitus. Unsurprisingly, then, 'you wanted to be on the right side of him, you wanted the warmth of that sunshine. He was *alluring*.'

It is noteworthy that this 'rugby master' diligently produced 'match reports' for each player in the team, for every game played. Fundamental to the athleticist enterprise is the disposition to monitor and record. The 'breaking' of records carries exceptionally high volumes of cultural capital which generally increases relative to the level of competition (although in the symbolic economy of sport this is never a straightforward equation and is always intersected by gender, ethnicity, disability, etc.). The scientific measurement of sports performance is fundamental – *doxic* – to the field and entry to the field. Thus, in childhood, entry to the field is increasingly based on scientific measurement which is imposed on children at increasingly earlier stages. Reflecting on the use of these match reports, Will's comment is profound: 'This is what you waited for – *praise*. We were all slaves to this praise and we were willing to do all sorts of things, *because it meant so much*.' That he retains these evaluations, decades later, seems to emphasize the claim that this mechanism had on him. To put it another way, this boy was both thoroughly invested in this 'game' and beholden to it.

Fundamental to initiation into the *game* is the code that members reproduce, faithfully and diligently, the logic of the game. Player's commitment to this logic is perhaps not inevitable, nevertheless, silence is 'part-and-parcel' of the game and for those with *a feel for the game* – it goes without saying. Hence, speaking publically (to non-members) about what is said in the 'dressing room' is profoundly condemned and will likely lead to isolation and exclusion. The borders of the field are guarded by idioms such as 'what-goes-on-tour-stays-on-tour' and the sanctity of the 'changing room', a sort of spiritual centre of sport, is paramount. More potently, initiation rituals, common to sports teams, are designed to engender complicity – intoxication, nudity and engagement in activities that one would otherwise not participate in are practices employed to secure allegiance to the group. Through participation in 'games' specific to the group, collusive bonds based on shared, illicit, experience, are generated. In other terms, it is a strategy to comprehensively align habitus and field, to ensure the *investment* in the field is sufficient to ensure the continuance of the field.

This is the significance of the 'ritual' of pouring out measures of whisky and positioning the boys in close proximity. The objective is, not simply inebriation or close physical contact, but *participation*, investment, and complicity in the illicit act. This is a world – a *game* – of exploitation, in which young boys are offered special access to an illicit masculinist world occupied by powerful men whom they have been taught to respect and desire. Thus, a secretive world is created and maintained, by consent. It is the emotional hold – a bondage – that this shared world creates that severely limits the boy's capacity to resist and to tell.

References

Bourdieu, P. (1989) Social space and symbolic power. *Sociological Theory*, 7(1): 14–25.

Deer, C. (2012) Reflexivity. In M. Grenfell (ed.) *Pierre Bourdieu: key concepts* (2nd ed.). Durham: Acumen, 195–210.

Grenfell, M. (2012) (ed.) *Bourdieu: key concepts* (2nd ed.). London: Routledge.

Chapter 6

A relational account of child sexual exploitation in sport

Fields are generally semi-autonomous, overlapping in myriad ways and as the accounts presented above illustrate, the early lives of these children were lived predominately within three fields that shaped their developing habitus: *family*, *education* and *sport*. In addition, the more dispersed but particularly dominant field of *patriarchy* (and its ideology of masculinism) can also be observed (with the possible exception of Stephen), chiefly through its effects within each of these three fields. Within these intersections, is the *field of power* within which all these children encountered *men* of power. These men, without exception, influenced not only the child, but the adult community around the child. It is quite clear that the seven main perpetrators within these accounts were collectively responsible for the sexual subjection of many children, possibly hundreds. It is also clear that their actions were not somehow hermetically sealed (concealed) from the community in which they abused children.

Typically, this is expressed as an extension of individual 'grooming' (e.g. Leberg, 1997) by a malevolent, 'clever' and manipulative 'groomer' or 'predator' who 'groomed' or 'fooled' not only the child, but also the community or environment around the child. However, such explanations are, sociologically at least, unsatisfying as they rely on a sort of 'super criminal' operating within, but also above and outside, a community of well-meaning but naïve, 'culturally dopey' adults. Yet a persistent finding in cases of 'institutional abuse', illustrated again by these accounts, is that other adults 'knew' and either did nothing or actively concealed the abuse:

PAUL: it was kind of understood that whichever boy was in his car at practice was the boy he was sleeping with. And that was right in front of your face, everybody knew it, but nobody said anything.

Similarly, an assistant swimming coach who worked with Rick Curl, convicted in 2013 for sex offences against elite female swimmers in the USA, said, 'It seemed like everyone knew at Maryland, but it was something you didn't talk about' (Brittain and Trevino, 2013). The notion of 'grooming' serves to pathologize the man that subjects a child to sex as well as negating the agency of a child who becomes simply and completely a 'victim' of the 'perpetrator'. It also fails to recognize, or disguises, the gendered culture of the social space that permitted the abuse to continue.

Given Jenks' (2005b) criticism that face-value positivism offers only simplistic explanations of child abuse, the sociological approach of Pierre Bourdieu (also a fierce critic of positivism) has been proposed as a substantive means by which the problem may be approached. Rather than conducting a thematic analysis of the data, I have presented condensed 'narratives' of the life stories of the research participants, so that they may 'breathe' (Frank, 2010) as stories in their own right. This is to treat them seriously as accounts that offer insight that may engender deeper understanding about the problem of sexual exploitation in sport through providing the space (in both actual time and on the page) to allow these stories to be told, and then brought to the reader, in sufficient depth and detail, well beyond the 'act' itself. Hopefully, this meets, in some way, Brackenridge's recommendation that analyses 'encompass life histories as a whole, and not just in sport, for it is in the total narrative account of someone's life that their predilections and susceptibilities begin to make sense' (Brackenridge, 2001: 135).

Specifically, I have sought to situate the individual stories with the *fields* in which these childhoods were lived. Therefore, this analysis does not simply elucidate the relationship between the 'perpetrator' and 'victim' – and the strategies and techniques that a perpetrator may employ in his (or her) subjection of a child to sex (already well documented). Rather I have attempted to *situate* the relation between child and adult by considering these stories through the notions of *habitus*, *capital* and *field*. In this chapter, I extend this analysis to offer a theoretical account of child sexual exploitation in sport.

Recalling the point that there are general mechanisms of fields, I begin with a focus on such mechanisms, situated within the athleticist field. Bourdieu's notions of 'symbolic violence' and more particularly 'gift exchange' are explicitly intended to reveal mechanisms of domination and subordination in a manner consistent with his relational approach to action. I then focus more specifically on *habitus*, developing ideas trailed in the preceding analyses of the individual stories, as well as Bourdieu's ideas on sexual relations and masculine domination, in order to develop a theoretical account of the sexual exploitation of children and young people *in sport*.

Field mechanisms and effects

Symbolic domination and gift exchange

Symbolic capital is an ordinary property (physical strength, wealth, warlike valour, etc.) which, perceived by social agents endowed with the categories of perception and appreciation permitting them to perceive, know and recognize it, becomes symbolically efficient, like a veritable magical power.

(Bourdieu, 1998: 102)

Titles such as *coach, athlete* and *sportsman*; but also *fly-half, centre-forward, opening-batsman* and *quarterback*; not to mention *captain, champion* and (in a slightly different universe) *Olympian*, are just some examples of sporting titles heavily laden with symbolic capital. Such capital is accrued instantaneously (almost magically) by those who have legitimate claim on such roles and titles, permitting them to 'exert symbolic effects'. Recognition of this process, or its effects, can be detected among the participants' reflections:

SIMON: ...there was that whole thing of *mindlessly* complying...

PAUL: ...going along with the whole coaching thing – discipline and loyalty and becoming a success – all those things can be used against you...

WILL: He wrote match reports for every player! This is what you waited for – *praise*. We were all slaves to this praise and we were willing to do all sorts of things, because it meant so much. He was treated with a mixture of hero-worship and fear.

Thus, ordinary properties – such as an ability to perform certain sports skills to a proficient level or the ability to teach such skills, and implement strategies that result in (team or individual) success in sport – when perceived by others endowed with the dispositions to value such properties, are indeed transformed, through a kind of social alchemy, into a 'magical power.' What could be more ordinary than writing a match report? Or teaching a jump shot? Or a rugby tackle? Or the 'offside' rule? However, in the symbolic economy of athleticism, such ordinary things are, indeed, highly valued capital. Thus, ordinary properties, indeed ordinary individuals, are endowed with symbolic capital – *athleticist* capital – materially signified in some instances through 'professional' credentials such as 'coaching badges' – that affords the power to distribute or confer similar capital (e.g. certificates, awards): a veritable magical power – a kind of enchanted relation – which infers a debt of gratitude. Bourdieu (1998: 109) argues:

> In order for intergenerational exchanges to continue despite everything, the logic of debt as recognition must also intervene and a feeling of obligation or gratitude must be constituted. Relations between generations are one of the sites *par excellence* of the transfiguration of the recognition of debt into recognition, filial devotion, love.

Sport, since its inception, has persistently functioned as a site of masculinist intergenerational 'filial devotion' and 'love', where the initiated (typically adult males) have constructed certain practices (or rites) as central to the achievement of recognition for the un-initiated. Achieving entry presupposes a demonstration of commitment. There have always been large numbers of young people, especially males, committed to a *game* which renders them in a dominated state, misrecognized as such. Therefore, 'symbolic violence acts ... to maintain a relation of domination ... works when subjective structures – the habitus – and objective structures are in accord with each other' (Krais, 1993: 172).

The child in sport, then, or rather a 'young athlete', is perhaps, almost by definition, an exemplar of accord between subjective and objective structures. Indeed, it seems reasonable to observe, if one brackets a whole discourse that proclaims the 'potential' of sport, that the aim of 'sport' (particularly in its objectified state, e.g. a 'governing body' of sport) is singular – to turn the child into an 'athlete' or 'player', more precisely, to *reconstitute* the child *as* the field. Indeed, it is such ordained agencies and their affiliated agents that possess the power to carry out this work of reconstitution. This fundamental and totalizing objective, then, has the effect of rendering the child in a dominated, objectified state, providing her with the capacity to do little else *other* than apply, in their thought and action, the categories of the dominant. Action that includes the act of 'silence', but also the act of finding virtue in the necessity to contribute to one's own domination. According to Bourdieu (1998: 103):

> Symbolic violence is the violence which extorts submission, which is not perceived as such, based on 'collective expectations' or socially inculcated beliefs ... [not] in relation to a possibility of non-belief, but rather an *immediate adherence* ... achieved when the mental structures of the one to whom the injunction is addressed are in accordance with the structures inscribed in the injunction addressed to him. In this case, one says that it went without saying, that there was nothing else to do [emphasis added].

In such a fashion we may be able to understand the situation of children subjected to sexual abuse – 'what *could* I do? ... I felt helpless' [Simon].

PAUL: He took four of us on an away-trip – we were all 13 – and he just took us, one after the other, out of our motel room. And none of us said a word. Each of us got fucked and none of us said a word to each other – what was there to *say*? By the time I figured it out it was too late, I was too deep in, there was too much at stake.

Were you told not to say anything?

WILL: *No, never!* Never, never. That was never, ever suggested. He knew perfectly well I wasn't going to say anything.

Of course the participants in this study *could* have done/said something. They should not be (theoretically) reduced to inertia, somehow non-cognisant of the events engulfing them. As Simon stated: 'He put me in a situation where I knew I was doing something profoundly wrong. That didn't escape me.' Undoubtedly, they acted in multiple and complex ways, to 'manage' their abuse and their abuser – to calm them, to appease them, to resist and challenge them, to reduce the impact on others (especially parents), to maintain the *status quo*. Indeed, the scale of the challenges facing them meant that they had to bring all their powers of ingenuity, creativity and fortitude to bear on their environment. The image of Mary Jo, lying silently on her bed in the dark during the day, persistently remaining silent in order to protect her parents, presents a powerful image of the challenges these children had to resolve. They did *act*, they were agents in this encounter, and they could have acted differently. Simon's depiction of his situation is interesting in this regard:

SIMON: ...there was kind of a – what could be better than being a rugby hero? It's literally a *Faustian Pact*. But you have to sign you know, it's not a choice, you have to sign...

Through the notion of striking a 'deal' or 'bargain' with a malevolent being, Simon evocatively and explicitly raises the notion of an *active* agent, complicit in the bargain, desiring a special power in exchange for his 'soul'. However, he quickly retracts and replaces this notion with a subject that has no choice *but* to sign. It seems important to address this point substantively. The 'gift exchange' is a process explored by many anthropologists (e.g. Mauss, 1954) and one which Bourdieu developed within his theoretical scheme.

Gift exchange and the *athlete obligatus*

Simon also stated that the experiences he was subjected to were ultimately about power, rather than simply sexual gratification. This is a well-established position within feminist and sociological theorizing of sexual violence. Bourdieu's interpretation of 'gift exchange' provides a means of exploring this further. Both Bourdieu and Alex Hyde (1983) observe that *gift exchange* is a fundamental feature of social life. That is, all cultures place considerable significance on the exchange of 'gifts'; thus, we come to understand this as a fundamental cultural practice from a very young age (obvious examples within some cultures include birthdays, *Christmas*, *Easter*, Thanks*giving*). Thus, we are 'immersed from childhood in a universe where gift exchange is socially instituted in dispositions and beliefs' (Bourdieu, 1998: 95).

Hyde (1983) offers a thorough exploration of gift exchange within traditional societies which may help to further illuminate contemporary youth sport: 'in the simplest examples, gifts carry an identity with them, and to accept the gift amounts to incorporating the new identity. It is as if such a gift passes through the body and leaves us altered' (Hyde, 1983: 46). This notion chimes with the dominant narrative of sport – indeed perhaps the dominant experience of sport – where the fundamental premise is the notion that something extremely valuable (character building, even 'life-changing') is being given to the child. However, while he pays them less attention, Hyde (1983: xix) acknowledges that there are also 'gifts that leave an oppressive sense of obligation, gifts that manipulate or humiliate'. Bourdieu develops this aspect:

> …the initial act is an attack on the freedom of the one who receives it. It is threatening: it obligates one to reciprocate … beyond the original gift; furthermore, it creates obligations, it is a way to possess, by creating people obliged to reciprocate.
>
> (Bourdieu, 1998: 94)

Bourdieu's insight allows for a problematization of sport. Arguably, children find themselves in a deeply obliged state simply by virtue of their engagement in the athleticist field. In essence, the culturally valuable, widely recognized, *gift* of sport – athleticist capital – establishes a debt that obligates one to reciprocate. The athleticist field, as it places increasingly specific demands upon children through prescription and prohibition, institutes 'correct' modes of physical skill, performance and behaviour. Consequently, appropriate adults – those recognized for their recognition of such modes – are recruited to provide (*give*) such culturally valuable knowledge to those who are 'prepared to listen', 'do as they are told' and dedicate themselves fully and without complaint. Thus, the child that exhibits 'commitment' – who properly recognizes the value of the gift – accrues athleticist capital and is permitted, gradually, to enter the athleticist field.

In other words, this is a conditional investment – conditional, in the first instance, upon the child embodying the disposition to obey, ideally without question, and subsequently upholding the injunctions of the field. Conditional in the second instance on an understanding that what is being given can also be withdrawn, thus, to appreciate fully the value of the 'gift'. Indeed, 'appreciation', or 'recognition', is the objective of 'the game' as it is through appreciation that a social agent recognizes the true value of the gift and, therefore, their obligation to the field – and the field agent. Thus, children are rewarded, incrementally, with trinkets (certificates, badges, medals) or rather *credits*, that serve as a means to both chart their gradual recognition towards fully endorsed agents of the field, as well as a register of what they owe – their debt – to the field. Therefore, it is possible to note the frequent expressions of athletes who want to 'give something back' to the sport that *gave* them so much. Indeed, Jack's adult reflections on skating and his abuser are illustrative:

JACK: I still feel somewhat guarded about that period, and letting anybody in to my world that gave me so much. If I told anybody [about the abuse], I would lose that altogether and I would have betrayed myself and what skating had given me.

It is only possible to speculate at the effect of each instance of *receiving* in the participants' childhoods, but it would not seem unreasonable to assume that with each 'gift' – such as team selection and various ranking systems – the child was drawn deeper into the 'game' and also the debt of those 'players' ordained as the gatekeepers to such gifts:

ELAINE: Tony had promised the world. It was up to my mum and dad – they paid – so I just went to Tony's squad when I was 11 ... I was having lessons with his squad, lessons with him at regional level and I was having lessons at his home as well. It was great to have him as a coach...

PAUL: After practice I would go home for dinner and then go back to the gym, and he would have several of us there working out. Eventually other guys dropped out and I was the only one there. So he spent a lot of time developing me.

Sport is, then, (like other fields) an economy – an exchange of symbolic goods where the dominant can be identified through their capacity to acquire and control the most valuable *capital*. With each descending step into the field, tangibly represented by the extrinsic rewards that youth sport is so visibly and ritually adorned (colours, titles, trophies, etc.), so their habitus is shaped increasingly according to the structures of the field. Thus, a social agent, from childhood, comprehends and intuitively obeys 'the logic of reciprocity'. Jack's account highlights this aspect particularly explicitly:

JACK: At the door he stopped and told me that I need not worry about those guys again. He would protect me for as long as I can keep our secret safe. I understood and I agreed. It seemed like a small trade to get what I wanted.

The *gift* (however it is constituted) is something to be *given back*. Therefore, the adult-child exchange in sport may be viewed as 'an act of giving beyond the possibilities of return, which puts the receiver in an obliged, bound and dominated state' (Bourdieu, 1998: 100): or *athlete obligatus*.

Sports mechanisms for achieving this obligation and conformity are central to its operation – corporeal instruction or 'training' – essentially bodily repetition, directed by dominant agents, in the pursuit of symbolic capital. Children are *drilled*, not only in the technical aspects of their sport, but also to recognize the stakes of the game in which they are caught up:

WILL: If you fucked up he'd put you through circuits, circuit training. So you knew if you played crap … you were put through the mill, it was *hell*.

Anyone who has played sport competitively, regardless of level, will recognize this account. Yet to profess a 'love' for the game, is the staple diet of any serious sportsman or woman; to speak out, or act, against the game would be to 'crack the game asunder', to disregard or discard the stakes of the game. This is close to impossible for the child characterized by the *athleticist habitus* – a child who has been taught to recognize the stakes of the game and is 'ready to die' for those stakes. That is, it simply would not occur to him/her to do such a thing, such is the manner in which the game has been introduced to her or his mind.

This is perhaps well-illustrated by Simon when he recounts being given the explicit opportunity to disclose his abuse:

SIMON: Anyway, so I walk in and my dad's there and I go 'oh my god what's going on here?'… 'oh, I need to talk to you,' so we walked out … and he said 'so did [abuser] ever interfere with you?'… and without really much of a second thought I said 'no he never touched me.' So something had gone so wrong with my brain that I was prepared to defend the abuser against my own flesh and blood. And that makes no logical sense to anybody who hasn't been abused, but everybody who's been abused goes 'yeah I absolutely understand that'.

According to my account, there was nothing wrong with Simon's brain, at least nothing that could not be explained by the hold that his adjustment to *the game* had on him. That is, through the investment he had made in the game, and it in him – the embodiment of which was his abuser.

Bourdieu uses the term 'alchemy' to refer to an enchanted relation which masks or 'transforms the truth of relations of domination'. If nothing else, there is certainly an enchantment with sport in contemporary society and as Bourdieu (1998: 101) argues, for this enchantment to work 'it must be sustained by the entire social structure, therefore, by the dispositions produced by that social structure'.[1] It is evident, then, that our societies include a range of mechanisms for sustaining our collective enchantment with sport, not least the promotion of sport as central to a healthy, if not moral, childhood. Bourdieu (1998: 102) elaborates on this mechanism:

> One of the effects of symbolic violence is the transfiguration of relations of domination and submission into affective relations, the transformation of power into charisma or into the charm suited to evoke affective enchantment ... The acknowledgment of debt becomes recognition, a durable feeling toward the author of the generous act, which can extend to affection or love, as can be seen particularly well in relations between generations.

It may be argued, that 'youth sport' is an ideal vehicle for this transfiguration of relations of domination. Ideal in the sense that a moral judgement is built-in to the coach-athlete relation or exchange; indeed, the very terms 'sportsman' and 'athlete' are *a priori* moral designations: 'he's a good *sport*' (albeit the struggle to maintain this discourse has perhaps become more apparent given continuing evidence of widespread use of performance enhancing drugs in sport). Even in the professionalized (paid) role of 'coach' or 'sports development officer', there is implicit the act of 'giving', of generosity. Thus, 'the gift' of sport (skill, techniques, strategy, team selection, family/fraternity, etc.) assumes increasing importance for the 'sports child' and is immediately acknowledged as such, indeed perhaps as a gift beyond all others, 'the keys to the kingdom' (interview with Sheldon Kennedy, 2005). Therefore, despite the situation they faced, the children remained cognisant of what their relationship with their abusers could offer:

SIMON: I was helpless ... but one side of me was quite happy ... I had good status at the school – I was in the *Colts*, and I was in the *first fifteen*...

'Why didn't I say something?' (Kennedy and Grainger, 2006) is perhaps a perpetual question of the adult survivor; they knew they could have, yet when they say, 'I just couldn't', this is in fact exactly the point – 'saying something' was theoretically possible, yet *literally* impossible. This is the symbolic violence to which Bourdieu refers, an enchanted relation to the game – *athlete obligatus* – the young athlete in a bound and obliged state.

Developing the notion of *athlete obligatus*, an enchanted relation secured through the socially constituted mechanism of gift exchange, in the following section I explore the notion of habitus in relation to sexual practices within the athleticist field.

The *athleticist habitus* and the sexual subjection of children in sport

Following Kelly (1988), Cossins (2000), Brackenridge (2001) and Jones (2012) among others, it is important to approach the issue of sexual violence and child sexual abuse from an understanding of 'normative sexual practices'. Within Bourdieu's analysis of 'masculine domination', sex is a central feature:

> A political sociology of the sexual act would show that, as is always the case in a relation of domination, the practices and representations of the two sexes are in no way symmetrical ... the sexual act itself is seen by men as a form of domination, appropriation, 'possession'.
>
> (Bourdieu, 2001: 20)

While such analysis may fall foul of some criticism regarding a lack of appreciation for multiple gender/sexual identities, it also bears a strong resemblance to much feminist writing on sexual violence (see Chapter 1). Such a position both accords with the overwhelming prevalence of males as perpetrators of sexual crimes and also resonates strongly with critical accounts of male sexual practice within the sociology of sport literature (e.g. Benedict, 1997; Brackenridge, 2001, 2002; Curry, 1991, 1998; Messner and Sabo, 1994). However, in considering Brittan's (2001) observation that masculine and masculin*ist* should not be confused (any more than feminine and feminist), it would seem that the notion of a 'masculin*ist* habitus' perhaps more appropriately reflects Bourdieu's (2001) observation. Certainly, in considering the (hyper-) masculinist field of athleticism, this seems particularly apt.

Furthermore, bearing in mind feminist critique (see Chapter 2), it is necessary to ensure that the 'destabilising' aspect of *field* is thoroughly activated in order to make visible or 'yield a differentiated and dynamic model of power relations' (McNay, 2000: 57) through the conceptualization of agency as 'inscribed potential' or 'regulated liberties which escapes from the binary of domination-resistance' (McNay, 2000: 56). Therefore, to reflect a mobilization of *field* that meets Bourdieu's emphasis on history and social space, the notion of an *athleticist habitus* offers a situated, or contextualized, notion of habitus. At this point, Maton's description of habitus as a 'structured structuring structure' is worth repeating:

> It is 'structured' by one's past and present circumstances ... It is 'structuring' in that one's habitus helps to shape one's present and future practice. It is a 'structure' in that it is systematically ordered rather than random or unpatterned. This 'structure' comprises a system of dispositions which generate perceptions, appreciations and practices.
>
> (Maton, 2012: 50)

Sexual relations in the masculinist field: *libido dominandi*

The *desire* for command over capital (indeed to determine what counts *as* capital, illustrated well in the historic representation of sport as unsuitable for females) does not differentiate social agents along any collective lines, including gender. However, habitus is always a product of history and the legacy of patriarchal masculinism deposits a particular conceptualization of sexual activity and, therefore, a particular disposition towards sexual relations. According to Bourdieu (2001: 20): 'men are *inclined* to compartmentalize sexuality, which is conceived as an aggressive and essentially physical act of *conquest* oriented towards penetration and orgasm' (Bourdieu, 2001: 20, emphasis added). Sex is conceptualized, then, fundamentally as an instrument of power.

As Bourdieu always insists, each field is constituted by 'struggles' for power, and the dominant agents will endeavour to impose their version of the field upon all others. The field of masculinity is dominated by the masculinist vision – potently symbolized within art, literature, theatre, poetry, radio, film, TV and many other mediums of cultural production – and is generative of a masculinist habitus that generates the field. Masculinism, in accord with the patriarchal endeavour, is a field constructed to assure the reproduction of gendered power relations in favour of males, but not equally so. Therefore, Bryson (1999: 47) is correct to argue that 'to learn masculinity or femininity is, therefore, to learn about subordination and domination', but this is clearly not a straightforward algorithm that situates males outside of or beyond exploitation, sexual or otherwise. Indeed, according to Bourdieu (2001: 21):

> Penetration, especially when performed on a man, is one of the affirmations of the *libido dominandi* that is never entirely absent from the masculine libido. It is known that in a number of societies homosexual possession is conceived as a manifestation of 'power', an act of domination (performed as such, in some cases, in order to assert superiority by 'feminizing' the other).[2]

This is demonstrated from research in male prison populations where entitlement to (anal and oral) penetration (or perhaps possessing a 'wife') is the ultimate symbol of domination – part of the symbolic economy of an all-male, hyper-masculinist environment (e.g. Schwartz, 2004). Similarly, reports of widespread rape and sexual humiliation in war/conflict zones (e.g. in Bosnia and Rwanda, and the US army's 'interrogation' practices of male prisoners in Abu-Graib prison during the Iraq occupation) and within totalitarian regimes (e.g. BBC, 2009a; see Jones, 2012) illustrates that sexual activity (forced or otherwise) with either the wife and children of one's adversary – or most potently, the adversary *himself* – is a demonstration of power that symbolizes the ultimate masculinist conquest: feminization of the other.

The centrality of this disposition to the masculinist habitus is also visible (leaving aside statistics on sexual violence) through the widespread sexual objectification of women, recently encapsulated through common and celebrated (western) expressions such as 'mother-fucker' and 'MILF' ('mother-I'd-like-to-fuck') and through myriad forms of popular culture that operate to instil a masculinist vision, not least the semi-naked ('topless') images of (near emaciated, surgically altered) women in national newspapers, street advertising, pop-culture magazines, music videos and sports events. All of which and more (even leaving aside the exponential growth in and availability of images of sexual exploitation and child sexual abuse via the internet) serve as regular and powerful reminders of what *is*, and *should* be, valued 'in women'. In other words, the *libido dominandi* appears as a central disposition of the *masculinist* field. As such, this applies (and perhaps multiplies) in its potent, culturally dominant, *athleticist* form.

The athleticist libido

According to Pronger (1999: 386–387):

> The triumphant pleasure of competitive sport is the violent phallocentric pleasure of adding to oneself by subtracting from another.... One takes one's delight in the vulnerability of one's competitor, in one's phallic ability to pry open their otherwise closed openings against their will, and specifically because it is against their will ... The convention of most players consenting to play also serves to legitimate sport's brutal libidinal economy ... Competitive sport, therefore, is a profoundly unethical way to organize desire.

Expressions of this libidinal economy can be very clearly observed in the common, phallocentric, 'hazing' practices conceived for 'new recruits', 'freshers' ('fresh meat'), 'virgins' or 'rookies' common to many male-sports (Johnson and Holman, 2004). Such 'rites' are of the same order and their design, of which the aim is 'initiation' (effectively a submission to the will of the group) is far from accidental. Bryshun and Young (1999: 269) argue 'throughout sport-related rituals, veterans "test" rookies and evaluate whether they have sufficiently adopted behaviours and beliefs required for membership'. Similarly, Brackenridge (2001) notes such 'testing of the water' among the 'grooming' techniques of perpetrators of CSA in sport; interestingly, one convicted abuser remarked that 'boys were much better at keeping quiet' (Brackenridge: 2001: 106). As Bourdieu (1993: 74) argues, 'one of the factors protecting the various games from total revolutions, which could destroy not only the dominant agents and their domination, but the game itself, is the very size of the investment, in time, effort and so on, presupposed by entry into the game.' The sexualized element to this entry, or *investment*, is evident from the cases of 'hazing' that are officially documented. For example, Bryshun and Young (1999: 273) cite a number of cases; in one instance: 'four members of a male hockey team in Chatham, Ontario, reported that they were forced to masturbate publicly. Thirteen people were charged with over 100 sexual offences.' In September 2008, it was reported that six high school football players in the USA were accused of sodomizing younger boys on the team, and one youth later pleaded guilty to rape (Fox News, 2008).

Curry (1991: 119) observed that 'the men's locker room is enshrined in sports mythology as a bastion of privilege and a center of fraternal bonding'. Using ethnographic methods, Curry collected 'talk fragments in locker rooms from athletes on two teams participating in contact sports' in the USA. He found that talk about 'sex and aggression … [were] of paramount importance in the locker room':

> Locker room talk about women … promotes harmful attitudes and creates an environment supportive of sexual assault and rape. Competition among teammates, the emphasis upon women as objects, sexual conquest as enviable achievement, peer group encouragement of antisocial comments and behaviour, and anxiety about proving one's heterosexuality – all of these ideas are combined … to promote a selfish, hostile, and aggressive approach to sexual encounters with women.
>
> (Curry, 1991: 132)

His later work found that such dispositions went beyond 'talk' and were in fact played out in practice (Curry, 1998). The rape-culture of fraternities and sports teams has now become much more apparent as the problem of sexual assaults within universities, and its relation to masculinist cultures, has become more widely recognized (see Sanday, 2007). Thus, in 2012, two Steubenville High School football players in the USA raped an unconscious 16-year-old female and distributed nude images of the girl among their peer group, some of whom were captured on video seemingly celebrating the attack (*The Guardian*, 2013). Such cases demonstrate that sexual violence is recognized as a legitimate practice within the panoply of domination-strategies available to the athleticist habitus. According to Pronger (1999: 382):

> Boys raised on competitive sport learn to desire, learn to make connections according to the imperative to take space away from others and

jealously guard it for themselves ... this is the conquest logic of competitive sport: to penetrate the other as an expression of the impenetrable self.

'Homosexual' possession, then, (or 'man-boy sex') is not anathema to the athleticist field; sexual activity with a boy is in no way contrary to the *libido dominandi*, indeed, it is in perfect accord:

JACK: The only rumours that, on occasion, circulated were those of other girls the current girlfriend was not comfortable with. He was known as a 'player' ... He preferred I be passive and I would only comply with something if he had a request...

However, to be clear again, the suggestion here is not that organized sport somehow generates, in any straightforward, necessary fashion the desire to engage children and young people in sex. It would be bizarre to consider sport as somehow generative of a *paedo*sexual desire (or 'Minor-Attracted Adult' Goode, 2010). But sport – born out of the patriarchal endeavour, has at its centre the athleticist field, which is generative of, and generated by, the *athleticist habitus*, fundamental to which, I argue, is the *libido dominandi*. This libido refers to an economy of practice in which *capital* is acquired through the corporeal domination of others. In this 'libidinal economy' (Pronger, 1999), sex is a strategy of acquisition and a means of elevating and demonstrating ones position. Penetration, as the ultimate symbol of domination, is the most potent form of capital accessible to the *libido dominandi*:

MARY JO: He was well known for having sex with other women. A female coach that started working with us had a relationship with him; he was involved with a high-ranking official of the sport; with international judges. He was a dandy, a womaniser. He liked women around him ... Sometimes ... he would pick me up in his car and take me for a drive. He would grab me at the back of my head and force me down.

WILL: ...he was alluring, a bit of a chap about town, with a flat [in affluent area] ... which he'd call 'my fuck-box'.

ELAINE: There was all this talk about how he was the one who was going to *transition* me into becoming a woman – by having sex with me ... He only had intercourse with me once, but the abuse went on for about two or three years after that. He always wanted oral sex and so any opportunity he got, that was the thing.

The inherent risk to the less powerful within a field that revolves around the master-apprentice (or servant) relation, where childhood and masculinism collide and reside in close proximity, is therefore considerable and brought into sharp relief by the experiences these children were subjected to.[3]

This might be considered a precursor to a psychological offender profile – a sort of typical *sports-offender*. The offenders described in the accounts offered here certainly lend support to previous studies in sport (Brackenridge, 1997; Kirby *et al.*, 2000; Toftegaard Nielsen, 2001) which found 'sexually abusing coaches [to] have good social skills, high visibility, popularity and a high level of sexual confidence and assertiveness' (Brackenridge, 2001: 109). Brackenridge (2001: 108) therefore suggests 'the predator' model (developed from and as a mirror-image to Wolf's (1984) 'paedophile cycle of offending') and this model seems applicable to the men described here. Certainly the notion of a *libido dominandi* seems to resonate with the 'predator' model. However, Brackenridge (2001: 112) also advocates caution in attempting to classify or 'profile' perpetrators (as does Cowburn, 2005, in addition to much feminist theory on sex offending). Via the athleticist habitus, *libido dominandi* expresses the gender-sex economy of a field rather than a profile of a perpetrator. It is a contextualized expression of collective habitus enacted by individuals, recalling that:

> Within certain objective limits (the field), habitus engenders a potentially infinite number of patterns of behaviour, thought and expression that are both 'relatively unpredictable' but also 'limited in their diversity'.
>
> (McNay, 2000: 38)

More importantly, it is also just one expression of sexuality and sexual practice, which is not constituted simply in terms of the 'perpetrator', but as agents within a relation, acting within specific cultural contexts or fields. Crucially, the child is *also* a social agent whose *agency* is closely related to, or bound-up with, his/her – dynamic, creative – adjustment to the field. This enables the incorporation of the reflections of 'survivors' who both recognize their victimization but see no reason to deny their active engagement in the sexual activity (which neither implies nor denies 'affection' or 'pleasure'). Indeed, it might be said that what 'survivors' most want others to understand is not the violation itself, but the relation that constituted and facilitated their violation. The following section, then, introduces the counterpart to *libido dominandi*.

Libido dominantis

According to Bourdieu (2001: 79–80):

> Masculine domination finds one of its strongest supports in the misrecognition which results from the application to the dominant of categories engendered in the very relationship of domination and which

can lead to that extreme form of *amor fati*, love of the dominant and of his domination, a *libido dominantis* (desire for the dominant) which implies renunciation of personal exercise of *libido dominandi* (the desire to dominate).

This clearly needs to be carefully considered, but seems particularly appropriate for the cases of sexual subjection presented above. Children in sport, from their first entry into the field, are closely instructed in, and through, the narrative of a *libido dominantis*. In their apprenticeship (or servitude), children (perhaps especially boys) are taught to value domination and, therefore, to exalt the dominant. They 'desire' that which they wish to replicate: the 'heroic rugby teacher', 'the legendary coach'. This is not to imply an explicit or conscious desire (or indeed a sexualized desire) – symbolic violence is 'exercised only through an act of knowledge and practical recognition which takes place below the level of the consciousness and will' (Bourdieu, 2001: 42). The notion of *illusio* helps to further illuminate this process.

'*Illusio* is the fact of being caught up in and by the game, of believing the game is "worth the candle", or, more simply, that playing is worth the effort' (Bourdieu, 1998: 77):

> ... If your mind is structured according to the structures of the world in which you play, everything will seem obvious and the question of knowing if the game is 'worth the candle' will not even be asked ... the *illusio* is the enchanted relation to a game that is the product of a relation of ontological complicity between mental structures and the objective structures of social space ... games which matter to you are important and interesting because they have been imposed and introduced in your mind, in your body, in a form called the feel for the game.

This is evident in the early childhoods of all the participants interviewed. With the possible exception of Stephen, all the participants were raised in an environment which encouraged them to feel, from a very early age, that *the game* was definitely 'worth the candle'.

ELAINE: From the age of 10, I was on the tennis court about 7 hours a day. I would get up around six in the morning and play from 6:15 a.m. to 7:30 a.m. before school. When school finished I would be straight back on the tennis court for 4 to 5 hours every single afternoon.

Their childhood was punctuated with powerful symbols related to sporting achievement from which they derived their identity and status; it's what they 'danced for' (as Will put it), and it's what they desired above all else.

This 'game', then, is clearly productive of corporeal practices – a *bodily hexis* (Bourdieu, 1977) – and this was a 'game' introduced in very explicit terms in the early childhoods of all the participants. They had a *feel for the game*; they were 'caught up in and by the game' so that, it might be said, there was an 'ontological complicity' between their mental structures and the objective structures of the field.

ELAINE: My friends were all elite tennis players. I never really had much time out of tennis so I never experienced the full privileges of child-hood. I didn't know what it was like to have a *social* life. But I always got a good feeling from winning. I have an intense desire to win...

MARY JO: I started training there when I was 8 or 9. I left for school at 7:30 a.m. and I didn't get back home until 11 or 11:30 p.m. At 5 o'clock I would rush to the gym and train for 5 hours every day. You can only do that if you really, really, *really* like it.

JACK: I knew this was my destiny. All I did was eat, sleep, school and skate. I didn't apply myself at school – I had to skate – I had to conquer myself and be a success with this. I put everything into it. I also wanted to make my mum proud.

They had been taught, explicitly, persistently and bodily to *desire* the field of athleticism and, therefore, those agents that most closely embodied it. Where the child is constructed or labelled as (and aspires to be) an 'elite athlete' it is clear that their (new) identity demands that they be 'an athlete' and little else. That is, it is not simply the case that the child desires to *be* an athlete, rather, they have been explicitly depicted, often from a very young age, *as* 'an athlete':

MARY JO: He would call us all kinds of things, like 'whore! – you only come here for the boys'. But my family were very happy and I was quite famous. I was on TV and so girls would stop me on the street.

Thus, while the narratives the participants told regarding their sometimes difficult parental relationships are important, these were not neglected, *unloved* children, or (especially) unhappy children. They cannot reasonably be described as abnormally 'emotionally deprived' and certainly not intellectually deficient. In many ways, these were all *relatively* privileged children who appear to have had well developed cognitive, social and (par-ticularly) physical capacities. They were, however, distinguished by their 'love' of, or more substantively, *immersion in*, the athleticist field. Thus, Sheldon Kennedy observes: 'in fact, most of my earliest memories seem to occur on a long, white ice surface. My parents brought me to one of the outdoor rinks when I was two years old' (Kennedy with Grainger, 2006: 11). From early in life, then, the *game* of athleticism had been introduced to their minds and prioritized in their boyhood or girlhood. Unsurprisingly, they had invested in it to the extent that, it might be said, they resembled it, they became the 'field made flesh':

MARY JO: The workout was hard. But we liked it. I was very obedient and if he told me to do 100 sit-ups then I would do 101. I didn't miss one. If he told me to go on the beam and do a flip I would do it. I was very disciplined and very obedient.

Similarly, Will remarked on his abuser's skills as a rugby coach: '[we] were *like thirty pieces of blotting paper on a pitch*' (my emphasis). Childhood in sport, then, perhaps under the euphemisms of 'discipline' and 'respect', engenders a habitus disposed towards the desire for, and exaltation of, the dominant. Children literally 'soak-up', absorb, the social space and 'desire' those who most closely embody it. Therefore, the 'reason' immanent in practice refers not simply to the *libido dominandi* (a central constituent of the *athleticist habitus*), but also to the *libido dominantis*, represented here by the child who has developed the capacity to find virtue (expressed through obedience, compliance and silence) in the sexual activity s/he is subjected to.

The *athleticist habitus* constitutes a contextualized expression of sexual practice structured, according to the logic of the field: a zero-sum/win-lose, *binary* 'game'. It follows that there are two libidinal *moments* to this habitus – *dominandi* and *dominantis*: the desire for domination and the desire for the dominant. The 'survivor' stories recognize and illustrate this. For example:

PAUL: He would take you in the back room off the gym ... and he would grab you by the balls and spank you. It was kind of a Litmus Test: if you can put up with that you can go to the next level. The thing is you want to play basketball for the best team in the City and go on to have a career. So you put up with it.... I let it continue ... I loved him. People cannot *stand* to hear that, but that's what happened. I was so psychologically dependent, and sexually dependent and *materially* dependent.

SIMON: ...a lot of us tried to excel in the sport, and in the training, and in the coaching – in the whole thing – to be more and more attractive to our abusers. I think there was that feeling of – you know, it was almost a sexual experience when you did something good, a good tackle or something, they would give you a smile or pat you on the back – it would be like, 'oh my god' that's just like, *that thing*.

ELAINE: ...after the abuse began I think I was trying to hang onto something that I suppose wasn't really there. I think that I might have even become a little bit jealous of him as I was always wondering where he was. I do remember seeing him with other girls and seeing them in the car and wondering what the hell was going on.

Bourdieu's observation on sport is that:

> It is perhaps by thinking what is most specific about sport, that is, the regulated manipulation of the body, about the fact that sport, like all disciplines in total or totalitarian institutions, convents, prisons, asylums, political parties, etc., is *a way of obtaining from the body an adhesion that the mind might refuse*, that one could reach a better understanding of the usage made by most authoritarian regimes of sport … 'The Soldier's Tale' reminds us of the old popular tradition: making someone dance means possessing them (my emphasis).
>
> (Bourdieu, 1990: 167)

Sport is centred on the principle of manipulating the body, of obtaining from it that which the mind would refuse. While 'making someone dance' indicates possession of them, under the terms of the *libido dominandi*, possession is infused with eroticism and the erotic relates explicitly to domination and control. This is perhaps to express, in different terms, Simon's insight:

SIMON: Sometimes he'd come and get me from home in the school holidays and it was almost like he didn't want sex, he just wanted someone to touch his bits.… Sex is not that important, it's not about sex itself, it's more about control, absolute control.

JACK: My role in these encounters was an object for display, I think. It felt as if he was showing me off. Initially I was very fearful but … he set limits for them and he always showed he was in control.… One guy was a bit more aggressive and it all came to an abrupt halt. The two of them left the bedroom and Coach returned alone and he continued as if nothing happened. The same guy did return two or three times, but he was not aggressive at all. That showed me just how much control he had…

The notion of *athleticist habitus*, then, is used to depict a 'generative principle' derived from and active upon the *athleticist field*. The field is characterized broadly by instrumentalism and masculinism, and the adult-child relation is constructed through discourses of respect and obligation (*athlete obligatus*). Fundamental to the athleticist field is a binary form of sexual practice comprising two positions or moments: the *libido dominandi* – the desire for domination, conquest and adding to oneself by the taking from (or simply 'taking' *of*) others; and the *libido dominantis* – a desire for, and to do the will of, the dominant. Through this *libido*, sexual subjection is an 'inscribed potentiality' between two agents (man *and* child) acting within the field and through its economy of practices. The 'perpetrator' is neither imbued with an especially developed psychological capacity to identify and manipulate 'vulnerable' children, nor is the child-victim designated as distinctively impoverished in some way that predisposes him or her to victimization.

Reproducing the field

In the previous sections, I set down my explanatory account of sexual subjection in sport. In this final section, I will explore my thesis further by considering the broader sociocultural and political context of organized sport in light of the notion of an *athleticist habitus*. In particular, I will consider how sport as a field reproduces itself as a wholesome and virtuous activity through processes of denial and misrecognition (Bourdieu, 1998). I will argue that the *athleticist habitus* (the field made flesh) and its corollary, the *sports illusio* (an enchanted belief in the game generative of the *athlete obligatus*), serves to facilitate a denial of the symbolic economy of sport – the logic of sport – and thus to deny the symbolic violence done to children in its midst, a symbolic violence that facilitates, among other things, sexual violence. I will argue that sport has a largely untroubled representation of itself as a context and institution that operates in the best interests of children – a 'fact' perhaps only enhanced by its engagement with 'child protection'/'safeguarding' agendas. I argue that the logic of athleticism – embodied in *athleticist habitus* – is a logic that objectifies and commodifies children, efficiently separating those who *can* from those who *can't*, and those who *will* from those who *won't*, ranking and fetishizing bodies whose performance most consistently meets institutional priorities, while binding and incorporating them in an enchanted relation.

Denial and misrecognition in reproducing the field

The overwhelming silence around sex, especially sexual subjection, in organized sport disguises a sexually charged environment (sexual storytelling/jokes, sexualized banter, sexualized rituals, etc., see Curry, 1991; Messner and Sabo, 1994; Pronger, 1990). Sex is simultaneously ever-present and utterly denied in dominant discourse, where sport is resolutely about character development, teamwork, discipline, responsibility, achievement, health, etc. Indeed, organized sport is about anything (and everything) *but* sex. Despite decades of feminist and pro-feminist critique, advocacy and policy development, arguably, the hyper-masculinist sports enterprise has never been stronger. Yet while sex is central to the male changing room/bar-room environment, the rules of the *game* are clear: what happens in the dressing room/locker room stays there. The unwritten law of 'Omertà' prevails and to be an *athlete* is to understand this implicitly, to incorporate it and embody it; as one child protection officer at an English junior rugby league club said, 'I don't think you tend to get issues like bullying and things like that cos it gets sorted in-house' (Hartill and Prescott, 2003). This is a code central to the *athleticist habitus*.

It is useful to consider Bourdieu's comments on 'the Church' in relation to such denial in sport. For Bourdieu (1998: 113), the contemporary social universe is characterized by 'the generalization of monetary exchanges [where] the maximization of profit has become the basis of most ordinary practices' so that all social agents implicitly or explicitly place a monetary value on their work or time. He argues that the 'Catholic Church [is an] enterprise with an economic dimension founded on the denial of the economy' so that those agents of the church (but not confined to the church) simultaneously play 'the religious game' by thoroughly rejecting any possibility of an association between the religious enterprise and the economic one (113). Although the forces of commercialism are evident in abundance within sport, nevertheless, where 'youth sport' is concerned, the 'athleticist game' might be considered in a similar light. For Bourdieu, this is not necessarily a disingenuous rejection; agents in fact believe, *bodily*, in the games they 'play.' Instead, he argues:

> Here again we find the problem which is provoked by the making explicit of the truth of institutions (or fields) whose truth is the avoidance of rendering their truth explicit. Put more simply: rendering explicit brings about a destructive alteration when the entire logic of the universe rendered explicit rests on the taboo of rendering it explicit.
>
> (Bourdieu, 1998: 113)

Adult-organized, childhood/youth sport displays very clearly these characteristics. That is, it can be argued that the 'truth' of youth sport is the avoidance of rendering its truth explicit. From its inception, the *athleticist field* has been constituted as an economy of symbolic goods constructed according to the (economic) interests of the dominant, most obviously in terms of economic status ('class'), ethnicity and gender. But this symbolic economy must be denied, as the whole functioning of the field (the logic of that universe) rests on the denial of that truth. Thus, (youth) sport is resolutely anchored in the discourse of public good – community cohesion, social inclusion, equality, health benefits, including psychological (e.g. increased confidence), crime reduction – it is about children's *welfare* (thus Brackenridge *et al.*, 2007 refer to sport as the 'sixth social service').

Therefore, the symbolic (and actual) violence done to children through rendering them *athlete obligatus* – objectified, instrumentalized and commodified – to be trained in the pursuit of adult-generated goals, is persistently denied (and reconstituted as a public 'good'). Children are initiated, at increasingly younger ages, within this athleticist frame. As the proud Thai-boxing coach of a 9-year-old said, shortly after he had fought, and won, in a 'cage-fight': 'The earlier the better. Get them when they're young. Show me the boy at seven and I'll show you the man' (*Channel 4*, 2008). These achievement-performance goals are more accurately represented as symbolic capital which is accrued by adults in various ways through children's sports participation. Such capital is clearly manifest as both economic, social and cultural (Messner, 2009). As the father of another child boxer said: 'I always wanted to be the champ ... but it's as good them saying it to my son' (*Channel 4*, 2008). Thus, in the wake of *Lawn Tennis Association* coach Claire Lyte's 2007 conviction for sexually abusing a 13-year-old girl in her charge, Alan Jones, a successful but not 'mainstream' tennis coach in the UK, observed:

> I don't think all these scandals will harm tennis' image, because what drives the sport is money. These scandals make no difference to making money. A lot of parents look to possibly making money from their children. That's the real scandal, that children are being denied a childhood. Children are pushed early, and often don't have the talent, but parents won't listen if you say that. There are graveyards out there full of children's childhoods.
>
> (Hodgkinson, 2007)

However, a 'structural double game' occurs – 'a double consciousness' (Bourdieu, 1998) – in which the economic dimension is 'denied as such through a systematic usage of euphemism' (Bourdieu, 1998: 115). Thus, boxing becomes the 'art of pugilism', football – the 'beautiful game' (or even 'the *more* beautiful game' in the case of *Euro2005* women's tournament), and the field regenerates itself through representations of a strong and moral masculinity ('it's just not cricket'), preferably accompanied with an inspiring hero (e.g. Tiger Woods, Lance Armstrong).

Yet for Bourdieu, this denial and misrecognition should not be regarded as a cynical act because 'agents believe in what they are doing and they do not accept the strict economic definition of their action and their function' (1998: 115), however:

> ...to be able to do what one does by making people (and oneself) believe that one is not doing it, one must tell them (and oneself) that one is doing something other than what one is doing, one must do it while saying (to oneself and others) that one is not doing it, as if one were not doing it.
>
> (Bourdieu, 1998: 115)

Therefore, while adult's (overwhelmingly, but not exclusively, men) train children how to use their bodies as 'weapons' to defeat other children (as is the case in the major sporting forms for males, see Messner, 1990, 1992) they must tell themselves and others that they are doing something very different, so that to all intents and purposes, they *are* doing something different. Hence, rugby union's 'core values' are 'teamwork, respect, enjoyment, discipline, and sportsmanship' (RFU, 2009).[4] Like religious institutions, sport institutions 'work permanently, both practically and symbolically, to euphemise social relations, including relations of exploitation, by transfiguring them into relations of spiritual kinship … [particularly] through the logic of volunteerism' (Bourdieu, 1998: 116). 'We are thus dealing with enterprises which, functioning according to the logic of volunteer work and offering, have a considerable advantage in economic competition (among these advantages, the effect of the label)' (Bourdieu, 1998: 118). As in organized religion, 'Christian' or 'Vicar' has 'the value of a guarantee of quasi-domestic morality' (Bourdieu, 1998: 118); so the label 'sport' and 'sports coach' is similarly imbued with notions of those who give freely, of a charitable element that denotes a moral character grounded in the spirit of volunteerism, fraternity and selflessness. In a similar fashion, 'sportsman' or 'athlete' speaks to endeavour, dedication, obedience, abstinence and bodily discipline, all of which denotes moral discipline and fortitude. Thus, Coakley (2006: 160) suggests that 'the achievements of children in an activity as visible and highly publicized as sports come to symbolize proof of one's moral worth as a parent. Talented child athletes, therefore, become valuable moral capital.' According to Bourdieu (1998: 119):

> …objectively economic enterprises can only benefit from these advantages provided that the conditions of the misrecognition of their economic dimension are continually reproduced, that is, as long as agents succeed in believing and making others believe that their actions have no economic impact.

It might be argued, that like 'religious work,' sport work 'includes a considerable expenditure of energy aimed at converting activity with an economic dimension into a sacred task' (Bourdieu, 1998: 119). Thus, sporting events are converted into seemingly sacred rituals, at the centre of which, in extending the religious metaphor, it might be said, is the pilgrimage, where hugely profitable rituals (e.g. the 'Olympic' Games, the 'Ashes', the 'State of Origin', the 'Theatre of Dreams', etc.) are imbued with the sanctity of the holy, and agents of the field are transformed into quasi-religious spiritual leaders (sometimes commanding the devotion of huge congregations or followers) whose wisdom must be sought and carefully considered.

The tools or strategies operationalized in this process of *misrecognition* would include the ritualized initiation ceremonies (formal and informal, explicit and implicit) prevalent in organized male-sport (especially team sports) where young initiates are endowed with a clear understanding of what that universe entails and what it means to be a part of it. Thus are rank and privilege bestowed – to be 'in the club', 'one of the boys', in 'the team' – processes that seek to cement or fraternalize relations of power so that each member implicitly recognizes another and understands ('it goes without saying') that retaining membership depends on abiding by, and actively maintaining, the codes (written and unwritten) of the game. The following situation, if not typical, is arguably illustrative of the economy of practices within masculinist youth sport:

> I had a lady phone me this year … her 12 year old son went to a birthday party, and they were watching hockey [on TV], and then they started playing this game where you basically just choke the other kid until he passes out; and her son had been choked unconscious three times in one evening, at the coach's house! And so she was phoning me asking like what I felt they should do. And the parents are still really scared of 'what if I get blacklisted as being a potential trouble-maker here, will my kid's entire career in hockey be done?' And there's still a lot of problems with that … and she is just sobbing on the phone describing this situation but then with the caveat of, 'well, please don't tell him because I don't want anything to happen to my son's career'…
>
> (Interview with Hockey Youth Leader, North America)[5]

It is not by chance then that the initiation rite or ceremony is at the heart of organized male-sport and that this resembles the religious ritual or ceremony in its emphasis on embodiment. Indeed, commentators often remark on the 'sanctity' of distinguished sports venues, 'inner sanctums' of powerful sports organizations, and the 'religious fervour' displayed by sports spectators (especially in traditional games). Again, it is also crucial to acknowledge the gender-sex dimension of these symbolic 'mythico-ritual' practices – they are overwhelmingly male dominated, explicitly heterosexualized and often misogynist. They are absolutely not for girls or 'gays' yet simultaneously highly sexualized, homosocial encounters (Bird, 1996; Burstyn, 1999; Pronger, 1999). Indeed, one such symbol of North American masculinism, Maple Leaf Gardens in Toronto, housed not only one of the most successful professional hockey teams of its generation, it was also the site of systematic sexual abuse of young boys for many years (Vine and Challen, 2002). Similarly, a bastion of athleticism in the USA, the Pennsylvania State University football programme bestowed many privileges upon one of its star coaches, Jerry Sandusky, while apparently failing to prevent his sexual activities with young boys (Freeh *et al.*, 2012).

Sportsmen, self-deception and bad faith

Bourdieu (1998: 119) claims 'what is valid at the lay level is true to the *nth* degree for the level of the clerics who are always in the logic of self-deception'. For the athleticist field we might replace 'cleric' with any number of official roles, but perhaps above all we would say 'athlete', 'coach', or perhaps 'sportsman'. Such is the coherence between mental structures and objective structures (of the field) that it is possible to observe that those agents would not think to consider the activities (*training*) they devise and arrange in the language of banality or arbitrariness, let alone as de-humanizing. The game and all it comprises is paramount, is *'worth* the candle' and an end-in-itself. To ensure the continuity of the game is the chief and overriding disposition of the *athleticist habitus* that structures and is structured by the *athleticist field*.

In late modernity the task of sustaining the field, then, has become much more determined as agents move increasingly from the position of interested lay-person (volunteer) to professionalized 'agent', financially remunerated in the explicit service of 'the game'. Sports coaching and administrating is no longer simply a 'calling' but a *profession*, requiring and receiving (in some cases) state funding. When 'the game' sustains livelihoods (as well as identities), it might be argued that there can be little or no room afforded to genuine reflection or fundamental criticism. This would be to explicitly risk 'destroying' the game (and the immediate fortunes of the individual agent). And so we can note the immense amount of energy and expense that goes into securing 'the future of the game', particularly through the ongoing struggle to reconstruct athleticism as a panacea for all manner of social ills and moral panics around childhood, typically *health* (e.g. childhood 'obesity') and *crime* (e.g. youth 'delinquency'). However, it is crucial to reiterate Bourdieu's position regarding social action and self-deception:

> To speak of self-deception may lead one to believe that each agent is responsible for deceiving himself. In fact, the work of self-deception is a collective work, sustained by a whole set of social institutions ... functioning with the support of a group which benefits from it: collective bad faith is inscribed in the objectivity of language (in particular euphemisms, ritual formulae, terms of address) ... and also in the bodies, the habitus, the ways of being, of speaking, and so forth; it is permanently reinforced by the logic of the economy of symbolic goods which encourages and rewards this structural duplicity.
>
> (Bourdieu, 1998: 121)

Therefore, when brought forward to condemn (usually in very opaque terms) the latest revelation of (sexual) misconduct, it is possible to note the unflinching resolve with which any number of 'sport agents' will simultaneously *defend* 'sport', especially if the scandal relates to *their* sport. As soon as an individual agent, however firmly embedded within the logic of the field, jeopardizes the 'integrity' of 'the sport' by effecting a sort of pulling-back of the curtain – they are cast out, ex-communicated and, where possible, expunged from official records. The example of the cyclist Lance Armstrong illustrates the point. It is instructive, then, to consider sexual subjection in sport from Bourdieu's perspective of 'self-deception'. Indeed, it may tell us a great deal about the initial 'collective denial' within sport to concerns raised about child sexual abuse (see Brackenridge, 2001). The example of the chief administrator of one US swimming coaches organization refusing to accept allegations of sexual abuse against a coach unless it was made by another coach, on the grounds that to do otherwise would incite a raft of 'spurious' allegations, seems to represent the embodiment of 'collective bad faith' (BBC TV, 1993). Thus, writing in the *Irish Independent* on 31 January 1998, about her ex-swimming coach and prolific sex offender Derry O'Rourke, Michelle Smith de Bruin asks:

> Why did no one question if he should be allowed to take young girls on their own into the gym in the dark to hypnotise them, or to the pool for special attention? Why did no one question when he made lewd comments about the young girls?
>
> (McCarthy, 2010: 190)

The recognition that the abuse was known about but not acted upon by other adults is often very difficult for 'survivors' to come to terms with. According to Sheldon Kennedy:

> Players and coaches on other teams constantly accused me of being gay during games … I was taunted … The other coaches would shout, 'Hey it's Graham's girlfriend!' The opposing players called me 'faggot' and 'Graham's little wife' every chance they got. After news of Graham's abuse became public, everyone in the league acted surprised, as if they'd had no idea what was going on. Well they sure had *acted* like they knew what was going on.
>
> (Kennedy and Grainger, 2006: 89–90)

The collective bad faith inscribed within fields has served to deny children subjected to sex by agents of the field – the religious field perhaps being the most palpable illustration of this. The following extract from Will illustrates clearly this disposition – habitus – within the athleticist field:

WILL: ...[perpetrator] ended up coaching the under 14s at a very good rugby club, a mile down the road. I said to the President of the club ... '[perpetrator] used to coach the Under 14s at [name of club]. You may not know this but he's a career paedophile and has been cited in complaints to the police. Were you aware of that?' 'Don't know [perpetrator]' I said, 'but John, it's in the papers', 'No we've never had anyone called [perpetrator]' I said 'Oh John ... speak to [reporter] on the local paper, *he* remembers [perpetrator]'. 'No we've never had anyone called [perpetrator]'. That immediately – when you hear the president of a club speaking like that – don't they realise that all they're doing is completely discrediting the organisation. But they don't! Which is why I have no respect for people in authority at all, because very few of them have the moral fibre to say, 'well we've got a problem here, let's get to the bottom of it'. Until you let the light in onto the problem it will never heal. *Why? I don't get it*. It makes no sense. It's beyond me – *why*? It's about surely the people ... the children who are there. *It's about them*! It's not about reputation.

Notes

1 This enchantment might also be considered in relation to organized religion, particularly given the extent of the covering-up of CSA in the Catholic Church reported recently (Isely and Isely, 1990; Murphy Report, 2009).
2 For clarity, this is in no way to confuse homosexual relations with child sexual abuse or to limit CSA to acts of penetration only.
3 Interestingly, the Latin *puer* translates as male child or servant.
4 Coincidentally produced in the wake of 'blood-gate' where one of the sport's iconic figures (Dean Richards) was found guilty of instructing one of his ('Harlequins') players to bite on a blood capsule in the last minutes of a major cup game in order to fake a blood-injury so they could substitute him for a goal-kicker in an attempt to win the match. After the plan was discovered, he then instructed his assistants to lie to a disciplinary panel to cover-up his involvement (see BBC Sport, 2009b).
5 Despite his concern, this General Manager with official responsibility for child welfare in youth hockey in a North American city appeared happy to acquiesce to the parent's request that the incident go unreported.

References

BBC (British Broadcasting Corporation) Television (1993) *On the line: secrets of the coach*. Documentary. 25 August.
BBC (2009a) Amnesty condemns Iranian rights abuses. *News*, [online] available at: http://news.bbc.co.uk/1/hi/world/middle_east/8405063.stm [accessed 11 December 2014].
BBC (2009b) Richards hit by damning judgement. *Rugby Union*, [online] available at: http://news.bbc.co.uk/sport1/hi/rugby_union/my_club/harlequins/8233248.stm [accessed 5 September 2009].

Benedict, J. (1997) *Public heroes, private felons: athletes and crimes against women*. Boston: Northwestern University Press.

Bird, S. (1996) Welcome to the men's club: homosociality and the maintenance of hegemonic masculinity. *Gender and Society*, 10: 120–132.

Bourdieu, P. (1977) *Outline of a theory of practice*. Cambridge: Cambridge University Press.

Bourdieu, P. (1990) *In other words: essays towards a reflexive sociology*. Cambridge: Polity Press.

Bourdieu, P. (1993) *Sociology in question*. London: Sage.

Bourdieu, P. (1998) *Practical reason: on the theory of action*. Cambridge: Polity Press.

Bourdieu, P. (2001) *Masculine domination* [translation by R. Nice]. Cambridge: Polity Press.

Brackenridge, C.H. (1997) 'He owned me basically': women's experience of sexual abuse in sport. *International Review for the Sociology of Sport*, 32(2): 115–130.

Brackenridge, C.H. (2001) *Spoilsports: understanding and preventing sexual exploitation in sport*. London: Routledge.

Brackenridge, C.H. (2002) Men loving men hating women: the crisis of masculinity and violence to women in sport. In S. Scraton and A. Flintoff (eds.) *Gender and sport: a reader*. London: Routledge, 255–270.

Brackenridge, C., Pitchford, A., Russell, K. and Nutt, G. (2007) *Child welfare in football: an exploration of children's welfare in the modern game*. London: Routledge.

Brittan, A. and Trevino, C. (2013) *The Washington Post* [online]. Ex-swimming coach Rick Curl gets 7 years in child sex abuse case. Available at: www.washington post.com/local/ex-swimming-coach-rick-curl-to-be-sentenced-in-child-sex-abuse-case/2013/05/23/d80320f2-c3a5-11e2-9fe2-6ee52d0eb7c1_story.html [accessed 6 March 2014].

Brittan, A. (2001) Masculinities and masculinism. In S.M. Whitehead and F.J. Barrett (eds.) *The masculinities reader*. Cambridge: Polity, 51–55.

Bryshun, J. and Young, K. (1999) Sport-related hazing: an inquiry into male and female involvement. In P. White and K. Young (eds.) *Sport and gender in Canada*. Ontario: Oxford University Press, 269–292.

Bryson, V. (1999) *Feminist debates: issues of theory and political practice*. Hampshire: Macmillan.

Burstyn, V. (1999) *The rites of men: manhood, culture and the politics of sport*. London: University of Toronto Press.

Channel 4 Television Corporation (2008) *Strictly baby fight club*. Documentary. Available at: www.channel4.com/programmes/strictly-baby-fight-club.

Coakley, J. (2006) The good father: parental expectations and youth sports. *Leisure Studies*, 25(2): 153–163.

Cossins, A. (2000) *Masculinities, sexualities and child sexual abuse*. The Hague: Kluwer Law International.

Cowburn, M. (2005) Hegemony and discourse: reconstruing the male sex offender and sexual coercion by men. *Sexualities, Evolution and Gender*, 7(3): 215–231.

Curry, T.J. (1991) Fraternal bonding in the locker room: a profeminist analysis of talk about competition and women. *Sociology of Sport Journal*, 8(2): 119–135.

Curry, T.J. (1998) Beyond the locker room: campus bars and college athletes. *Sociology of Sport Journal*, 15: 205–215.

Fox News (2008) *Horrific High School Football Hazing Case Shakes New Mexico Town*, [online] available at: www.foxnews.com/story/2008/09/24/horrific-high-school-football-hazing-case-shakes-new-mexico-town.html [accessed 25 October 2008].

Frank, A.W. (2010) *Letting stories breathe: a socio-narratology*. Chicago, IL: University of Chicago Press.

Freeh, L.J., Sporkin, S. and Sullivan, E.R. (2012) *Report of the investigative counsel regarding the actions of the Pennsylvania State University related to the child sexual abuse committed by Gerald A. Sandusky*. Washington D.C.: Freeh, Sporkin & Sullivan, LLP. Available at: www.freehsporkinsullivan.com/news/23 [accessed 24 July 2014].

Goode, S.D. (2010) *Understanding and addressing adult sexual attraction to children: a study of paedophiles in contemporary society*. London: Routledge.

Guardian, The (2013) *Two Steubenville football players found guilty of raping teenage girl at party*, [online] available at: www.theguardian.com/world/2013/mar/17/steubenville-football-players-guilty-rape [accessed 6 March 2014].

Hartill, M. and Prescott, P. (2003) Safeguarding children in sport: a critical approach to policy implementation. *Conference of the European Sociological Association* (ESA), Murcia, Spain, 22–26 September.

Hodgkinson, M. (2007) Scandals that soil tennis' garden party. *The Telegraph*, Tennis. Available at: www.telegraph.co.uk/sport/tennis/2324829/Scandals-that-soil-tennis-garden-party.html. [accessed 3 November 2011].

Hyde, L. (1983) *The gift: how the creative spirit transforms the world*. Edinburgh: Canongate.

Isely, P.J. and Isely, P. (1990) The sexual abuse of male children by church personnel: intervention and prevention. *Pastoral Psychology*, 39(2): 85–99.

Jenks, C. (2005b) *Childhood* (2nd ed.). London: Routledge.

Johnson, J. and Holman, M.J. (2004) *Making the team: inside the world of sport initiations and hazing*. Toronto: Canadian Scholars Press.

Jones, H. (2012) On sociological perspectives. In J.M. Brown and S.L. Walklate, (eds.) *Handbook on sexual violence*. Oxon: Routledge, 181–202.

Kennedy, S. with Grainger, J. (2006) *Why I didn't say anything: the Sheldon Kennedy story*. Toronto: Insomniac Press.

Kelly, L. (1988) *Surviving sexual violence*. Cambridge: Polity.

Kimmel, M. (2005) *The gender of desire: essays on male sexuality*. Albany, New York: State University of New York Press.

Kirby, S.L., Greaves, L. and Hankivsky, O. (2000) *The dome of silence: sexual harassment and abuse in sport*. London: Zed Books.

Krais, B. (1993) Gender and symbolic violence: female oppression in the light of Pierre Bourdieu's theory of social practice. In C. Calhoun, E. LiPuma and M. Postone (eds.) *Bourdieu: critical perspectives*. Cambridge: Polity, 156–177.

Leberg, E. (1997) *Understanding child molesters: taking charge*. London: Sage.

Maton, K. (2012) Habitus. In M. Grenfell (2012) (Ed.) *Bourdieu: key concepts* (2nd ed.). London: Routledge, 48–64.

Mauss, M. (1954/1990) *The gift: the form and reason for exchange in archaic societies*. London: Routledge.

McCarthy, J. (2010) *Deep deception: Ireland's swimming scandals*. Dublin: The O'Brien Press.

McDonald's (2015) *Football*, [online] available at: www.mcdonalds.co.uk/ukhome/Sport/Football.html [accessed 23 November 2015].

McNay, L. (2000) *Gender and agency: reconfiguring the subject in feminist and social theory*. Cambridge: Polity.

Messner, M.A. (1990) When bodies are weapons: masculinity and violence in sport. *International Review for the Sociology of Sport*, 25: 203–218.

Messner, M.A. (1992) *Power at play: sports and the problem of masculinity*. Boston: Beacon.

Messner, M.A. (2009) *It's all for the kids: gender, families and youth sports*. University of California Press.

Messner, M.A. and Sabo, D. (1994) *Sex, violence and power in sports: rethinking masculinity*. California: The Crossing Press.

Murphy Report (2009) Commission of investigation into Catholic archdiocese of Dublin, July 2009. *Irish Department of Justice, Equality and Law Reform*.

Pronger, B. (1990) *The arena of masculinity: sport, homosexuality and the meaning of sex*. Toronto: University of Toronto Press.

Pronger, B. (1999) Outta my endzone: sport and the territorial Anus. *Journal of Sport & Social Issues*, 23(4): 373–389. DOI:10.1177/0193723599234002.

Sanday, P.R. (2007) *Fraternity gang rape: sex, brotherhood, and privilege on campus*. New York University Press.

Schwartz, J. (2004) *Turned out: sexual assault behind bars*. Documentary. USA: Interlock Media Inc.

Toftegaard Nielsen, J. (2001) The forbidden zone: intimacy, sexual relations and misconduct in the relationship between coaches and athletes. *International Review for the Sociology of Sport*, 36(2): 165–183.

Vine, C. and Challen, P. (2002) *Gardens of shame: the tragedy of Martin Kruze and the sexual abuse at Maple Leaf Gardens*. Vancouver: Greystone Books.

Wolf, S.C. (1984) A multifactor model of deviant sexuality. Paper presented to the third international conference on victimology, Lisbon, cited by C. Brackenridge (2001) *Spoilsports*. London: Routledge.

Conclusion

The sexual abuse and exploitation of children and young people is a persistent and deeply gendered social practice. As feminist writers have long observed, this aspect must be central to explanatory accounts. I have argued that a comprehensive account of sexual abuse must be able to account for its historical persistence as well as its gendered dimensions. The recognition of sexual violence against children within sport has been underpinned, indeed driven, by feminist criticism, theory and advocacy from the start. Brackenridge (2001) set out the key debates that critical sport researchers must engage with, identifying key differences and weaknesses between psychology-based and sociology-based conceptualizations of sexual exploitation: 'Both disciplines … tend to over-emphasise aspects of sexual exploitation that can most easily be accommodated and explained within their particular parameters and to ignore those that cannot' (Brackenridge, 2001: 107). This remains a challenge, and currently, there is no agreed theoretical or conceptual framework within the field of sexual violence or sex offending (Brown and Walklate, 2012; Smallbone and McKillop, 2015; Ward, 2014). Some of the most ardent advocates for theoretical development have come from within the psychology-focused disciplines. Tony Ward and Anthony Beech are two of the most notable and have contributed to the field immeasurably. However, while they, and others, insist that social and cultural influences must be included in any universal theory of child sex offending, they do not offer the theoretical or methodological tools through which the sociocultural might be appropriately interrogated and incorporated into theories of 'causation'. Of course, introducing sociocultural structures into such theories makes a challenging area much more so. The work of Celia Brackenridge recognizes this explicitly and combines positivist/psychological approaches with critical feminist perspectives. In doing so, Brackenridge (2001) makes clear that theoretical accounts must 'account for the complexities of gender-power relations' (Brackenridge, 2001: 107) yet also noting that 'socio-cultural analyses of power often lack the specificity of understanding that can come from looking at individual perpetrator and victim experiences ... within specific sporting circumstances' (Bracken-ridge, 2001: 127). Bourdieu's 'theory of practice' perhaps offers an episte-mological framework for the development of empirical studies that may allow for the individual *and* sociocultural to be more cohesively and robustly accounted for.

In this text, I have attempted to incorporate both these dimensions, but prioritized the accounts of those who know most about the experience of sexual violence, not only the act of abuse itself, but the entire experience of sexual subjection and its aftermath. In doing so, I have indicated that while such experiences are important in and of themselves, recounting them in detail also contributes a great deal to uncovering the logic of a field, the *reason immanent in practice* or in David Gil's (1975) terms 'the particular quality of human relations prevailing in the society, which derives from its philosophy, values, and institutions' (in Donnelly and Oates, 2000: 65). As a central and powerful institution of global society, the quality of human relations that prevail within sport is particularly important for sociological investigation.

I have explored the narratives of men and women who experienced sexual subjection in boyhood and girlhood, in a sport-related context, and through the application and extension of Bourdieu's theory of social prac-tice, I have offered a sociocultural, relational account of this social problem. I have suggested that this approach avoids the problems identi-fied by critics of earlier psychological, feminist and sociological theories. Arguably, it facilitates an explanatory account of CSA that avoids patholo-gizing the perpetrator yet, connects sexual subjection to the sociocultural context and normative aspects of masculinist sexual practice in a manner that incorporates an 'active and determinate sense of agency' (McNay, 2000: 71).

Bourdieu's insistence that the social world can be explored via the notion of *field* and *habitus* enables an approach to sexual abuse and exploitation which requires us to situate this phenomena in its historical and sociocultural context, while providing the conceptual means to link social forces to practice. Such an approach cannot replace psychological perspectives, which enable the development of therapeutic strategies that can assist the individual to cope with the impact of sexual exploitation or prevent recidivism in known offenders. But such perspectives should be couched within a coherent theoretical framework that understands that 'Social reality exists, so to speak, twice, in things and in minds, in fields and in habitus, outside and inside of agents' (Bourdieu in Wacquant, 1989: 43).

Brackenridge (2001: 241) concludes that:

> ...much more work is required to develop a seamless theoretical ana-lysis of sexual exploitation in sport. There is also a need to draw

together much more neatly the now familiar gender critique ... with
the social-psychological models ... any theoretical resolution will have
to incorporate both the organisation sexuality of sport and its interpersonal sex-gender relations in ways which expose the problem
of men.

I agree that much more work is still required. However, I have suggested
and employed a theoretical and conceptual approach that, arguably,
addresses the problems Brackenridge identifies. I have offered a depiction
of the masculinist social forces at play within organized sport – conceptualized as the *athleticist field* – while illustrating the ways in which such
forces may impact upon children who encounter (enter) this field and the
dominant habitus within it. The notion of habitus refers to an 'inscribed
potentiality' which permits a wide range of action within the contextual
limits of the field. In sport, when an adult (male) chooses to subject a child
to sex, they do so of their own free will, but this *will* is not simply an
expression of a deranged, rabid, mind, but rather the expression of a
potentiality, embedded within the practical reason or logic of the field. To
illustrate this in more particular terms, I have utilized the notion of *athleticist habitus*, characterized by masculinism and the principle of corporeal
domination, which gives expression to two opposite but conjoined libidinal moments: *dominandi* (desire for domination) and *dominantis* (desire
for the dominant). Equally, while emphasizing and illustrating the action
(agency) of the child subjected to sex, I have tried to depict the social
forces and mechanisms (such as *gift exchange*) that undermine children's
autonomy and render them 'bound' and obliged – *athlete obligatus* – thus
vulnerable to exploitation from those who embody the athleticist field.
Such ideas may provide grounds for further research in this field and certainly require much more investigation.

I have prioritized the habitus as the source of the practice of CSA while
presenting the social agent as one who determines the field that determines
him; in other words, as an agent with the capacity for choice, whose action
is intimately connected to the sociocultural universe. This not only seems
to represent accurately what is known about offenders from 'survivor' testimony such as that presented here, but also seems necessary for an
accurate representation of the historically persistent practice of childhood
sexual abuse; the conditions for which we persistently reproduce.

In the stories of sociosexual encounters between man and child presented here, all the elements of the field, as I have identified them, can be
seen to be present. It is a field which structures a perception of children's
bodies as means-to-an-end, things or *tools* to be used, 'talent' or material
to be recruited and exploited in the pursuit of adult ends; a field underpinned by patriarchal interests that structures the perception that the masculine is primary and that masculinity is principally demonstrated through

bodily conquest and domination – the exemplar being *sexual* conquest; a homosocial field that is thoroughly immersed in sexualized symbolism yet denies any relation to sexuality or sexual/erotic practices; a field where hierarchy and rank is central and the relation between man and child is one of master-to-servant, where the servant's body may be idolized or fetishized but where her/his 'voice' is generally in-valid; a field where the adult role (coach, etc.) is consecrated by the scientification and professionalization of the sport environment, and the infantilization and disempowerment of the child-athlete position; and a field that works hard to keep itself separate from wider political structures, that revels in and exhorts its idiosyncrasies and mythologies and that jealously guards its autonomy and exclusiveness, patrolling its boundaries vigorously, encouraging membership while delineating clear separation between members and non-members, where everyone is welcome, but only the initiated have access to its privileges and 'secrets.'

Thus, for the child-athlete (if not also his/her mature self) to speak out about the violation is an act that risks revealing the true nature of the universe that has structured his/her cognitive structures. Such a revelation would place the individual at odds with the athleticist economy that is so fundamental to her/his habitus. Such an act, for the young athlete, characterized by the sport *illusio*, enchanted by the game, is virtually unthinkable and they labour, endure and remain silent.

The sexual subjection of children occurs across society, but not outside of it. Endorsing theoretical accounts that fail to authentically evaluate and incorporate social structures, allows the institutions that constitute the social space to remain relatively free from the deep interrogation and elucidation of 'rape-supportive' cultures (Sanday, 2007) that is required. Applying a field analysis enables the logic of practice – the practical reason – of our social institutions to be explored and the mechanisms of domination within them, to be more fully illuminated. If this risks a particularly disenchanting view of our much treasured institutions and practices, not least the beloved world of sport, the volume of revelations about child sexual abuse in those institutions over the past decade should perhaps indicate that such an approach – indeed, disposition – is vital.

Finally, having been granted such privileged and generous access to the lives of my participants, and the experiences which continue to burden them, and having delivered these stories – regardless of my success or otherwise in generating a coherent theoretical account of this practice – it seems that the most important 'truth' is how we locate *ourselves* in these stories, how we locate our lives and our practice through the narratives they offer. It is perhaps possible to hope, then, that these stories may operate (in some way) to affect the habitus that structures the field in a manner that holds much greater potential for the empowerment and wellbeing of children and young people than currently seems to be the case. As Will observed:

Until you let the light in onto the problem it will never heal.

Hopefully this book has let a little more light in.

References

Brackenridge, C.H. (2001) *Spoilsports: understanding and preventing sexual exploitation in sport*. London: Routledge.

Brown, J.M. and Walklate, S.L. (eds.) (2012) *Handbook on sexual violence*. Oxon: Routledge.

Donnelly, A.C. and Oates, K. (2000) *Classic papers in child abuse*. Thousand Oaks, CA: Sage.

Gil, D.G. (1975) Unraveling child abuse. *American Journal of Orthopsychiatry*, 45(3): 346–356.

Smallbone, S.W. and McKillop, N. (2015) Evidence-informed approaches to preventing sexual violence and abuse. In P.D. Donnelly and C.L. Ward (eds.) *Oxford handbook of violence prevention*, 177–181.

Ward, T. (2014) The explanation of sexual offending: from single factor theories to integrative pluralism. *Journal of Sexual Aggression*, 20(2): 130–141.

Appendix I

Relevant concepts and definitions according to statutory guidance within the UK

Sexual Abuse:

> Involves forcing or enticing a child or young person to take part in sexual activities, not necessarily involving a high level of violence, whether or not the child is aware of what is happening. The activities may involve physical contact, including assault by penetration (for example, rape or oral sex) or non-penetrative acts such as masturbation, kissing, rubbing and touching outside of clothing. They may also include non-contact activities, such as involving children in looking at, or in the production of, sexual images, watching sexual activities, encouraging children to behave in sexually inappropriate ways, or grooming a child in preparation for abuse (including via the internet). Sexual abuse is not solely perpetrated by adult males. Women can also commit acts of sexual abuse, as can other children.
>
> (HM Government, 2015: 93)

Sexual Exploitation (SE) is defined as a particular form of child sexual abuse:

> Sexual exploitation of children and young people under 18 involves exploitative situations, contexts and relationships where young people (or a third person or persons) receive 'something' (e.g. food, accommodation, drugs, alcohol, cigarettes, affection, gifts, money) as a result of them performing, and/or another or others performing on them, sexual activities ... In all cases, those exploiting the child/young person have power over them by virtue of their age, gender, intellect, physical strength and/or economic or other resources. Violence, coercion and intimidation are common, involvement in exploitative relationships being characterized in the main by the child or young person's limited availability of choice resulting from their social/economic and/or emotional vulnerability.
>
> (HM Government, 2009: 9)

Appendix 2

Participant information and consent form

The title of this project is: *Childhood sexual exploitation and abuse in sport*
This project is led by **Dr Mike Hartill**
Department of Sport & Physical Activity
Edge Hill University

Approval for this project has been granted by: Edge Hill University Research Ethics Committee

Background information

Thank you for showing an interest in this project. This is obviously a sensitive piece of research, and I hope I have already answered any queries or concerns you may have. The information included here is intended to be a recap and written record of our previous discussion(s). However, please read all the information carefully and take further time to consider your participation in this project. If you decide to take part, you will be asked to sign this form.

As already discussed, you do not have to take part, but if you do your participation will be confidential. Your identity will be safeguarded in any published material that may result from the research and all identifying details (names, dates, etc.) will be removed or altered. Therefore, the interview will be conducted in the understanding that your identity will remain confidential.

If you decide that you do not want to participate, there will be no disadvantage to you nor will you be asked to explain your decision.

What are the aims of the project?

The main aims of the project are to develop understanding about:

- the nature of child sexual abuse in sport;
- the impact of sexual abuse on those who experience abuse in sport;
- the contexts in which abuse takes place.

The information you provide may also be used for educational and training purposes within the sports community.

Summary of procedure

If you agree to participate, we will arrange an interview(s). This will be audio-recorded and then transcribed. You will be provided with a digital copy. The topic of these interviews will be your life history, particularly your childhood experiences of sexual abuse within sport/PE.

You can change your mind and decide not to take part at any time during the interview. If you decide to stop, you do not have to give any reasons for your decision. There is also a 'cooling-off' period of eight weeks during which you can withdraw any and all data collected.

The amount of time spent on this is entirely up to you, however, I would anticipate at minimum one interview of approximately three hours. Several interviews are often more appropriate. The time and location of the interviews is entirely up to you, although a quiet/discreet location is preferable, and (if you are in the UK), I would expect to travel to meet you. If you are not in the UK, alternative means are readily available, such as telephone interviews and/or video interviews (e.g. Skype).

There are no direct rewards from participating in this study, however, by taking part, it is anticipated that you will help to increase knowledge of an issue that is often hidden and is also under-researched. It is intended that this knowledge be used to help develop understanding of this issue, to inform policy and ultimately to help prevent children from experiencing abuse in the future. There will be opportunities to become involved in outreach work should you so wish, and I would be very happy to discuss this.

Security of data

The audio recording will be stored on a password protected computer, laptop and/or a USB stick stored in a locked draw. The recording will be transcribed, verbatim, by myself or a research assistant who will also be bound by the conditions of this agreement. The assistant will not retain a copy of the original recording or transcript. The original recording and transcript (version 1) will be sent to you.

Any identifying information (i.e. names) will be removed from the research transcript (version 2). This transcript will be assigned a code and stored separately from the coding system/key.

Version 2 (anonymized transcript) may be available to other researchers in the future under a carefully controlled and restricted process and according to best practice in research ethics. Extracts from this transcript may be used within research publications, such as journal articles, reports or books and these may be accessible via the internet.

Extracts that appear in any resulting publications will be thoroughly anonymized, including the identity of people you refer to and place names, etc. However, if specific evidence is given that authorities may use to prevent harm to a child, I will be bound by the terms of this agreement to ensure this information is reported to the appropriate authorities. It is, then, entirely your choice to provide such evidence. If you did, I would encourage you to officially disclose this type of information. If you did not wish to do so, I would pass on the relevant detail, but your identity would not be disclosed. However, it is important to note that research data given in confidence do not enjoy legal privilege and may be liable to subpoena by a court.

What information will be collected, and how will it be used?

While not exhaustive, the points below illustrate the sorts of topics/areas we might discuss:

- family background and general childhood experiences;
- what sport(s) you were involved in;
- the perpetrator(s) and their relationship to you;
- how the sexual activity/abuse began and what it entailed;
- how you dealt with it;
- how it affected you and those around you;
- whether you told anyone;
- whether you received any professional help;
- how you reflect upon it now.

Risks and benefits

There are no extrinsic or material benefits to participating in this research. However, there is the possibility that you may experience distress through your involvement in this research, and you should consider this carefully before proceeding to the interview stage. We have discussed available sources of professional support as well as your feelings towards participating in this study and how it might impact upon you and how you might deal with this.

Agreement and statement of consent to participate

I have read this form and I consent to participate in this research study on the basis that:

- My participation is voluntary and without material benefit to me;
- I know I can stop taking part at any time without being disadvantaged;

- I understand that any information disclosed by me that could reasonably be used to prevent the abuse of a child will be passed on to the relevant authorities;
- I understand that research data given in confidence do not enjoy legal privilege and, although unlikely, could be liable to subpoena by a court;
- I have been informed of the arrangements for storage of my interview data, I am satisfied with those arrangements, and I participate on the understanding that these arrangements will be followed exactly;
- The research may be published, but it will not be linked to me;
- I will receive the original recording and transcript of my interview;
- There will be a 'cooling-off' period of eight weeks following which I will be given the opportunity to withdraw;
- I have been able to discuss the possible risks involved;
- I have been provided, where appropriate, with contact details for sources of professional support;
- I agree to inform the researcher if I feel unduly distressed or wish to stop or take a break;
- I have had the opportunity to ask questions.

Participant

Name (printed):

Signature: Date:

Researcher

Name (printed):

Signature: Date:

Appendix 3

Obituaries listed under 'sport' in *The Telegraph* newspaper (online) according to order of publication and sport: 1 March 2014–29 December 2015

	Name	Gender	Sport
1	Eileen Gray	F	cyclist
2	Dean Potter		base jumper
3	John Dewes		cricketer
4	Philip Carter, Sir		businessman, football club owner
5	Brian Bellenger		golf caddie
6	Geoff Duke		motorcyclist
7	Calvin Peete		golfer
8	Valentine Lamb		editor, horse racing
9	Chris Plumridge		golf correspondent
10	Mario Wallenda		high-wire artiste
11	Richie Benaud		cricketer, journalist
12	Ruth Guler	F	Swiss hotelier, skiing
13	Bob Braithwaite		trap-shooter
14	Bob Appleyard		cricketer
15	Derek Day, Sir		diplomat, hockey
16	Clive Freshwater		entrepreneur (canoeing)
17	Dave Mackay		footballer
18	Brian Manley		engineer, swimmer
19	Mick Lunn		river keeper
20	Brian Gardener		cricket enthusiast
21	Daniel Topolski		rowing coach
22	The Marquis of Waterford		Polo
23	John Cox		boatbuilder
24	Billy Casper		golfer
25	Christopher Sporborg		banker, horse enthusiast
26	Jack Hayward, Sir		philanthropist, football
27	Richard Meade		horseman
28	Leslie Silver		entrepreneur (football)
29	Geoff Pullar		cricketer
30	Bill Shand Kydd		businessman, jockey
31	Richard Graydon		jockey, daredevil
32	John-Macdonald-Buchanan, Cptn.		horse-racing
33	David Mackay		architect, Olympics
34	Horace Batten		bootmaker, show-jumping, horse
35	Ernie Terrell		boxer
36	Brian Lister		sports car designer
37	Norman Mair		rugby union player & rugby journalist
38	Jack Kyle		rugby union player
39	Lady Herries of Terregles	F	racehorse trainer

	Name	Gender	Sport
40	Ian Thomson		rugby union
41	Phillip Hughes		cricketer
42	Mary Glen Haig, Lady	F	fencer
43	Ian Craig		cricketer
44	Dorian 'Doc' Paskowitz		surfer
45	William Dugdale, Sir, Bt		football club chairman, landowner
46	Dessie Hughes		jockey, racehorse trainer
47	Vic Braden		tennis player, coach
48	John Solomon		croquet
49	Len Terry		racing car engineer
50	Eric Parker, Sir		industrialist, race horse owner
51	Douglas 'Ox' Baker		wrestler
52	Dick Bromley Gardner, Lt-Col		soldier, hunter
53	Nelson Bunker Hunt		racehorse owner
54	Hans Lobenhoffer		mountaineer
55	Tony Priday		bridge player, correspondent
56	Andrea de Cesaris		F1 driver
57	Dorothy Tyler	F	high jumper
58	Andreas Fransson		extreme skier
59	Toby Balding		race horse trainer
60	Giovanni Pinarello		cyclist, bike builder
61	Norman Gordon		cricketer
62	Hashim Khan		squash
63	James Alexander Gordon		broadcaster, football results
64	Arthur Clarke		rifleman, shooting
65	James Murphy-O'Connor		rugby union
66	Louis 'Red' Klotz		basketball
67	Gary Gilmour		cricketer
68	Alice Coachman	F	high-jump
69	Michael Scudamore		jockey, trainer
70	Alfredo Di Stefano		footballer
71	Don Bennett		cricketer
72	Lousi Zamperini		athlete
73	Olga Kotelko	F	nonagenarian athlete
74	Tom Moran		fishing rod builder
75	Johnny Leach		table tennis
76	Esm Jack	F	dressage, horse
77	Jamie Douglas-Home		racehorse trainer, writer
78	David Allen		cricketer
79	Billie Fleming	F	cyclist
80	Malcolm Glazer		football club owner
81	Charlie Porter		adventurer
82	Peter Kirwan-Taylor		skier, financier
83	Phil Sharpe		cricketer
84	Jack Brabham		F1 driver
85	Hugh McLeod		rugby union
86	John Page		real tennis
87	Walter Walsh		shooting
88	Billy Robinson		wrestler
89	Elena Baltacha		tennis player
90	Ray Colledge		climber
91	Gurth Hoyer Millar		rugby union
92	Julian Wilson		horse racing correspondent
93	Rubin 'The Hurricane' Carter		boxer
94	The Ultimate Warrior		wrestler, USA
95	Hobart 'Hobie' Alter		designer, surfer

	Name	Gender	Sport
96	Mickey Duff		boxing promoter
97	John Tyson		explorer
98	Ken Gregory		F1 driver
99	John Mortimore		cricketer
100	Nick Bevan		school rowing coach

Index

Page numbers in *italics* denote tables.